Mechanics

29
Manuscript and
Letter Form

ms

30
Underlining
for Italics

ital

31
Spelling

sp

32
Hyphenation
and
Syllabication

~

33
The
Apostrophe

'

34
Capital
Letters

cap

35
Abbreviations

ab

36
Numbers

num

Diction and Style

37
Standard
English and
Style

d

38
Wordiness

w

39
Repetition

rep

40
Abstract and
General Words

abst

41
Connotation

con

42
Figurative
Language

fig

43
Flowery
Language

fl

Composition

44
Clear and
Logical
Thinking

log

45
Writing
Paragraphs

¶

46
Writing
Papers

47
Writing About
Literature

48
Writing the
Research
Paper

Glossaries

49
Glossary
of Usage

gl/us

50
Glossary of
Grammatical
Terms

gl/gr

PRACTICAL ENGLISH HANDBOOK

Instructor's Annotated Edition

PRACTICAL ENGLISH HANDBOOK

SEVENTH EDITION

Floyd C. Watkins
Emory University

William B. Dillingham
Emory University

Houghton Mifflin Company   Boston
Dallas   Geneva, Ill.   Lawrenceville, N.J.   Palo Alto

Authors of works quoted in the text are identified with the quotations.

Grateful acknowledgment is made to the following publishers and authors for permission to reprint from their works:

American Heritage Dictionary. Definition of *double.* © 1980 by Houghton Mifflin Company. Reprinted by permission from the *American Heritage Dictionary of the English Language, New College Edition.*

Stanley Milgram. From "Reflections on News." Copyright © 1977 by The Antioch Review, Inc. First appeared in *The Antioch Review,* Vol. 35, No. 2-3 (Spring-Summer, 1977). Reprinted by permission.

Walter Pritchard. From "Up the Attic." Originally appeared in *The Virginia Quarterly Review,* 21 (Spring 1945). © 1945. Reprinted by permission.

Theodore Roethke. "My Papa's Waltz," Copyright 1942 by Hearst Magazines, Inc., from *The Collected Poems of Theodore Roethke.* Reprinted by permission of Doubleday & Company, Inc.

Gay Talese. From "New York." Copyright by Gay Talese. Reprinted by permission of the author.

Elinor Wylie. From "The Eagle and the Mole." *Collected Poems of Elinor Wylie,* © 1932 by Alfred A. Knopf, Inc. Reprinted by permission.

Cover by Hannus Design Associates

Printed in the U.S.A.

Library of Congress Catalog Card Number 85-81206

Student's Edition ISBN: 0-395-35745-4

Instructor's Edition ISBN: 0-395-40283-2

ABCDEFGHIJ-M-898765

Contents

Sentence Errors 29

Sentence Structure   81

Preface

Generations of students have used the *Practical English Handbook*, both in classes and as a reference tool. Many who encountered it for the first time in college classes are now teaching from it themselves; others use it in their businesses or professions. It wears well because it is marked by simplicity and practicality. It remains a standard for its type because it is concise, clear, sure of hand, always up to date. In preparing this seventh edition, we have gone over every word to make sure that those qualities that have long been associated with the book still prevail. We remain most fundamentally concerned with students themselves, for we feel that only by keeping them constantly in mind and forming an imaginary and sympathetic link with them can the authors of a handbook of English produce a truly helpful work. To all those students—those we have known firsthand and those countless others whose presence we have felt as we worked through the various editions—we dedicate this seventh edition with respect and affection.

In this edition, we have rethought every sentence in the book, sharpening the grammar chapter, expanding the chapter on paragraphs, and adding new examples and exercises. A new student paper, "The Animal Factor," is presented in three drafts to show the revision process. In the Writing About Literature chapter, we have included a short story by Saki, "The Open Window," and an accompanying sample essay. We have expanded the dictionary section, adding an annotated sample dictionary entry so that students can learn what each part of the entry means and how to use the entry correctly. Finally, the student research paper, "Hope Through Fantasy in James Thurber's Drawings," has been documented according to the new MLA style.

In addition to the student edition of *Practical English Handbook*, seventh edition, an instructor's annotated edition, a new edition of *Practical English Workbook*, a separate reference/correction chart, and three forms of the diagnostic test are available. There is now a computerized version of the diagnostic test as well as duplicating masters.

A handbook of writing is a collaborative effort in many ways. We have profited immeasurably from correspondence and conversations with many composition professors, and the seventh edition incorporates a great number of their excellent suggestions. They have helped us identify materials that were not as practical as we had hoped they would be and to make substitutions that are more suitable. For their spirit of kinship in the mutual effort to improve our students' writing, we are grateful, and we wish that we could thank by name each one who has offered assistance and suggestions. The list would be almost as long as the book, so we must content ourselves with mentioning a few who have been especially helpful in preparing this edition: Eric and Marie Nitschke, Peter W. Dowell, and Trudy Kretchman of Emory University. We would also like to thank the following individuals for their helpful suggestions: Ray Anschel, Normandale Community College; Norma Bailey, Newport College—Salve Regina; Jay Balderson, Western Illinois University; Manuel B. Blanco, Laredo Junior College; Edith C. Blankenship, Alexander City State Junior College; Richard Charnigo, Cuyahoga Community College; Ronald Davis, Plattsburgh State University College; Vivian I. Davis, Tarrant Junior College South; Harriette Dodson, Florida Junior College; Susan Popper Edelman, Long Island University; Patricia H. Graves, Georgia State University; Patsy R. Gray, North Harris County College; Betty Lu Heimbold, University of Cincinnati; T. Mark Ledbetter, Emory University; Emily M.

Liebman, St. Louis Community College; Twila Yates Papay, Rollins College; Prudence Perry, Marquette University; William Reynolds, Hope College; Joel Roache, University of Maryland; Mary A. Wood, Santa Ana College; and Stephen F. Wozniak, Palomar College.

F.C.W.
W.B.D.

To the Student

Using this Book

Your instructors may use this book as a basis for class discussions and for various kinds of exercises in writing, or they may simply ask you to buy a copy of the book to use on your own. The *Practical English Handbook*, seventh edition, is designed to be equally useful in class and as a reference book. Either way, you need to know how to use the book. Thumb through it. Consider how it is organized. Use the reference numbers and the index. Learn where you can find the help you need on particular and general problems. As you make plans to write a paper, the following list of sections will be of special help to you:

Selecting a topic	Sections **46a** and **46b,** pp. 260–261
Organizing	Section **46d,** pp. 262–265
Writing and rewriting	Section **46e** and **46f,** pp. 265–280
Avoiding errors in sentences, mechanics, diction, and style	Sections **1–43,** pp. 30–217
Avoiding errors in thinking	Section **44,** pp. 220–228
Check before turning in paper	p. 280

Writing and Revising Papers

Good writers develop a well-planned system of working. Generally, they think hard, search diligently for information, set certain times aside for writing, and shape and reshape their work.

Take your writing seriously. If you write only to satisfy a requirement, your papers probably will lack thoughtfulness and conviction. Earnestness of purpose and true interest show in all types of writing. Conversely, casualness and lack of interest are also easily apparent.

Once you have written the first draft of a paper, study it impersonally and critically as if you were seeing it for the first time. Good writers strive to look at their writing as their readers will see it. Imagine that you are two people—the writer and the stranger who will read what you write. The process of writing involves a series of questions and answers from both perspectives. When you learn to find your own problems and correct them before another reader sees the paper, you will then be well on the way to realizing your full capabilities as a writer.

Give your paper a final check for errors. The value of a clean and correct manuscript is based partly on the impression it conveys. A final draft marred by careless errors bespeaks a sloppy writer (and, by implication, perhaps a fuzzy thinker). If a writer submits a paper that is riddled with the kinds of mistakes proofreading can catch, everything in the paper is questionable.

Whether or not your instructor applies a penalty for late papers, you should allow nothing short of a dire emergency to prevent you from completing and submitting your work on time. By establishing sensible priorities, using what time you do have wisely, and then meeting your responsibilities, you are learning how a mature writer works under pressure. Definite deadlines neither dilute nor destroy the creative impulse.

The process of revising and the act of learning do not come to an end when you submit your paper. Sadly, some students pay little attention to anything on a returned paper but the grade. Most teachers take care to mark strengths and weaknesses on papers, and many write comments in the margins and at the end. Their purpose in doing so is to offer constructive advice about future writing. Learn to accept and use criticism. It can be a valuable tool in helping you improve your writing.

F.C.W.   W.B.D.

PRACTICAL ENGLISH HANDBOOK

Grammar

Anyone who can use a language, who can put words together to communicate ideas—even an illiterate—knows something about grammar without necessarily being aware of it. Grammar is the methodology of the way a language works. It is also the formal study of that system, its laws or rules. For example, a person who says "They are" is using grammar. A person who says that *they* is a plural pronoun and takes the plural verb *are* is using terms of grammar to explain the proper use of the language. The technical study of grammar may be pursued almost for its own sake, for the pleasure of a scholar, a grammarian. Much of this system is helpful in discussions about *how* to speak or to write. It is a tool.

This book introduces a minimum amount of the grammatical system—all that is needed—to develop effective writing and speaking.

The Parts of Speech

Knowing the part of speech of a word may be the most basic aspect of grammar.

The eight parts of speech are **nouns, pronouns, verbs, adjectives, adverbs, conjunctions, prepositions,** and **interjections.** Each of these is explained and illustrated below.

NOTE: Much of the time, the function of a word within a sentence determines what part of speech that word is. For example, a word may be a **noun** in one sentence but an **adjective** in another.

noun
↓
She teaches in a *college.*

adjective
↓
She teaches several *college* courses.

Nouns

Nouns are words that name. They also have various forms which indicate **gender** (sex—masculine, feminine, neuter), **number** (singular, plural), and **case** (see **Glossary of Grammatical Terms**). There are several kinds of nouns.

(a) **Proper nouns** name particular people, places, or things (*Thomas Jefferson, Paris, Superdome*).

   Meet me in *San Francisco* at *Fisherman's Wharf.*

(b) **Common nouns** name one or more of a class or a group (*reader, politician, swimmers*).

   The *women* stared hard and listened intently.

(c) **Collective nouns** name a whole group though they are singular in form (*navy, team, pair*).

   It has been said that an *army* moves on its stomach.

(d) **Abstract nouns** name concepts, beliefs, or qualities (*courage, honor, enthusiasm*).

   Her *love* of *freedom* was no less obvious than her *faithfulness.*

(e) **Concrete nouns** name tangible things perceived through the senses (*rain, bookcase, heat*).

   The *snow* fell in the *forest.*

Pronouns

Most **pronouns** stand for a noun or take the place of a noun. Some pronouns (such as *something, none, anyone*) have general or broad references, and they do not directly take the place of a particular noun.

Pronouns fall into categories which classify both how they stand for nouns and how they function in a sentence. (Some of the words listed below have other uses; that is, they sometimes function as a part of speech other than a pronoun.)

(a) **Demonstrative pronouns** point out (see **demonstrative adjectives,** p. 9). They can be singular (*this, that*) or plural (*these, those*).

demonstrative pronoun
↓

Many varieties of apples are grown here. *These* are winesaps.

(b) **Indefinite pronouns** do not point out a particular person or thing. They are usually singular, though sometimes plural. (See **8d.**) Some of the most common are *some, any, each, everyone, everybody, anyone, anybody, one,* and *neither.*

indefinite pronoun
↓
Everyone knows that happiness is relative.

(c) **Intensive pronouns** end in *-self* (singular) or *-selves* (plural). An intensive pronoun is used to emphasize a word that precedes it in the sentence.

intensive pronoun
↓
The clown *himself* refused to walk the tightrope.

intensive pronoun
↓
I *myself* will carry the message.

(d) **Reflexive pronouns** end in *-self* or *-selves* and indicate that the subject acts upon itself.

reflexive pronouns ————
↓
I hurt *myself.*

Members of an athletic team sometimes defeat *themselves.*

(e) **Interrogative pronouns** are used in asking questions: *who, whom, whose,* and *which. Who* and *whom* combine with *ever: whoever, whomever.*

interrogative pronoun
↓
Who was chosen?

(f) **Personal pronouns** usually refer to a person, sometimes to a thing. (See **9h.**) They have many forms, which depend on their grammatical function.

	SINGULAR	PLURAL
First person	I, me, mine	we, us, ours
Second person	you, yours	you, yours
Third person	he, she, it, his, hers, its	they, them, theirs

(g) **Relative pronouns** are used to introduce dependent adjective or noun clauses: *who, whoever, whom, whomever, that, what, which, whose.* (See **9i** and **7j.**)

relative pronoun
↓
The director could not decide *who* was to act the role of the hero.

They may function as connectives as well as stand for a noun.

relative pronoun—connective
↓
The director said *that* he was resigning.

■ Exercise 1

Identify and distinguish between the nouns and pronouns in the following sentences.

　　　　 P　　　　　　　**N**　　　　　 **N**　　　 **P**
1. Everyone knew the adage but the teacher, and she asked a
　　N　　　　 **P**
   student to recite it.

　　 P　　　　　　　 **P**　　 **N**　 **P**
2. Someone has said that a person who works hard and plays

   little will be dull.

　　　　　　　 N　　　　　　　　　　　　　　　　 **N**
3. Yosemite National Park is far west of the Mississippi River.

　　　　　　 N　　　　 **P**　　 **N**　 **P**
4. The two speakers said that a person who completes
   N　　　　　　　　 **P**　　　　　 **P**　**P**　**P**
   college is educated, but they should have said that one who
　　　　　 N　　　　　　　　　　 **N**
   completes college has been exposed to knowledge.

   P　　　　　　 **P**　 **P**　 **P**　　　 **N**
5. It is also possible that those who go to school for only a few
   N
   years may be intelligent and even learn a great deal by them-

   selves.

Verbs

Verbs can assert an action or express a condition. (See **3.**)

action
↓
Twenty-seven mallards *flew* south.

condition
↓
The twenty-seven birds *were* mallards.

A main verb may have helpers, called **auxiliary verbs,** such as *are, have, will be, do,* and *did.*

auxiliary verb ⟍   ⟋ *main verb*
Twenty-seven mallards *did fly* south.

auxiliary verbs   *main verb*
↙ ↘   ↓
Leif Erickson *may have preceded* Columbus to America.

Linking verbs express condition rather than action: *appear, become, feel, look, seem, smell, sound,* and *taste.* The most common linking verbs, however, are the many forms of the verb *to be (is, are, was, were,* etc.). See p. 404.

linking verb
↓
The child *appeared* joyful in the presence of so many toys.

linking verb
↓
The woman with the wax fruit on her hat *is* not an actress.

Verbs are either **transitive** or **intransitive** (see pp. 47, 404, 406). For **verb tenses,** see **4.** For **verbals,** see pp. 22–23, 407.

■ Exercise 2

Identify the verbs in each of the following sentences.

1. The boys <u>found</u> the long-forgotten recluse's diary.

2. The flight attendant <u>walked</u> among the passengers and <u>looked</u> for the lost purse.

3. The symphony <u>was performed</u> by a renowned orchestra, but the audience <u>was</u> not enthusiastic.

4. Eight of the ten windows and doors <u>were</u> open during the hard rain and strong wind.

5. An appointment with a famous person <u>can be</u> an anxious experience.

Adjectives

Adjectives modify a noun or a pronoun. They limit, qualify, or make more specific the meaning of another word. Generally, they describe. Most adjectives appear before the word they modify.

adjective
↓
Sour apples are often used in cooking.

Predicate adjectives follow linking verbs and modify the noun or pronoun that is the subject of the sentence.

subject   predicate adjective

A nap in the afternoon is *restful.*

The three **articles** (*a, an, the*) are classified as adjectives.

Some **possessive adjectives** have forms which are the same as some possessive pronouns: *her, his, your, its, our, their.* (*Your, our,* and *their* have endings with *-s* in the pronoun form.)

Demonstrative adjectives, which have exactly the same forms as demonstrative pronouns, are used before the nouns they modify.

this dog or *that dog; these dogs* or *those dogs*

Indefinite adjectives have the same form as indefinite pronouns: for example, *some, any, each, every.*

(See **10.**)

Adverbs

Adverbs, like adjectives, describe, qualify, or limit other elements in the sentence. They modify verbs (and verbals), adjectives, and other adverbs.

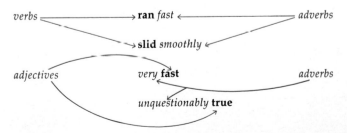

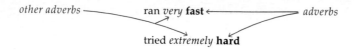

other adverbs ——— ran *very* **fast** ←——————→ *adverbs*

tried *extremely* **hard**

Sometimes adverbs modify an entire clause:

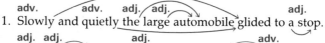

Frankly, *she did not speak the truth.*

Many adverbs end in *-ly (effectively, curiously),* but not all words that end in *-ly* are adverbs *(lovely, friendly).*

Adverbs tell how *(slowly, well);* how much *(extremely, some-what);* how often *(frequently, always);* when *(late, afterward);* where *(there, here).* These are the main functions of adverbs, but not the only ones. Adverbs must be identified by their use in the sentence; that is, they cannot all be memorized. (For a discussion of the degrees of adverbs, see **10.**)

■ Exercise 3

Identify the adverbs and adjectives in the following sentences. Tell what each one modifies. (A, an, *and* the *are adjectives.)*

    adv.   **adv.**   **adj.** **adj.**   **adj.**
1. Slowly and quietly the large automobile glided to a stop.
   adj. **adj.**   **adj.**   **adv.**
2. The huge sign was a warning. "Drive carefully and live
   adj. adj.
   a long time."

            adj.   **adv.**   **adj.**
3. Knowing that all things eventually come to an end, one
              adj.
   should try to profit by every moment of life.

    adj. / adj. / adj. /   adv.   adj.
4. Two small frantic dogs ran quickly over the cloth where

    adj.   adj.   adj.
the food for the afternoon picnic had been spread.

    adj. / adj.   adv.   adj.
5. Many young couples are carefully restoring the beauties of

    adj.   adv.   adv.
old homes which have been almost entirely ignored for

    adj.
many years.

Conjunctions

Conjunctions connect words, phrases, or clauses. They are classified as **coordinating, subordinating,** or **correlative.**

    Coordinating conjunctions connect elements that are—grammatically speaking—of equal rank. Those most frequently used are *and, but, or, nor, for,* and *yet.*

coordinating conjunction

The orchestra played selections from *Brahms, Beethoven,* **and** *Wagner.*

coordinating conjunction

The angry candidate left the podium, **and** *he did not return.*

    Subordinating conjunctions introduce a subordinate or dependent element of a sentence. Examples are *although, because, if, since, though, unless, when, where, while.*

subordinating conjunction

Although *many painters sell their work,* few become wealthy.

Some words (such as *before, after*) may function as conjunctions and also as other parts of speech.

Correlative conjunctions are always used in pairs. Examples are *both . . . and, either . . . or, not only . . . but also, neither . . . nor.* (See **18.**)

correlative conjunctions

Not only a well-balanced diet *but also* adequate sleep is needed for good health.

▨ Exercise 4

Identify all conjunctions in the following sentences, and tell whether each is coordinating or subordinating or correlative.

1. After a tiring night a sentry leaves his post. <u>As</u> he prepares to [subordinating]

   rest, he discards from his memory the long hours
   <u>and</u> the loneliness. [coordinating]

2. <u>When</u> the sun comes up, the world takes on an entirely new [subordinating]

   appearance, <u>and</u> hope seems to bloom again. [coordinating]

3. The ceilings of the old room were high, <u>but</u> the windows [coordinating]

   were narrow, <u>and</u> the wind blew hard <u>and</u> whistled through [coordinating] [coordinating]

   the cracks around the door.

4. <u>After</u> the electricity came on again, the manager discovered [subordinating]

correlative   **correlative**
that <u>neither</u> the meats <u>nor</u> the vegetables were spoiled

coordinating
<u>or</u> even discolored.

      coordinating   **correlative**
5. Inquiries <u>and</u> investigations were conducted <u>not only</u> by

      correlative
agencies of the city <u>but also</u> by representatives of the courts.

Prepositions

Prepositions connect a noun or a pronoun (the **object of the preposition**) to another word in the sentence.

Most prepositions are short single words: *above, across, after, against, along, among, at, before, behind, below, beneath, beside, between, by, from, in, into, of, on, over, through, up, upon, with, without.*

Groups of words may also serve as prepositions: *along with, according to, in spite of.*

A preposition introduces and is part of a group of words, a phrase, that includes an object. The phrase is used as a unit in the sentence, a single part of speech—usually an adjective or an adverb.

above the clouds	*across* the tracks	*after* the game
by the creek	*through* the hallways	*under* the floor

(See **37e** for a discussion of the idiomatic use of prepositions.)

■ Exercise 5

Identify prepositions, objects of prepositions, and prepositional phrases in the following sentences.

   P   **O**   **P**   **O**

1. For several days Achilles sulked in his tent, and then he

   joined the battle.

        P   **O** **P**   **O**   **P**   **O**

2. According to the rules of the game, the contestant at the front

 P   **O**   **P**   **O**

   of the line must turn quickly and race toward the rear.

        P   **O**

3. There on the table was the book the hostess had borrowed

  P   **O**

   from her friend.

       P   **O** **P**   **O**

4. Never in the history of the province had so devastating an

   event occurred.

                         P   **O**   **P**   **O**

5. The guest handed the object to the person on his left.

Interjections

Interjections are words that exclaim; they express surprise or strong emotion. They may stand alone or serve as part of a sentence.

Ouch!
Well, that was a shame.

Because of their nature, interjections are most often used in the spontaneity of speech, not writing, which is generally more planned than exclamatory.

■ Exercise 6

Name the part of speech of each word underlined and numbered in the following sentences.

$$\begin{array}{cccccccc} 1 & 2 & 3 & 4 & 5 & 6 & 7 & 8 & 9 \end{array}$$

<u>Well</u>, <u>questions</u> <u>do</u> <u>not</u> <u>always</u> <u>have</u> <u>answers</u>, <u>but</u> <u>that</u> does not

mean we should stop asking.

$$\begin{array}{cccccc} 10 & 11 & 12 & 13 & 14 & 15 & 16 \ \ 17 \ \ 18 \end{array}$$

<u>In</u> a <u>brown</u> <u>bottle</u>, <u>she</u> <u>discovered</u> a <u>note</u> composed <u>long</u> <u>ago</u> <u>in</u> a

$$\begin{array}{cc} 19 & 20 \end{array}$$

<u>far</u> <u>country</u>.

1. interjection	6. verb	11. adjective	16. adverb
2. noun	7. noun	12. noun	17. adverb
3. verb	8. conjunction	13. pronoun	18. preposition
4. adverb	9. pronoun	14. verb	19. adjective
5. adverb	10. preposition	15. noun	20. noun

The Parts of Sentences

A sentence, a basic unit of language, has a complete meaning of its own. The essential parts of a sentence are a **subject** and a **predicate**.

A **subject** does something, has something done to it, or is identified or described.

subject	*subject*	*subject*
↓	↓	↓
Birds sing.	*Songs* are sung.	*Birds* are beautiful.

A **predicate** expresses something about the subject.

predicate	*predicate*	*predicate*
↓	⌐——⌐	⌐———⌐
Birds *sing.*	Songs *are sung.*	Birds *are beautiful.*

Simple subjects, complete subjects, compound subjects

The essential element of a subject is called the **simple subject.** Usually it consists of a single word.

simple subject
↓
The large *balloon* burst.

The subject may be understood rather than actually stated. A director of a chorus might say "Sing," meaning, "You sing." But here one spoken word would be a complete sentence.

understood subject   predicate
↘   ↙
[You] sing.

All the words that form a group and function together as the subject of a sentence are called the **complete subject.**

complete subject
┌─────────┴─────────┐
The large balloon burst.

(When any similar units of a sentence—subjects, verbs, adjectives—are linked together and function together, they are said to be **compound.**)

compound subject
↙   ↘
The large *balloons* and the small *bubbles* burst.

Of course pronouns as well as nouns may make up compound subjects.

compound pronoun subject
↓   ↙
She and *I* sang.

■ **Exercise 7**

Identify the subjects and the complete subjects. Tell whether each sentence has a single subject or a compound subject.

s   1. In the middle of the campus stood a tall, beautiful tower.

s   2. Swimming against the current, the otter returned to her young.

s   3. The workers, distracted from their tasks, laid down their tools and stared.

c   4. The George Washington Bridge and the Golden Gate Bridge are both well known.

s   5. All the slender trees swayed gracefully in the wind.

Simple predicates, complete predicates, compound predicates

The single verb (or the main verb and its auxiliary verbs) is the **simple predicate.**

simple predicate
↓
Balloons *soar.*

simple predicate
Balloons *are soaring.*

The simple predicate, its modifiers, and any complements form a group that is called the **complete predicate.**

complete predicate

Balloons *soared over the pasture.*

When two verbs in the predicate express actions or conditions of a subject, they are a **compound predicate**—just as two nouns may be a **compound subject.**

compound predicate

Balloons *soar and burst.*

compound predicate

Balloons *soared over the pasture and then burst.*

(For errors in predication, see **15.**)

■ **Exercise 8**

Identify the verbs (including auxiliaries) and the complete predicates. Tell whether each sentence has a single verb or a compound verb.

C 1. The scientist left the laboratory and walked to the library.

S 2. All day long the caravan moved through long valleys and over steep hills.

S 3. Build beautiful and lasting buildings.

C 4. People of wisdom exercise their bodies and use their minds.

C 5. A good writer frequently composes a first draft, revises it, and then revises again.

Complements

Complements, usually a part of the predicate, complete the meaning of the sentence. They are nouns, pronouns, or adjectives. They function as predicate adjectives or predicate nominatives (both sometimes called **subjective complements**) and direct or indirect objects.

Predicate adjectives

A **predicate adjective** follows a linking verb and modifies the subject, not the verb.

```
             linking
   subject   verb    predicate adjective
      ↓        ↓            ↓
The boots    were       muddy.
```

Predicate nominatives

Predicate nominatives follow linking verbs and rename the subject. (Compare **predicate adjectives** above and **appositives,** p. 400.)

```
           predicate
           nominative
              ↓
Bears are omnivores.
```

Direct objects

A **direct object** receives the action indicated by a transitive verb. Naturally, it is always in the objective case. See **9.**

```
    verb  direct object
     ↓      ↓
Bears eat honey.
```

Indirect objects

An **indirect object** receives the action of the verb indirectly. The subject (through the verb) acts on the direct object, which in turn has an effect on the indirect object (that is, *it is given to,* or *it is done for*).

	indirect	*direct*
verb	*object*	*object*
↓	↓	↓

Rangers *fed*   the *bears honey.*

The sentence can be rearranged to read

			indirect
verb	*object*	*understood*	*object*
↓	↓	↓	↓

Rangers *fed honey*   [to]   the *bears.*

When the preposition (*to,* as above, or *for*) is understood, the word is an indirect object. When the preposition is expressed, the word is an object of a preposition:

prepositional phrase

preposition   object of preposition
↓   ↓

Rangers fed honey *to* the *bears.*

(Grammatically the sentence above has no indirect object.)

Objective complements accompany direct objects. They may modify the object or be synonymous with it.

The editor considered the manuscript *publishable.*

The corporation named a former clerk its *president.*

■ Exercise 9

Underline and identify the predicate adjectives, predicate nominatives, direct objects, and indirect objects in the following sentences.

                                     DO

1. The librarian suggested a <u>book</u> which was a popular
   PN
   <u>autobiography</u>.

              PA   **IO**   **DO**

2. The brick wall was <u>high</u>, but my friend threw <u>me</u> an <u>apple</u>

   straight over the top.

              PA   **PA**

3. Good peaches are <u>sweet</u> and <u>juicy</u>.

    IO   **DO**   **DO**

4. Give each of the men and the women a <u>book</u> and a <u>candle</u>

                DO   **DO**

5. Whoever wins the <u>contest</u> will receive a <u>trophy</u>.

Phrases

A **phrase** is a cluster of words that does not have both a subject and a predicate. Some important kinds of phrases are **verb phrases, prepositional phrases,** and **verbal phrases.**

Verb phrases

The main verb and its auxiliary verbs are called a **verb phrase:** *were sitting, shall be going, are broken, may be considered. Were, shall be, are, may be,* and verbs like them are often auxiliary verbs (sometimes called ''helping'' verbs).

               verb phrase
       ┌─────┴─────┐

The bear *had been eating* the honey.

Prepositional phrases

Prepositional phrases function as adjectives or adverbs.

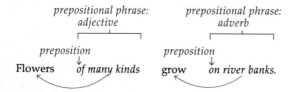

prepositional phrase: adjective

preposition

prepositional phrase: adverb

preposition

Flowers *of many kinds* grow *on river banks.*

Verbals and verbal phrases

A **verbal** is a grammatical form derived from a verb. No verbal is a complete verb. It may have an object and modifiers. (Adverbs modify verbals as they modify verbs.) A verbal and the words associated with it compose a **verbal phrase.**

There are three kinds of verbals: **gerunds, participles,** and **infinitives.** A gerund is always a noun; a participle is an adjective; an infinitive may be either a noun, an adjective, or an adverb, depending on its use in the sentence.

GERUNDS AND GERUND PHRASES

Gerunds always end in *-ing* and function as nouns.

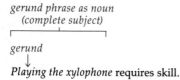

gerund phrase as noun
   (complete subject)

gerund

Playing the xylophone requires skill.

PARTICIPLES AND PARTICIPIAL PHRASES

Participles usually end in *-ing* or *-ed* (there are many irregular forms also) and always function as adjectives.

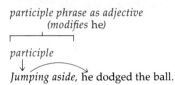

participle phrase as adjective
(modifies he*)*

participle

Jumping aside, he dodged the ball.

INFINITIVES AND INFINITIVE PHRASES

Infinitives begin with *to,* which may be understood rather than actually stated. They may be used as nouns, adjectives, or adverbs.

USED AS NOUN

infinitive phrase
used as subject

infinitive

To rescue the swimmer was easy.

USED AS ADJECTIVE

infinite phrase
modifies book *(noun)*

infinitve

Charlotte's Web is a good book *to read to a child.*

USED AS ADVERB

infinitive phrase
modifies eager *(adjective)*

infinitive

The novelist was eager *to read a story.*

■ Exercise 10

Identify phrases in the following sentences and tell what kind each is —infinitive, gerund, participle, preposition, or verb.

       gerund
1. Building the pyramids was an astonishing feat.

   participle   prepositional
2. Working through the night, they completed the musical score
  infinitive   prepositional
to be included in the play.

         verb   prepositional
3. Though she had been visiting the resort for many years, she

still enjoyed its pleasures.

   gerund   prepositional
4. Taking the census in modern times is not as simple as it was

two thousand years ago.

   participle   verb
5. Insisting that his vegetables had been grown organically, the
         infinitive   prepositional
gardener refused to sell them at a lower price.

Clauses

A **clause** is a group of words with a subject and a predicate. There are two kinds of clauses: **independent** and **dependent** (or **subordinate**).

Independent clauses

An **independent clause** can stand alone; grammatically it is like a complete sentence. Two or more independent clauses in one sentence may be joined by coordinating conjunctions, conjunctive adverbs, semicolons, and other grammatical devices or punctuation marks.

Some birds soar, but others must constantly beat their wings while in flight.
Some birds soar; others must constantly beat their wings while in flight.

Dependent clauses or subordinate clauses

Like verbals, **dependent clauses** function as three different parts of speech in a sentence: nouns, adjectives, and adverbs. Unlike independent clauses, dependent clauses do not express a complete thought in themselves.

DEPENDENT CLAUSE NOT IN COMPLETE SENTENCE
When the auction began.

USED AS NOUN (usually subject or object)
That the little child could read rapidly was well known.
   (noun clause used as subject)

The other students knew *that the little child could read rapidly.*
   (noun clause used as direct object)

USED AS ADJECTIVE

Everyone *who completed the race* won a shirt.
(modifying pronoun subject)

USED AS ADVERB

When spring comes many flowers bloom.
(modifying verb)

The Kinds of Sentences

A **simple sentence** has only one independent clause (but no dependent clause). A simple sentence is not necessarily a short sentence; it may contain several phrases.

Birds sing.
After a long silence, *the bird began to warble a sustained and beautiful*

song.

A **compound sentence** has two or more independent clauses (but no dependent clause).

independent clause   *independent clause*

Birds sing, and bees hum.

A **complex sentence** has both an independent clause and one or more dependent clauses.

dependent clause   *independent clause*
When spring comes and [when] new leaves grow, migratory birds return

north.

A **compound-complex** sentence has at least two independent clauses and at least one dependent clause. A dependent clause may be part of an independent clause.

*dependent adverb   independent   dependent noun clause
— clause —   — clause —   used as object*
— independent clause —
When heavy rains come, the streams rise; and farmers know that there

will be floods.

26   Grammar

■ Exercise 11

Underline each clause. Tell whether it is dependent or independent. Tell the use of each dependent clause in the sentence. Tell whether each sentence is simple, compound, complex, or compound-complex.

1. People in some towns are awakened in the morning when a
factory whistle blows to signal the change in a shift of
workers.

    complex / independent / dependent-adverb

2. Moving down the hills and around the curves, the procession
of cars was not able to proceed faster than twenty miles an
hour.

    simple / independent

3. That she had paid the five-dollar debt was proved beyond
doubt, so her friend apologized and bought her a red rose.

    compound-complex / dependent / independent / independent

4. The students who are straggling up the steps seem reluctant,
but they are really hoping that they will be allowed to enter
the museum.

    compound-complex / dependent / independent / independent / dependent / independent

5. The visitor politely asked to be allowed to speak, and the
moderator agreed.

    compound / independent / independent

Sentence Errors

1   Sentence Fragment   *frag*

Write complete sentences.

Fragments are parts of sentences written and punctuated as complete sentences. They may be dependent clauses, phrases, or any other word groups that violate the accepted subject-verb sentence pattern.

Notice how the fragments below are revised and made into complete sentences.

FRAGMENT (phrases)
Fear of heights, one of the most common phobias.

COMPLETE SENTENCE (verb added)
Fear of heights is one of the most common phobias.

FRAGMENT (dependent clause)
Although some graduates are well trained in the techniques used by debaters.

COMPLETE SENTENCE (dependent conjunction *although* omitted)
Some graduates are well trained in the techniques used by debaters.

FRAGMENT (noun and phrase—no main verb)
The green fields humming with sounds of insects.

COMPLETE SENTENCE (modifier *humming* changed to verb *hummed*)
The green fields hummed with sounds of insects.

Fragments are often permissible in dialogue when the meaning is clear.

"See the geese."
"Where?"
"Flying north."

Fragments are occasionally used for special effects or emphasis.

The long journey down the river was especially pleasant. A time of rest and tranquility.

■ Exercise 1

Make the following fragments complete sentences by deleting one word, adding one word or a verb phrase, changing one word, attaching a fragment to a sentence, or rewriting.

1. The various colors and designs of academic regalia revealing-ed

    the wearers' schools, degrees, and fields of learning.

2. ~~That~~ the bald eagle flies high over the mountaintops looking

    for prey.

3. An empty attic and an uncluttered basement suggest~~ive of~~ a

    life without a meaningful past.

4. ~~Because~~ learning may begin when one first understands that

    there is a problem to be solved.

5. The young artist ~~who~~ won first prize in the autumn exhibit of

    watercolors.

The o

6. Øffice furniture ~~that~~ is attractive and innovative.
   ⌃

7. Lakes provide a wide range of recreation. Wading, swim-   **, including w**
   ⌃

   ming, fishing, boating.

8. Meadows of deep green grass, hills with trees soaring almost

   into the white clouds, one superhighway, and a small dirt

   road─╱─a landscape of contradictions.   **make up**
   ⌃

9. ~~The fact that~~ writing appears in print considered authorita-   **Because**   **, it is**
   ⌃

   tive and accurate.

10. Although the range of her voice was limited. She had perfect   **, s**
    ⌃

    pitch.

2   Comma Splice and Fused Sentence   cs/fus

Join two independent clauses clearly and appropriately, or
write two separate sentences.

A **comma splice** or **comma fault** occurs when independent
clauses have a comma between them but no coordinating conjunction.

SPLICE OR FAULT
Human nature is seldom as simple as it appears, hasty judgments are
     therefore often wrong.

A **fused sentence** or **run-on sentence** occurs when the independent clauses have neither punctuation nor coordinating conjunctions between them.

FUSED OR RUN-ON

Human nature is seldom as simple as it appears hasty judgments are therefore often wrong.

Comma splices and fused sentences fail to indicate the break between independent clauses. Revise in one of the following ways:

1. Use a *period* and write two sentences.

Human nature is seldom as simple as it appears. Hasty judgments are therefore often wrong.

2. Use a *semicolon.* (See also **22.**)

Human nature is seldom as simple as it appears; hasty judgments are therefore often wrong.

Before *conjunctive adverbs* (see **20f** and **22a**) use a *semicolon* to join *independent clauses.*

The rare book had a torn flyleaf; *therefore,* it was advertised at a reduced price.

3. Use a *comma* and a *coordinating conjunction (and, but, or, nor, for, yet, so).* (See also **20a.**)

Human nature is seldom as simple as it appears, *so* hasty judgments are often wrong.

4. Use a *subordinating conjunction* (see pp. 11–12, 406) and a *dependent clause.*

Because *human nature is seldom as simple as it appears,* hasty judgments are often wrong.

■ **Exercise 2**

Identify (with CS or FS) and correct comma splices and fused sentences. Write C by correct sentences.

CS 1. Television sometimes offers worthwhile programs as well as
             and *or*. It *or*;
    trivia, it should not be condemned entirely.
         ^

C 2. After twelve years of silence, the composer finished two
    symphonies within six months.

                                      ;
FS 3. Conflicts almost always exist within a family however, it is
                                        ^
    still the most enduring of social units.

                                ; *or*. A *or* , and
FS 4. One ancient culture practiced the art of carving masks an-
                                       ^
    other expressed itself creatively by weaving elaborate tapes-
    tries.

FS 5. It is necessary to love roses in order to cultivate them success-
           . T *or* ;
    fully the gardener must have roses in the heart as well as in
      ^
    the garden.

■ **Exercise 3**

Identify each of the following as correct (C), a comma splice (CS), a fused sentence (FS), or a fragment (F).

CS 1. Vitamins are necessary for health, however, excessive amounts of some of them are dangerous.

C 2. Vitamins are necessary for health; however, excessive amounts of some of them are dangerous.

FS 3. Vitamins are necessary for health however, excessive amounts of some of them are dangerous.

F 4. Vitamins are necessary for health. Excessive amounts of some of them, however, dangerous.

C 5. Vitamins are necessary for health, but excessive amounts of some of them are dangerous.

▨ Exercise 4

Identify fragments (F), comma splices (CS), or fused sentences (FS) and correct them. Write C by correct sentences.

CS 1. Economy is a virtue up to a point, $\overset{; or. B or, but}{\wedge}$ beyond that it may become a vice.

C 2. Destroyers uproot trees and move vast quantities of earth but do not replace the soil.

C 3. Fresh seafood is plentiful even in inland cities; it can be flown in from the coasts without ever being frozen.

FS 4. Styles of clothing are not always planned for comfort $\overset{; or. B}{\wedge}$ belts and seams may be designed to look good rather than to fit natural contours of the body.

F 5. Paperback novels once cost so little that they were thrown away. Now $\overset{they\ are}{\wedge}$ often a permanent part of the home library.

C 6. New York's Washington Square has changed considerably since it was a haven for writers in the 1890s.

F 7. In remote villages on the seacoast, ~~where~~ the primitive beauty of nature survives.

FS 8. New buildings are springing up all over the city the skyline is
                                ; or. **A** *or,* **and**   *; or.* **T** *or,* **and**
rapidly changing.

C 9. For many, swimming is more pleasant than jogging, especially when the weather is hot.

CS 10. An adventurer will sometimes participate in a pastime de-
                       ; or . **S**
spite great danger/ sky diving, for example, is perilous.

■ **Exercise 5**

Follow the instructions for Exercise 4.

FS 1. In some parts of the world marriages are still arranged by
                ; (preferable) or . **C** *or,* **and**
parents consequently practical matters take precedence over love.

                                         ; or . **S** *or,* **so**
CS 2. After all, the student argued, any imbecile can punctuate,
studying the mechanics of composition is a complete waste of time.

CS 3. Most generous people are naive, $\overset{\text{; }or\text{ . T}}{\wedge}$ they simply do not realize

when they are being imposed upon.

F 4. Some say that nonconformity has become a fad/ $\overset{\text{, n}}{\text{Non-}}$
or rewrite: **Some say that nonconformity for its own sake has become a fad.**
conformity for its own sake.

CS 5. Science and art are not incompatible, $\overset{\text{; }or\text{ . S }or\text{ , and}}{\wedge}$ some learned scientists

are also philosophers or poets.   **(comma optional)**

F 6. The art of pleasing is very necessary/ $\overset{\text{, b}}{\text{But}}$ difficult to acquire.

FS 7. Kindness can hardly be reduced to rules $\overset{\text{. G }or\text{ ;}}{\wedge}$ good will and

thoughtfulness will lead to congenial relationships with

others.

C 8. Writing on a blackboard frequently creates a scraping sound

that causes an unpleasant sensation.

FS 9. Some hobbies are for rich people $\overset{\text{. O }or\text{ ;}}{\wedge}$ only the wealthy can collect

diamonds.

CS 10. Fossils and oil are often found in cold regions where ice and

snow never entirely melt. $\overset{\text{,e}}{\wedge}$ Evidence that the climate and the

earth change drastically over long periods of time.
or rewrite: **Finding fossils and oil in cold regions where ice and
snow never entirely melt proves that the climate and the earth
change drastically over long periods of time.**

3 Verb Forms vb

Use the correct form of the verb.

All verbs have three principal parts: the present infinitive, the past tense, and the past participle. Verbs are regular or irregular.

Regular verbs form the past tense and the past participle by adding *-d* or *-ed* or sometimes *-t*. If only the infinitive form is given in a dictionary, the verb is regular.

INFINITIVE	PAST TENSE	PAST PARTICIPLE
close	closed	closed
dwell	dwelled, dwelt	dwelled, dwelt
help	helped	helped
open	opened	opened
talk	talked	talked

Irregular verbs usually form the past tense and the past participle by changing an internal vowel. For irregular verbs a dictionary gives the three principal parts and also the present participle. For *see*, the dictionary lists *see, saw, seen,* and *seeing*. For *think*, it shows *think, thought* (for past and past participle), and *thinking* (the present participle). The present and past participial forms always have auxiliary (helping) verbs (see p. 7).

Know the following irregular verbs so well that you automatically use them correctly.

INFINITIVE	PAST TENSE	PAST PARTICIPLE
awake	awoke, awaked	awoke, awaked
be	was	been
begin	began	begun
bid (to offer as a price or to make a bid in playing cards)	bid	bid

INFINITIVE	PAST TENSE	PAST PARTICIPLE
bid (to command, order)	bade, bid	bidden, bid
blow	blew	blown
bring	brought	brought
build	built	built
burst	burst	burst
choose	chose	chosen
come	came	come
deal	dealt	dealt
dig	dug	dug
dive	dived, dove	dived
do	did	done
drag	dragged	dragged
draw	drew	drawn
drink	drank	drunk
drive	drove	driven
drown	drowned	drowned
fly	flew	flown
freeze	froze	frozen
give	gave	given
go	went	gone
grow	grew	grown
know	knew	known
lead	led	led
lend	lent	lent
lose	lost	lost
ring	rang	rung
run	ran	run
see	saw	seen
sing	sang	sung
sink	sank, sunk	sunk
slay	slew	slain
sting	stung	stung
swim	swam	swum
swing	swung	swung
take	took	taken
teach	taught	taught
think	thought	thought
throw	threw	thrown
wear	wore	worn
write	wrote	written

Some verb forms are especially troublesome. *Lie* is confused with *lay; sit,* with *set;* and *rise,* with *raise.*

Lie, sit, and *rise* are intransitive (do not take objects) and have the vowel *i* in the infinitive form and the present tense.

Lay, set, and *raise* are transitive (take objects) and have *a, e,* or *ai* as vowels.

TRANSITIVE	lay (to place)	laid	laid
INTRANSITIVE	lie (to recline)	lay	lain
TRANSITIVE	set (to place)	set	set
INTRANSITIVE	sit (to be seated)	sat	sat

In special meanings the verb *set* is intransitive (a hen *sets;* the sun *sets;* and so forth).

TRANSITIVE	raise (to lift)	raised	raised
INTRANSITIVE	rise (to get up)	rose	risen

■ Exercise 6

*Underline the incorrect verb and write the correct form above it. Write **C** by correct sentences.*

1. The lake had froze over, and the ice gleamed on the surface. **[frozen]**

2. The character in the story slowly lies the book on the floor **[lays]** and raises majestically to her feet. **[rises]**

3. Before the cement could sit, someone written a name in it. **[set] [wrote]**

4. The swimmer dove in the pond before anyone ~~spoken~~ **spoke** a

   warning.

5. The passenger ~~give~~ **gave** a tip to the cab driver, who frowned and
   ~~sunk~~ **sank** in his seat.

6. One person ~~bidded~~ **bid** fifteen dollars, and then another ~~setting~~ **sitting**
   in the front row ~~bidded~~ **bid** twenty.

7. The young woman raised the steaming coffee to her lips and
   ~~drunk~~ **drank** it quickly.

C 8. The artist laid the brush on the stand just after he had

   painted the portrait, and it has been lying there ever since.

9. The carpenter promised to ~~sit~~ **set** the bucket on the tile, but it has
   been ~~setting~~ **sitting** on the carpet for a week.

10. The balloon which ~~hanged~~ **hung** over the doorway suddenly
    ~~bursted~~ **burst**.

4 | Tense and Sequence of Tenses   *t / seq*

Use appropriate forms of verbs and verbals to express sequence. Avoid confusing shifts in tense.

The present tense expresses an action or condition occurring in the present time; the past, an action or condition that occurred in the past but is now completed; the future, an action or condition expected to occur in future time.

4a Tense forms

For each kind of time—present, past, and future—verbs have a different form: simple, progressive, and perfect.[1]

SIMPLE	REGULAR	IRREGULAR
Present	I walk	I go
Past	I walked	I went
Future	I shall (will) walk	I shall (will) go

PROGRESSIVE		
Present	I am walking	I am going
Past	I was walking	I was going
Future	I shall (will) be walking	I shall (will be) going

PERFECT		
Present	I have walked	I have gone
Past	I had walked	I had gone
Future	I shall (will) have walked	I shall (will) have gone

4b Consistency (see 15)

Relationships between verbs should be consistent:

---

[1] There are in addition the emphatic forms with the auxiliary *do* or *did* (I *do go* there regularly).

TWO PAST ACTIONS

The sailor *stood* on the shore and *threw* shells at the seagulls. (not *throws*)
He *turned* away when he *saw* me watching him.

TWO PRESENT ACTIONS

As the school year *draws* to a close, the students *are swept* into a whirl of
activities.

4c Special uses of the present tense

In general, the present tense or the present progressive expresses
present time, but there are exceptions:

TO EXPRESS FUTURE ACTION

The plane *leaves* for New York tomorrow. (present tense—future action)
The plane *is leaving* in ten minutes. (present progressive tense—future
action)

TO MAKE STATEMENTS ABOUT THE CONTENT OF LITERATURE AND
OTHER WORKS OF ART (HISTORICAL PRESENT). (See **15** and **47D**.)

In Henry James's *The Turn of the Screw,* a governess *believes* that the
ghosts are real.

TO EXPRESS TIMELESS TRUTHS

In 1851, Foucault proved that the earth rotates on its axis.

BUT

Ancient Greeks *believed* that the earth *was* motionless.

4d Perfect tenses

The three perfect tenses indicate one time or action completed before another.

PRESENT PERFECT WITH PRESENT
I *have bought* my ticket, and I **am waiting** for the bus.

The controlling time word may not be a verb.

I *have bought* my ticket **already.**

PAST PERFECT WITH PAST
I *had bought* my ticket, and I **was waiting** for the bus.
I *had bought* my ticket before the bus **came.**

FUTURE PERFECT WITH FUTURE
I *shall have eaten* by the time we **go.** (The controlling word, *go,* is present
    tense in form but future in meaning.)
I *shall have eaten* by **one o'clock.**

The future perfect is rare. Usually the simple future tense is used
with an adverb phrase or clause.

RARE
I shall have eaten before you go.

MORE COMMON
I shall eat before you go.

4e   Verbals and sequence

An infinitive (see p. 23) generally takes the present tense when it
expresses action which occurs at the same time as that of the controlling verb.

NOT
I wanted *to have gone.*

BUT
I wanted *to go.*

NOT
I had expected *to have met* my friends at the game.

BUT
I had expected *to meet* my friends at the game.

NOT
I would have preferred *to have waited* until they came.

BUT
I would have preferred *to wait* until they came.

The perfect participle expresses an action which precedes another action.

Having finished the manuscript, the aged author stored it away in her safe.

■ Exercise 7

Underline the incorrect verb or verbal and write the correction above it. Write C by correct sentences.

1. In looking back, public officials almost always say they
   to remain
   would have preferred to have remained private citizens.
                                         began or opens and begins
2. The actor opened the Bible and begins reading the Song of

   Solomon.

3. It was Goethe's feeling that genius **is** ~~was~~ simply "consummate industry."

4. Joseph Conrad was well into his thirties before **he began** ~~having begun~~ to write his novels.

5. In the old silent film, the comedian walks under a ladder and a bucket of paint **falls** ~~fell~~ on his head.

6. In Gerôme's painting "The Cadet," the young man **has** ~~had~~ a slight sneer on his face.

c 7. The fall semester begins this year in August.

8. Having written his paper, the author placed his pen on the table and **contemplated** ~~contemplates~~ what he **had** ~~has~~ said.

9. The heroine **is** ~~was~~ young throughout the novel.

10. Several years ago baseball batters demonstrated that aluminum bats **are** ~~were~~ usable.

5

Voice   _vo_

Use the active voice for conciseness and emphasis.

A transitive verb is either active or passive. (An intransitive verb does not have voice.) When the subject acts, the verb is active. In most sentences the actor is more important than the receiver.

PASSIVE   The entire book was read by only half the class.

USE THE ACTIVE   Only half the class read the entire book.

PASSIVE   Satisfactory solutions for economic problems are being sought by the governor.

USE THE ACTIVE   The governor is seeking satisfactory solutions for economic problems.

In the sentences above, the active voice creates a more vigorous style.

When the subject is acted upon, the verb is passive. A passive verb may be useful when the performer of an action is unknown or unimportant.

The book about motorcycles *was misplaced* among books about cosmetics.

The passive voice can also be effective when the emphasis is on the receiver, the verb, or even a modifier:

The police *were* totally *misled*

■ **Exercise 8**

Rewrite the following sentences. Change the voice from passive to active.

    The birds ate
    t
1. The insects which were destroying the leaves of the plants

~~were eaten by birds.~~

                  W

2. ~~The trucks were finally loaded by~~ Workers who used fork-
finally loaded the trucks.
lifts⟋

                                          The

3. ~~Some ancient objects of art were discovered by~~ The amateur
                discovered some ancient objects of art.
archaeologist⟋

  The reporter   **the road**

4. ~~The road~~ had ~~been~~ traveled⌃many times⸴ ~~by the reporter⸴~~ but
she   **the old house**
~~the old house~~ had never before ~~been~~ noticed ~~by her~~.

                     T   **had a safe trip**

5. ~~A safe trip was had by~~ The tourists⌃because ~~the dangers were~~
                       carefully explained the dangers.
~~carefully explained by~~ the guide⟋⌃

■ Exercise 9

*Change the voice of the verb when it is ineffective. Rewrite the sen-
tence if necessary. Write E by sentences in which the verb is effective.*

         T   **brought a worm**

1. ~~A worm was brought by~~ The mother bird⌃to feed its young.

E 2. Some young people are learning the almost lost art of black-

    smithing and shoeing horses.

E 3. The horse lost the race because the shoe was improperly

    nailed to the hoof.

                                    M

4. ~~Sharp curves are not well negotiated by~~ Many beginning
           do not negotiate sharp curves well.
drivers⌃

The gardener did not properly care for the rare plants.
5. ~~The rare plants were not properly cared for by the gardener.~~

   Subjunctive Mood   *mo*

Use the subjunctive mood to express wishes, orders, and conditions contrary to fact. (See **Mood,** p. 404.)

WISHES
I wish I *were* a little child.

ORDERS
The instructions were that ten sentences *be* revised.

CONDITIONS CONTRARY TO FACT
If I *were* a little child, I would have no responsibilities.
If I *were* you, I would not go.
Had the weather *been* good, we would have gone to the top of the mountain.

Often in modern English other constructions are used instead of the subjunctive, which survives mainly as a custom in some expressions:

SUBJUNCTIVE
The new manager requested that ten apartments *be* remodeled.

SUBJUNCTIVE NOT USED
The new manager decided to have ten apartments remodeled.

■ **Exercise 10**

Change the mood of the verbs to subjunctive when appropriate in the following sentences. Put a check by those sentences which already use the correct subjunctive.

             were
1. If this silver dollar ~~was~~ more worn, it would feel entirely

   smooth.

✓ 2. This coin would be worth more money if it were not smooth.

                          were
3. The coin dealer wishes that the ancient coin ~~was~~ less worn.

✓ 4. The dealer required that the catalog be reprinted.

✓ 5. He demanded that his money be refunded because he be-

   lieved that the coin was a fake.

7   Subject and Verb: Agreement   *agr*

Use singular verbs with singular subjects, plural verbs with plural subjects.

The *-s* or *-es* ending of the present tense of a verb in the third person *(she talks, he wishes)* indicates the singular. (The *-s* or *-es* ending for most *nouns* indicates the plural.)

SINGULAR	PLURAL
The dog barks.	The dogs bark.
The ax cuts.	The axes cut.

7a A compound subject (see p. 16) with *and* takes a plural verb.

Work and play **are** not equally rewarding.

Golf and polo **are** usually outdoor sports.

EXCEPTION: Compound subjects connected by *and* but expressing a singular idea take a singular verb.

A gentleman and a scholar **is** a man of manners and breadth.

When the children are in bed, *the tumult and shouting* **dies**.

7b After a compound subject with *or, nor, either . . . or, neither . . . nor, not . . . but,* the verb agrees in number and person with the nearer part of the subject. (See **8b**).

NUMBER
Neither the *consumer* nor the *producer* **is** pleased by higher taxes.

Either *fans* or an *air conditioner* **is** necessary.

Either an *air conditioner* or *fans* **are** necessary.

PERSON
Neither *you* nor your *successor* **is** affected by the new regulation.

7c Intervening phrases or clauses do not affect the number of a verb.

Connectives like *as well as* and *along with* are not coordinating conjunctions but prepositions which take objects; they do not form compound subjects. Other such words and phrases include *in addition to, together with, with, plus,* and *including.*

SINGULAR SUBJECT, INTERVENING PHRASE, SINGULAR VERB

The *pilot* as well as all his passengers *was* rescued.

Written with a coordinating conjunction, the sentence takes a plural verb.

The *pilot* **and** his *passengers were* rescued.

7d A collective noun takes a singular verb when referring to a group as a unit, a plural verb when the members of a group are thought of individually.

A collective noun names a class or group: *family, flock, jury, congregation.* When the group is regarded as a unit, use the singular.

The *audience* at a concert sometimes **determines** the length of a performance.

When the group is regarded as separate individuals, use the plural.

The *audience* at a concert **have** varying reactions to the music.

7e Most nouns plural in form but singular in meaning take a singular verb.

Economics and *news* are considered singular.

Economics **is** often thought of as a science.

The *news* of the defeat **is** disappointing.

Trousers and *scissors* are treated as plural except when used after *pair*.

The *trousers* **are** unpressed and frayed.

An old *pair* of jeans **is** sometimes stylish.

The *scissors* **are** dull.

That *pair* of scissors **is** dull.

Similar nouns are *measles, politics,* and *athletics.* When in doubt, consult a dictionary.

7f Indefinite pronouns (*each, either, neither, one, no one, everyone, someone, anyone, nobody, everybody, somebody, anybody*) usually take singular verbs.

Neither of his essays **was** acceptable.

Everybody **has** trouble choosing a subject for an essay.

Each student **has** chosen a subject for the essay.

7g Some words such as *none, some, part, all, half* (and other fractions) take a singular or a plural verb, depending on the noun or pronoun which follows.

singular

Some of the *sugar* **was** spilled on the floor.

plural

Some of the *apples* **were** spilled on the floor.

singular

Half of the *money* **is** yours.

plural

Half of the *students* **are** looking out the window.

When *none* can be regarded as either singular or plural, a singular or plural verb may be used.

plural   *singular*

None of the *roads* **are** closed. **OR** *None* of the *roads* **is** closed.

The number is usually singular:

singular

The number of people in the audience **was** never determined.

A number when used to mean *some* is always plural.

plural

A number of the guests **were** whispering.

7h In sentences beginning with *there* or *here* followed by verb and subject, the verb is singular or plural depending on the subject.

There and *Here* (never subjects of a sentence) are sometimes **expletives** used when the subject follows the verb.

There **was** a long *interval* between the two discoveries.

There **were** thirteen *blackbirds* perched on the fence.

Here **is** a *thing* to remember.

Here **are** two *things* to remember.

The singular *There is* may introduce a compound subject when the first noun is singular.

There is *a swing* and *a footbridge* in the garden.

In sentences beginning with *It,* the verb is always singular.

It **was** many years ago.

7i A verb agrees with its subject, not with a predicate nominative or predicate adjective.

NO

His horse and *his dog* **are** his main source of pleasure.

NO

His main *source* of pleasure **is** his horse and his dog.

7j   After a relative pronoun *(who, which, that)* the verb has the same person and number as the antecedent.

antecedent ⟶ *relative pronoun* ⟶ *verb of relative pronoun*

We →*who* →**are** about to die salute you.

The *costumes which* **were** worn in the ballet were dazzling.

He was the *candidate who* **was** able to carry out his pledges.

He was one of the *candidates who* **were** able to carry out their pledges.

BUT

He was *the* only *one* of the candidates *who* **was** able to carry out his pledges.

7k   A title or a word used as a word is singular and requires a singular verb even if it contains plural words and plural ideas.

The Canterbury Tales **is** a masterpiece of comedy.

''Prunes and Prisms'' **was** a syndicated newspaper column on grammar and usage.

Hiccups **is** a word that imitates the sound it represents.

7L   Expressions of time, money, measurement, and so forth take a singular verb when the amount is considered a unit.

Two tons **is** a heavy load for a small truck.

Forty-eight hours **is** a long time to go without sleep.

■ Exercise 11

Correct any verb which does not agree with its subject. Write C by a correct sentence.

1. The sound of hammers mingle ^s with the screech of seagulls and the crash of waves on the beach.

2. In O'Neill's *Long Day's Journey into Night,* Mary's smiles and laughter ~~is~~ **are** increasingly forced, her resentment is more obvious, and her journey into night is more plainly marked.

3. *The Aspern Papers* deal ^s with the subject of the right of privacy.

C 4. A large number of students are now moving away from housing provided by universities and colleges.

5. Some of the tailors ~~is~~ **are** unhappy with the scissors that cuts poorly.

6. Ethics ~~are~~ **is** the study of moral philosophy and standards of conduct.

7. Molasses ~~were~~ **was** used in a great number of early New England recipes.

8. This tribal custom is enforced by strict taboos, the violation of
   which bring ostracism.

(s inserted above: bring → brings)

9. Childish sentences or dull writing ~~are~~ **is** not improved by a
   sprinkling of dashes.

10. Neither money nor power ~~satisfy~~ **satisfies** the deepest human needs
    of those who seek to fulfill themselves.

■ **Exercise 12**

Follow the instructions for Exercise 11.

1. For a certain kind of American, a vacation of at least two
   weeks ~~have~~ **has** come to be looked upon as a panacea.

2. All year long, the worker who is shackled to his job ~~look~~ **looks** forward to the time when he can lounge upon the shore of a
   mountain lake or the white sands by the sea.

3. It is highly improbable that either the white sands or the
   mountain lake ~~are~~ **is** the answer for this tense city-dweller.

4. Anybody who ~~live~~ **lives** a life of quiet desperation for months or
   even years can hardly expect to forget anxieties at once.

5. Nevertheless, realizing a need to slow down, the American

   takes

   vacationer, along with his entire family, ~~take~~ a trip.

   has

6. Plan after plan ~~have~~ been made; nothing can go wrong.

   has (optional)

7. The trouble is that the family ~~have~~ made too many plans.

8. Father is determined to relax; he somehow fails to see that re-

   are

   laxation and two weeks of feverish activity ~~is~~ not compatible.

   is

9. This man's situation, like that of thousands of others, ~~are~~ the

   result of his desire on the one hand to slow down and on the

   haunt

   other to forget himself, to escape the thoughts that ~~haunts~~

   him for fifty weeks of the year.

C 10. Physical relaxation and at the same time escape from frustra-

   tions is impossible for him.

C 11. He returns to his job more weary or more worried or both

   than when he left.

12. The roots of this man's problem ~~goes~~ very deep, and he must

   go

   search deep within himself for the solution.

C 13. He must learn to stop frequently and to take account of him-

   self and his values.

14. He must identify himself with values which ~~has~~ **have** proved

    lasting.

15. Above all, he must learn that there ~~is~~ **are** much worse fates than

    falling behind the Joneses.

8	Pronouns: Agreement, Reference, and Usage *agr/ref/us*

Use singular pronouns to refer to singular antecedents, plural pronouns to refer to plural antecedents. Make a pronoun refer to a definite antecedent.

The *writer* finished **his** story.

The *writers* finished **their** stories.

8a   In general, use a plural pronoun to refer to a compound antecedent linked with *and.*

The *owner* and the *captain* refused to leave **their** distressed ship.

If two nouns designate the same person, the pronoun is singular.

The *owner and captain* refused to leave **his** distressed ship.

8b   After a compound antecedent linked with *or, nor, either . . . or, neither . . . nor, not only . . . but also,* a pronoun agrees with the nearer part of the antecedent. (See **7b.**)

Neither the *Secretary* nor the *Undersecretary* was in **his** seat.

Neither the *Secretary* nor his *aides* were consistent in **their** policy.

A sentence like this written with *and* is less stilted.

The Secretary and his aides were not consistent in their policy.

8c   A singular pronoun follows a collective noun antecedent when the members of the group are considered as a unit; a plural pronoun, when they are thought of individually. (See **7d.**)

A UNIT
The student *committee* presented **its** report.

INDIVIDUALS
The *committee* filed into the room and took **their** seats, some of **them** defiant.

8d   Such singular antecedents as *each, either, neither, one, no one, everyone, someone, anyone, nobody, everybody, somebody, anybody* usually call for singular pronouns.

Not *one* of the linemen felt that **he** had played well.

Be consistent in number within the same sentence.

AVOID   *singular*   *plural*

The committee *takes* **their** seats.

Everyone who is a mother sometimes wonders how **she** will survive the
   day.

   Traditionally the pronouns *he* and *his* have been used to
refer to both men and women when the antecedent has been unknown or representative of both sexes: "Each person has to face
his own destiny." *He* was considered generic, that is, a common
gender. Today this usage is changing because many feel that it ig-
nores the presence and importance of women: there are as many
"she's" as "he's" in the world, and one pronoun should not be
selected to represent both.
   Writers should become sensitive to this issue and strive to
avoid offense without at the same time indulging in ridiculous alternatives. Here are three suggestions:

1. Make the sentence plural.

   All *persons* have to face *their* own destinies.

2. Use *he or she* (or *his or her*).

   Each person has to face *his or her* own destiny.

NOTE: Be sparing in the use of *he or she, his or her.* Monotony results if these double pronouns are used more than once or twice
in a paragraph.

3. Use *the* or avoid the singular pronoun altogether.

   Each person must face *the* future.
   Each person must face destiny.

8e *Which* refers to animals and things. *Who* and *whom* refer to persons and sometimes to animals or things called by name. *That* refers to animals or things and sometimes to persons.

The *boy* **who** was fishing is my son.

The *dog* **which (that)** sat beside him looked happy.

Secretariat, **who** won the Kentucky Derby, will be remembered as one of the most beautiful horses of all time.

Sometimes *that* and *who* are interchangeable.

A mechanic *that (who)* does good work stays busy.
A person *that (who)* giggles is often revealing embarrassment.

NOTE: *Whose* (the possessive form of *who*) may be less awkward than *of which,* even in referring to animals and things.

The *car* **whose** right front tire blew out came to a stop.

8f Pronouns should not refer vaguely to an entire sentence or a clause or to unidentified people.

Some people worry about wakefulness but actually need little sleep. *This* is one reason they have so much trouble sleeping.

This could refer to the worry, to the need for little sleep, or to psychological problems or other traits which have not even been mentioned.

CLEAR
Some people have trouble sleeping because they lie awake and worry about their inability to sleep.

They, them, it, and *you* are sometimes used as vague references to people and conditions which need more precise identification.

VAGUE
They always get *you* in the end.

The problem here is that the pronoun *they* and *you* and the sentence are so vague that the writer may mean almost anything pessimistic. The sentence could refer to teachers, deans, government officials, or even all of life.

NOTE: At times writers let *this, which,* or *it* refer to the whole idea of an earlier clause or phrase when no misunderstanding is likely.

The grumbler heard that his boss had called him incompetent. *This* made him resign.

8g Make a pronoun refer clearly to one antecedent, not uncertainly to two.

UNCERTAIN
The agent visited her client before she went to the party.

CLEAR
Before the client went to the party, the agent visited her.

8h Use pronouns ending in *-self* or *-selves* only in sentences that contain antecedents for the pronoun.

CORRECT INTENSIVE PRONOUN

The cook *himself* washed the dishes.

FAULTY

The antique dealer sold the chair to my roommate and *myself.*

CORRECT

The antique dealer sold the chair to my roommate and *me.*

■ Exercise 13

Revise sentences that contain errors in agreement of pronouns.

1. The captain of the freighter let each member of the crew decide whether ~~they~~ wished to remain with the ship.

   (he)

2. On behalf of my wife and ~~myself~~, I welcomed the visitors.

   (me)

3. No matter what the detergent commercials say, no woman is
   really jubilant at the prospect of mopping ~~their~~ dirty kitchen
   floor.

   (her)

4. The drifter, along with his many irresponsible relatives,
   never paid back a cent ~~they~~ borrowed.

   (he)

5. Neither the batter nor the fans hesitated to show ~~his~~ ardent
   disapproval of the umpire's decision.

   (their)

6. In the early days in the West, almost every man could ride
   his
   ~~their~~ horse well.

                                                    it
7. The League of Nations failed because ~~they~~ never received

   full support from the member countries.

                                                    you
8. Did the dignitary hand the certificate to ~~yourself~~ or to your

   partner?

                                                    her
9. Neither of the two women ever accepted ~~their~~ prize from the

   advertising agency.

                        has
10. The political district ~~have~~ voted against additional taxes.

■ Exercise 14

Revise sentences that contain vague or faulty references of pronouns.

                                                    employers
1. The typical industrial worker is now well paid, but ~~they~~ have

   not been able to do much about the boredom.

   The government   s
2. ~~They~~ tell you that you must pay taxes, but most of the time

                        it   s
   you do not know what ~~they~~ use your money for.

                                    are inadequate
3. In most occupations, those who ~~do not have it~~ are soon

   passed over for promotions.

Mints
4. ~~They~~ use much less silver in modern coins; so the metal in

   them is worth less.

                                                                    postage
5. Mail service has not improved over the years though ~~it~~ has

   gone up.

■ **Exercise 15**

*Revise sentences that contain errors in reference of pronouns. Write C
by correct sentences.*

                who
1. The passerby ~~which~~ saved the two children did not know

   how to swim.

   His   **with**   **soles**
2. ~~The soles of his~~ shoes ~~were~~ worn ∧ ~~which~~ made him self-

   conscious.

                          who are not unusually poor
3. Lawyers generally charge their clients ∧ a standard fee ~~unless~~

   ~~they are unusually poor~~.

   Though small and inexperienced, David fought the giant Goli-
4. ~~David fought Goliath although he was much smaller in~~
   ath, who was an experienced warrior.
   ~~size. He was an experienced warrior, but he was not.~~

                              instructions were
5. The ~~instructions were~~ brief and clear ~~which was~~ helpful.

6. On the night of July 14, the patriots stormed the doors of the

                              them
   jail/ and ~~they were~~ immediately smashed ∧ open.

Since luck
7. ~~Luck~~ is a prerequisite to riches, ~~which is why~~ few people are

rich.

8. The poet is widely read, but it is very difficult indeed to make
by writing poetry.
a living ~~at it.~~

C 9. The osprey feeds on fish, which it captures by diving into the

water.

some students
10. Typing themes saves a great deal of time in school, but ~~they~~

do not wish to learn to type.

 Case   c

Use correct case forms.

Case expresses the relationship of pronouns *(me, I)* and nouns to
other words in the sentence by the use of different forms. Nouns
are changed in form only for the possessive case *(child, child's;* see
p. 400).
    Following is a chart of the cases of pronouns:

PERSONAL PRONOUNS

SINGULAR	SUBJECTIVE	POSSESSIVE	OBJECTIVE
First person	I	my, mine	me
Second person	you	your, yours	you
Third person	he, she, it	his, her, hers, its	his, her, it

PLURAL	SUBJECTIVE	POSSESSIVE	OBJECTIVE
First person	we	our, ours	us
Second person	you	your, yours	you
Third person	they	their, theirs	them

RELATIVE OR INTERROGATIVE PRONOUNS			
Singular	who	whose	whom
Plural	who	whose	whom

To determine case, find how a word is used in its own clause —for example, whether it is a subject or a subjective complement, or an object.

9a Use the subjective case for subjects and for subjective complements which follow linking verbs.

SUBJECTS

This month my *sister* and *I* **have** not been inside the library. (never *me*)

It looked as if my *friend* and *I* **were** going to be blamed. (never *me*)

SUBJECTIVE COMPLEMENTS

The guilty ones **were** *you* and *I*.

In speech, *you and me, it's me, it's us, it's him,* and *it's her* are sometimes used. These forms are not appropriate for formal writing.

9b Use the objective case for a direct object, an indirect object, or the object of a preposition.

Errors occur especially with compound objects.

FAULTY

The manager gave the jobs *to* **you and I.**

The manager had to choose *between* **he and I.**

RIGHT

The manager gave the jobs *to* **you and me.**

The manager had to choose *between* **him and me.**

Be careful about the case of pronouns in constructions like the following:

FAULTY

A few *of* **we campers** learned to cook.

RIGHT

A few *of* **us campers** learned to cook.

When in doubt, test by dropping the noun:

A few *of* **us** learned to cook.

RIGHT (when pronoun is subject)

We campers learned to cook.

9c Use the objective case for subjects and objects of an infinitive.

subject of infinitive

The reporter considered **him** *to be* the best swimmer in the pool.

9d Give an appositive and the word it refers to the same case.

The case of a pronoun appositive depends on the case of the word it refers to.

SUBJECTIVE
Two *delegates*—**Bill** and **I**—were appointed by the president.

OBJECTIVE
The president appointed two *delegates*—**Bill** and **me.**

9e The case of a pronoun after *than* or *as* in an elliptical (incomplete) clause should be the same as if the clause were completely expressed.

                    subject of understood verb
                            ↓
No one else in the play was as versatile as **she** *(was)*.

                    object of understood subject and verb
                                 ↓
The director admired no one else as much as *(he did)* **her.**

9f Use the apostrophe or an *of* phrase to indicate the possessive case. (See **33.**)

The club's motto was written in Latin.
The motto *of the club* was written Latin.

9g Use the possessive case for pronouns and nouns preceding a gerund.

My *driving* does not delight my father. (*My* here may be called a pronoun or an adjective.)
The **lumberman's** *chopping* could be heard for a mile.

A noun before a gerund (see p. 22) may be objective
    when a **phrase** intervenes:

Regulations prevented the family **of a sailor** *meeting* him.

    when the noun is **plural:**

There is no rule against **men** *working* overtime.

    when the noun is **abstract:**

I object to **emotion** *overruling* judgment.

    when the noun denotes an **inanimate object:**

The crew did object to the **ship** *staying* in port.

When a verbal is a participle and not a gerund, a noun or pronoun preceding it is in the objective case. The verbal functions as an adjective.

I heard **him** *singing*.
I hear **you** *calling* me.

9h The possessive forms of personal pronouns have no apostrophe; the possessive forms of indefinite pronouns do have an apostrophe.

PERSONAL PRONOUNS
yours   *its*   *hers*   *his*   *ours*   *theirs*

INDEFINITE PRONOUNS
everyone's   other's   one's   anybody else's

9i   The case of an interrogative or a relative pronoun is determined by its use in its own clause.

Interrogative pronouns (used in questions) and relative pronouns are *who (whoever), whose, whom, what, which. Who* is used for the subjective case; *whom,* for the objective case.

In formal writing always use *whom* for objects.

The hostess did not tell us **whom** she had invited to dinner.

In speech, *who* is usually the form used at the beginning of a sentence, especially an interrogative sentence.

Who were you talking to over there?

The case of pronouns is clear in brief sentences.

Who *defeated* the **challenger?**

But when words intervene between the pronoun and the main verb, determining the case may be difficult.

Who do the reports say *defeated* the **challenger?**

Mentally cancel the intervening words:

Who ~~do the reports say~~ *defeated* the challenger?

Do not confuse the function of the relative pronoun in its clause with the function of the clause as a whole. Pick out the relative clause and draw a box around it. Then the use of the pronoun in the dependent clause is more easily determined.

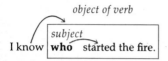

object of verb

I know | *subject* **who** started the fire.

Try to avoid writing sentences with elaborate clauses which make choice between *who* and *whom* difficult.

■ **Exercise 16**

Underline the correct word in each of the following sentences.

1. There was in those days in Paris a singer (<u>who</u>, whom) the secret police knew was a double agent.
2. On the platform stood the man (<u>who</u>, whom) they all believed had practiced witchcraft.
3. On the platform stood the man (who, <u>whom</u>) they all accused of practicing witchcraft.
4. The speaker defended his right to talk critically of (whoever, <u>whomever</u>) he pleased.
5. He (<u>who</u>, whom) would be great of soul must first know poverty and suffering.
6. Wise spending is essential to those (<u>who</u>, whom) have small incomes.
7. On skid row is a little mission which gives (<u>whoever</u>, whomever) comes a hot meal, a dry place to sleep, and a word of encouragement.
8. Will the delegate from the Virgin Islands please indicate (who, <u>whom</u>) she wants to support?
9. (Who, <u>Whom</u>) discovered the human fossils is not known.
10. Truth is there for (<u>whoever</u>, whomever) will seek it.

■ **Exercise 17**

Cross out the incorrect forms of pronouns and nouns, and write in the correct forms.

1. The director said that the stunt man and ~~myself~~ ^I were the ones most afraid of the white water on the trip down river.

2. After much discussion between the Navajo and ~~she~~ **her**, they agreed that the first chance to buy the turquoise bracelet was ~~her's~~ **hers** rather than the man's.

3. No one was able to make more intricate designs than ~~him~~ **he**.

4. "You and ~~me~~ **I**," the Chinese man said, "will construct intricate fireworks which will burst into colorful designs."

5. The physician said that he had not objected to the <u>employee</u>**'s** returning to work.

6. ~~Whom~~ **Who** it was rumored donated the money the board never heard.

7. Deep thinkers have motives and secrets that ~~us~~ **we** ordinary people can never fathom.

8. ~~Who's~~ **Whose** theory was it that matter can be neither created nor destroyed?

9. She had well described her heart͵'s desire as she talked about

   the vacation in the Alps.

10. I apologized because I wanted no ill feelings between ~~she~~ **her**

    and ~~I~~ **me**.

---

10   Adjectives and Adverbs   *adj / adv*

Use adjectives to modify nouns and pronouns, adverbs to
modify verbs, adjectives, and other adverbs.

Most adverbs end in *-ly*. Only a few adjectives (such as *lovely,
holy, manly, friendly*) have this ending. Some adverbs have two
forms, one with *-ly* and one without: *slow* and *slowly, loud* and
loudly. Most adverbs are formed by adding *-ly* to adjectives:
warm, warmly; pretty, prettily.

Choosing correct adjectives and adverbs in some sentences is
simple.

They stood *close.*
The barber gave him a *close* shave.
Study the text *closely.*

Adjectives do not modify verbs, adverbs, or other adjectives.
Distinguish between *sure* and *surely, easy* and *easily, good* and
well, real and *really, some* and *somewhat*.

NOT
Balloonists *soar* over long distances **easy.**

BUT

Balloonists *soar* over long distances **easily.**

10a Use the comparative to refer to two things, the superlative to more than two.

Both cars are fast, but the small car is (the) **faster.**
All *three* cars are fast, but the small car is (the) **fastest.**

10b Add *-er* and *-est* to form the comparative and superlative degrees of most short modifiers. Use *more* and *most* (or *less* and *least*) before long modifiers.

	COMPARATIVE	SUPERLATIVE
ADJECTIVES		
	-er/-est	
dear	dearer	dearest
pretty	prettier	prettiest
	more/most	
pitiful	more pitiful	most pitiful
grasping	more grasping	most grasping
ADVERBS		
	-er/-est	
slow	slower	slowest
	more/most	
rapidly	more rapidly	most rapidly

Some adjectives and adverbs have irregular forms: *good, better, best; well, better, best; little, less, least; bad, worse, worst.* Consult a dictionary.

Some adjectives and adverbs are absolute; that is, they cannot be compared *(dead, perfect, unique)*. A thing cannot be more or less dead, or perfect, or unique (one of a kind). Acceptable forms are *more nearly perfect* or *almost dead.*

10c Use a predicate adjective, not an adverb, after a linking verb (see p. 7) such as *be, seem, become, look, appear, feel, sound, smell, taste.*

ADJECTIVE

He feels **bad.** (He is ill or depressed. An adjective modifies a pronoun.)

ADVERB

He *reads* **badly.** (*Reads* is not a linking verb. An adverb modifies a verb.)

ADJECTIVE

The *tea* tasted **sweet.** (*Sweet* describes the tea.)

ADVERB

She *tasted* the tea **daintily.** (*Daintily* tells how she tasted.)

10d Use an adjective, not an adverb, to follow a verb and its object when the modifier refers to the object, not to the verb.

Verbs like *keep, build, hold, dig, make, think* are followed by a direct object and a modifier. After verbs of this kind, choose the adjective or the adverb form carefully.

ADJECTIVES—MODIFY OBJECTS

Keep your *clothes* **neat.**

Make my *bed* **soft.**

ADVERBS—MODIFY VERBS

Keep your clothes arranged **neatly** in the closet.

Make my bed **carefully.**

■ **Exercise 18**

Underline unacceptable forms of adjectives and adverbs, and write the correct form. If a sentence is correct, write **C.**

1. Socrates thought profound about the nature and purpose of

   humanity

   (profoundly)

2. The old clockmaker looked sadly when he spoke of the way

   the years whirl by.

   (sad)

3. The young coach was real angry about the controversial deci-

   sion to fine her.

   (really)

4. It sure cannot be denied that Tennyson was one of the popu-
   larest poets of his time.

   (surely) *(most popular)*

                                              rapidly

5. Hungry birds strip a holly bush of its berries <u>rapid</u> and swoop

              frantically

away seeking <u>frantic</u> for other food.

                  really   **a**

6. The computer, a <u>real</u> complicated mechanical mind, is <u>the</u>

<u>most</u> unique instrument of modern civilization.

C 7. The athlete played awkwardly and badly.

                                      more

8. Of the two factories, which one makes <u>the most</u> cars?

                                      logically

9. In times of tribulation, you must think <u>logical</u>.

10. The manager, a man of indecision, never knew which of two

                           better

possibilities was <u>the best</u>.

Sentence Structure

| **11** | Choppy Sentences and Excessive Coordination *chop* |

Do not string together short independent clauses or sentences. (See **19**.)

Wordiness and monotony result from choppy sentences or from brief independent clauses connected by coordinating conjunctions *(and, but, or, nor, for, yet, so)*. Excessive coordination does not show precise relationships between thoughts. English is rich in subordinating connectives, and skillful writers use them often.

STRINGY

Sugarloaf Mountain is four thousand feet high, and it is surrounded by fields and forests, and the air currents are favorable for hang gliding, and many gliding enthusiasts go there in the summer.

CHOPPY

Sugarloaf Mountain is four thousand feet high. It is surrounded by fields and forests. The air currents are favorable for hang gliding. Many gliding enthusiasts go there in the summer.

Consider the last clause or sentence the central idea, and improve by subordinating the other elements.

IMPROVED

Surrounded by fields and blessed with air currents favorable for hang gliding, four-thousand-foot-high Sugarloaf Mountain attracts many gliding enthusiasts in the summer.

■ **Exercise 1**

Improve the following sentences by subordinating some of the ideas. Combine choppy sentences into longer sentences.

Other choices possible.

1. ~~Pagodas are~~ ^{Sacred} temples or ~~sacred buildings, and they~~ ^{pagodas, which} are found

   in several Eastern countries, ~~and they~~ often have many

   stories and upward-curving roofs.

2. ~~Sharks are~~ ^{Although} ferocious/ ~~And they~~ ^{sharks} attack many bathers each

   year, ~~but~~ they seldom kill; so their reputation as killers is in

   part undeserved.

3. Some vacationers leave home in search of quiet/ ~~so they~~ ^{and} find

   a place without a telephone or television, but other people

   ^{who} want complete isolation/ ~~but they discover~~ ^{usually cannot} that it

   ~~is difficult to~~ find a park that is not crowded with trailers and

   tents.

4. The instructor gave the new student an assignment/ ~~and he~~

   ~~had~~ to write just one sentence/ [;] but ^{because} he could not think of an

   interesting subject, ~~and so~~ he did not do the required work.

5. Famous books are not always written by admirable people.

   Some authors are arrogant/ ^{or} ~~Some are~~ even immoral.

6. The manta ray has a wide, flat body, ~~and it is also called a de-~~ ^{graceful} ^{, also called a devilfish,}

   ~~vilfish, and it is graceful~~.

, **who are rapidly disappearing,**
7. Headhunters ∧ still exist in remote areas of the world/ ~~but they~~
even though
~~are rapidly disappearing, and~~ today we seldom hear of them.

8. Computers calculate rapidly, ~~and they~~ do more work than a

human being in the same time, and ~~they~~ threaten many jobs **;** /

but we must use them.

Although women have been discriminated against unjustly, they
9. ~~Women have been discriminated against, and they have~~
have been patient until recently.
~~been patient, but now they are complaining, and their cause~~

~~is just.~~

who
10. Benjamin Franklin, ~~was~~ an American/ ~~He~~ was at home wher-

ever he went **,** / ~~He~~ gained wide popularity in France/
and   became
~~He was~~ also ∧ well known in England.

---

12 Subordination *sub*

Use subordinate clauses to avoid excessive coordination
and to achieve emphasis and variety.

Putting the less important idea of a sentence in a subordinate
clause emphasizes the more important thought in the independent clause. Piling one subordinate clause on top of another awkwardly stretches out sentences and obscures meaning.

12a Express main ideas in independent clauses, less important ideas in subordinate clauses.

An optimistic sociologist wishing to stress progress despite crime would write:

Although the crime rate is high, society has progressed in some ways.

A pessimistic sociologist might wish the opposite emphasis:

Although society has progressed in some ways, the crime rate is very high.

Putting the main idea in a subordinate clause **(upside-down subordination)** places the stress on the minor instead of the major thought.

Although the patient recovered fully, the burn had been described as fatal.

12b Avoid excessive overlapping of subordinate clauses.

Monotony and even confusion can result from a series of clauses with each depending on the previous one.

OVERLAPPING
A watch is an intricate mechanism

    which measures time,

    which many people regard as a gift

    that is precious.

IMPROVED

A watch is an intricate mechanism made to measure time, which many
people regard as a precious gift.

■ **Exercise 2**

*The following is an exercise in thinking about relationships. The sen-
tences used are designed to point out differences in meaning that result from subordination. Read the pairs of sentences carefully, and
answer the questions.*

1. A. Although the lecturer had a speech defect, she was a
good teacher.
   B. Although the lecturer was a good teacher, she had a
speech defect.

   Which sentence stresses the lecturer's handicap? **B**
   Which stresses her accomplishment? **A**

2. A. Even though the nurse had a serious injury, she attended
to others.
   B. Even though the nurse attended to others, she had a serious injury.

   Which sentence stresses the selflessness of the nurse? **A**

3. A. Although a lifetime is short, much can be accomplished.
   B. Although much can be accomplished, a lifetime is short.

   Which of these sentences expresses more determination? **A**

4. A. When in doubt, most drivers apply the brakes.
   B. When most drivers apply the brakes, they are in doubt.

   With which drivers would you prefer to ride? **A**

5. A. While taking a bath, Archimedes formulated an impor-
        tant principle in physics.
    B. While formulating an important principle in physics, Ar-
        chimedes took a bath.

    Which sentence indicates accidental discovery? **A**
    In which sentence does Archimedes take a bath for relax-
    ation? **B**

■ **Exercise 3**

Rewrite the following sentences to avoid overlapping subordination.

       Shakespeare's play
1. ^Hamlet ~~is a play by Shakespeare that~~ tells of a prince who has

    difficulties making up his mind to avenge the murder of his

    father.

                                   performing
2. Each musician ~~who plays~~ in the orchestra ~~which performs~~ in
        on
    the club ~~that is on~~ the side of the lake has at least fifteen years

    of professional experience.

3. Lobster Newburg is ~~a dish which consists of~~ cooked lobster
                                 with
    meat ~~which is~~ heated in a chafing dish ~~which contains~~ a spe-

    cial cream sauce.

     Expensive paneling,   wormholes,
4. ^Chestnut ~~wood,~~ which has ~~holes that were made by worms~~

    ~~which is sometimes used as expensive paneling~~ comes from

                                    of 1925 that
trees ~~that were~~ killed in a blight ~~which~~ spread across eastern

America, ~~in 1925.~~
         ^

                              T   **stuck on the elevator**
  5. ~~The elevator stuck that had~~ ⌡the board member ~~who~~ could
                                                      ^
     have cast a vote that would have changed the future of the

     corporation.

13   Completeness   *compl*

Make your sentences complete in structure and thought.

Every element of a sentence should be expressed or implied
clearly to prevent inconsistency and misunderstanding.

13a Do not omit a verb or a preposition which is necessary to the structure of the sentence.

NOT
The baby was both frightened and attracted **to** the new kitten.

BUT
The baby was both frightened **by** and attracted **to** the new kitten.

BETTER
The baby was both frightened **by** the new kitten and attracted **to** it.

NOT
The *silver* coins **were** scattered and the *paper money* stolen. (Paper money *were* stolen?)

BUT
The *silver coins* **were** scattered, and the *paper money* **was** stolen.

When the same form is called for in both elements, it need not be repeated:

To err is human; to forgive, divine.

13b Omission of *that* sometimes obscures meaning.

INCOMPLETE
The labor leader reported a strike was not likely.

COMPLETE
The labor leader reported that a strike was not likely.

14 Comparisons   *comp*

Make comparisons logical and clear.

Compare only similar terms.

The *laughter* of a loon is more frightening than an **owl.**

This sentence compares a sound and a bird. A consistent sentence would compare sound and sound or bird and bird.

The *laughter* of a loon is more frightening than the **hoot** of an owl.

A *loon* is more frightening than an **owl.**

The word *other* is often needed in a comparison:

ILLOGICAL
The Sahara is larger than any desert in the world.

RIGHT
The Sahara is larger than any *other* desert in the world.

Avoid awkward and incomplete comparisons.

AWKWARD AND INCOMPLETE

The lily is *as white* if not whiter **than** any other flower. (*As white* requires *as,* not *than.*)

BETTER
The lily is *as* white **as** any other flower, if not whiter. (*Than any other* is understood.)

AWKWARD AND INCOMPLETE
Canoeing in white water is one of the most dangerous if not the most dangerous water sport. (After *one of the most dangerous,* the plural *sports* is required.)

BETTER
Canoeing in white water is one of the most dangerous water sports if not the most dangerous one.

OR
Canoeing in white water is one of the most dangerous water sports.

AMBIGUOUS

After many years my teacher remembered me better than my roommate.
(Better than he remembered my roommate, or better than my roommate remembered me?)

CLEAR

After many years my teacher remembered me better than my roommate
did.

OR

After many years my teacher remembered me better than he did my
roommate.

INCOMPLETE COMPARISON

Motion pictures of the 1930's were different.

COMPLETE COMPARISON

Motion pictures of the 1930's were different from those of other decades.
(or, even more exact, *more romantic than* . . .)

■ Exercise 4

*Correct any errors in completeness and comparisons. Write C by cor-
rect sentences.*

1. Exploring caves is more exciting than any ^other^ adventure.

2. Visitors to New Lawson discover that the summers there are
   as hot ~~if not hotter than~~ ^as^ any they have ever experienced/ ^if not hotter.^

3. Storms on the open ocean are usually more severe than ^those on^ small
   seas.

4. This sentence is a little ~~different.~~ ^unusual *or* different from the others.^

5. The baboons ate more ~~of the~~ bananas than ~~the~~ ants. *or* **The baboons ate more of the bananas than the ants did.**

6. Happy workers always have ~~and still do~~ produce ^d the best re-

   sults~~/~~ **, and they still do.**

7. The veterinarian read an article contending that horses like
                    they do *or* **cats do**
   dogs better than ^ cats.
                                              as
8. For good health, plain water is as good ~~if not better than~~ most

   other liquids~~/~~ **if not better.**
                                          of   as a
9. The lighthouse stood as a symbol ^ and ^ guide to safety.

C 10. Some laws are so broad that they allow almost unlimited in-

   terpretations.

■ Exercise 5

Follow the instructions for Exercise 4.
                                   other
1. The river was shallower than any ^ in the area.

2. A plant that lives in the air without roots is one of the stran-
                                        s
   gest ~~if not the strangest~~ form ^ of life, **if not the strangest one.**

3. The editors say that the headlines have been written and the
                has been
   type ^ set.

4. The children enjoyed singing songs about how we go over
   through
   the fields and ∧ the woods.

   that
5. The attorney saw ∧ the witness's composure was lost.

15 | Consistency   *cons*

Write sentences which maintain consistency in form and meaning.

15a Avoid confusing shifts in grammatical forms.

Tenses and Verbs

PRESENT AND PAST

SHIFT

The architect *planned* the new stadium, and the contractor *builds* it. (Use
planned . . . built or *plans . . . builds.*)

CONDITIONAL FORMS (*SHOULD, WOULD, COULD*)

SHIFT

Exhaustion after a vacation *could* be avoided if a family *can* plan better.
(Use *could . . . would* or *can . . . can.*)

Person

In felling a tree, *a good woodsman* **[3rd person]** first cuts a deep notch near
the bottom of the trunk and on the side toward which *he* **[3rd per-
son]** wishes the tree to fall. Then *you* **[2nd person]** saw on the other
side, directly opposite the notch.
(The second sentence should read *Then he saws. . . .* Or the first, *you
first cut . . . toward which you wish. . . .*)

Number

A *witness* may see an accident one way when it happens, and then *they* remember it an entirely different way when *they* testify. (Use *witness* and a singular pronoun or *witnesses* and *they*.)

Mood

SHIFT

$$\underset{\downarrow}{indicative} \qquad\qquad \underset{\downarrow}{imperative}$$

First the job-seeker *mails* an application; then *go* for an interview.

CONSISTENT

First the job-seeker *mails* an application; then he *goes* for an interview.
First *mail* an application; then *go* for an interview.

Voice

SHIFT

The chef *cooks* **(active)** the shrimp casserole for thirty minutes, and then it *is allowed* **(passive)** to cool. (Use *cooks* and *allows*.) See **5**.

Connectors

RELATIVE PRONOUN

She went to the chest of drawers *that* leaned perilously forward and *which* always resisted every attempt to open it. (Use *that . . . that* or *which . . . which*.)

CONJUNCTIONS

The guests came *since* the food was good and *because* the music was soothing. (Use *since . . . since* or *because . . . because*.)

Direct and Indirect Discourse

MIXED

The swimmer says that the sea is calm and why would anyone fear it?

CONSISTENT

The swimmer says, "The sea is calm. Why would anyone fear it?"
The swimmer says that the sea is calm and asks why anyone would fear it.

■ **Exercise 6**

Correct the shifts in grammar in the following sentences.

1. The florist explained that flowers wilt quickly/ and why ~~do~~ _asked_

   people wait so long to put them in water~~?~~.

2. A boy who writes an appealing letter to his girlfriend will
   seem to have personality, but the next time ~~you see~~ her ~~you~~ _he sees_ _he_
   should be as interesting in person as ~~you are~~ when ~~you write.~~ _he is_ _he writes._
   or was when he wrote.

3. The failures in the experiments will be avoided this time if
   the assistants ~~would~~ follow the instructions precisely. _will_

4. The retreating actor backed out of the door, jumped on a
   horse, and ~~rides~~ off into the sunset. _rode_

5. ~~It is wise to start~~ a fire with a wood like pine, and then a _Start_ _use_
   heavier wood like oak.~~is used.~~

6. Use pine first to start a fire ~~since~~ it ignites easily and because _because_
   it will then make the oak burn.

7. Dedicated joggers run every day; ~~you should~~ **they do** not get flabby.

8. Dedicated joggers want to run every day, but occasionally the weather ~~would be~~ **is** too bad to get outside.

9. For days the engaged couple plans a picnic, but then he decides to go bowling; so she gets angry and call~~ed~~**s** (*or* use all past tense) off the wedding.

10. For days the engaged couple planned a picnic which would be by a cool stream and ~~that~~ **which** would give them some precious moments alone.

15b Make subjects and predicates fit together. Avoid faulty predication.

Test the consistency of a sentence by mentally placing the subject and predicate side by side. If they do not fit together **(faulty predication),** rewrite for consistency.

FAULTY PREDICATION

Tragedy, according to Aristotle, *is when* a person of high estate falls. (*Tragedy . . . is when* makes no sense.)

CONSISTENT

Tragedy, according to Aristotle, *occurs when* a person of high estate falls.

FAULTY

After *eating* a large meal is a bad *time* to go swimming.

CONSISTENT

The *period* immediately after eating a large meal is a bad *time* to go swimming.

FAULTY

The *use* of a mediator *was hired* so that a compromise could be achieved.

CONSISTENT

A *mediator was hired* so that a compromise could be achieved.

■ **Exercise 7**

Correct faulty predication in the following sentences.

1. Not planning one's free time wisely is ~~where many~~ <ins>a common error among</ins> students. ~~err.~~

2. His <ins>love for his</ins> beautiful Irish setter ~~was the reason he~~ <ins>caused him to</ins> decided to become a veterinarian.

3. ~~By means of~~ <ins>A</ins> fast ferry ~~it~~ could shorten the time it takes to cross the English Channel.

4. Happiness ~~is~~ <ins>results from</ins> the sound of rain at night on a tin roof.

5. ~~The question of~~ _Ccensorship is ~~the answer~~ often ^{regarded}~~given to~~
   as the solution to the problem of language in
   ~~the objectionab~~le language of many modern novels.

16

   Position of Modifiers   *po*

Attach modifiers clearly to the right word or element in the sentence.

A misplaced modifier can cause confusion or misunderstanding. Usually a modifying adjective precedes its noun, whereas an adverb may precede or follow the word it modifies. Prepositional phrases usually follow closely, but may precede; adjective clauses follow closely; and adverbial phrases and clauses may be placed in many positions. (See pp. 22–23, 25)

16a   Avoid dangling modifiers.

A verbal phrase at the beginning of a sentence should modify the subject.

DANGLING PARTICIPLE

Hearing the good news, my *mood* was filled with joy.

CLEAR

Hearing the good news, *I* was filled with joy.

OR

After I heard the good news, my mood was joyful.

DANGLING GERUND

After **searching** around the attic, a *Halloween mask* was discovered. (The
passive voice in the main clause causes the modifier to attach
wrongly to the subject.)

CLEAR

After **searching** around the attic, *I* discovered a Halloween mask.

DANGLING INFINITIVE

To enter the house, the *lock* on the back door was picked. (*To enter the
house* refers to no word in this sentence.)

CLEAR

To enter the house, *he* picked the lock on the back door.

DANGLING PREPOSITIONAL PHRASE

During childhood, *my mother* was a consul in Italy. (In whose childhood?)

CLEAR

During **my** childhood, *my mother* was a consul in Italy.

DANGLING ELLIPTICAL CLAUSE

While still sleepy and tired, the *counselor* lectured me on breaking rules.

CLEAR

While I was still sleepy and tired, the counselor lectured me on breaking rules.

Loosely attaching a verbal phrase to the end of a sentence is unemphatic:

UNEMPHATIC
Every member of the infield moved closer to the plate, thus preparing for
    a double play.

Revise by using simple coordination:

BETTER
Every member of the infield moved closer to the plate and prepared for a
    double play.

Some verbal phrases that are **sentence modifiers** do not need to
refer to a single word:

Strictly speaking, does this sentence contain a dangling construction?
To tell the truth, it does not.

16b   Avoid misplaced modifiers.

Placement of a modifier in a sentence affects meaning.

He enlisted after he married *again.*
He enlisted *again* after he married.

Almost anything which comes between an adjective clause and
the word it modifies can cause confusion.

MISLEADING
Some insecticides are still used on crops that are suspected of being dan-
    gerous.

CLEAR
Some insecticides that are suspected of being dangerous are still used on
    crops.

16c A modifier placed between two words so that it may modify either word is said to squint.

UNCLEAR

The horse which was pawing *violently* kicked its owner.

CLEAR

The horse which was *violently pawing* kicked its owner.

OR

The horse which was pawing *kicked* its owner *violently*.

■ **Exercise 8**

Correct the faulty modifiers in the following sentences.

1. After studying biology, a student sees a bug becomes as a more complex

   organism.

2. Looking through a magnifying glass, the flaw in the diamond

   appeared as a dark spot.

3. The courageous patient was able to walk. about two
   About two weeks after the accident, t
   Two weeks . . . was able to walk about.
   weeks after the accident.

4. This computer is seldom used even though it is most effective.
   Because of the high cost t

   because of the high cost.

5. To be absolutely certain. the answer must be checked.
   Check the answer   *(or* You must check the answer . . .)

6. The restaurant offers meals for children _∧ ~~that are inexpensive.~~

   inexpensive

7. Serve one of the melons for dessert at lunch; keep one of
   them ~~for the picnic~~ in the refrigerator _∧.

   for the picnic.

8. ~~The carpenter inspected the board before sawing for nails.~~

   Before sawing, the carpenter inspected the board for nails.

9. ~~Slowly and relentlessly~~ **T**he lecturer said that _∧ witches attempt

   slowly and relentlessly

   to gain control over the minds of others.

10. The woman who was ⟵writing (hastily) rose⟶ from the desk and

    or

    left the room.

■ **Exercise 9**

Follow the instructions for Exercise 8.

1. ~~The manager gave~~ personal names to every doll, enabl~~ing~~ the

   By giving   **the manager**   **ed**

   shop to appeal to the children.

2. ~~Without shoes,~~ **T**he rough stones cut the feet of the _∧ hikers.

   T   **barefoot**

3. Although hindered by the weather, _∧ the bridge. ~~was still built~~

   the workers still built

   ~~by the workers.~~

4. ~~To taste delicious,~~ **T**he chef should prepare a dressing pre-

   T

   cisely suitable to _∧ the raw spinach salad/ **taste delicious.**

   make

only

5. The editor ~~only~~ told me that ⋀lighthearted materials would be

accepted for the column.

 Separation of Elements   *sep*

Do not needlessly separate closely related elements.

Separation of subject and verb, parts of a verb phrase, or verb and object can be awkward.

AWKWARD

At last the trapper had after many weeks of isolation and hard trudging through the snow returned to civilization.

IMPROVED

At last the trapper had returned to civilization after many weeks of isolation and trudging through the snow.

PUZZLING

She is the man who owns the service station's wife.

CLEAR

She is the wife of the man who owns the service station.

Do not divide a sentence with a quotation long enough to cause excessive separation.

AVOID

Stephen Clarkson's opinion that "politicians always create their own reality; during campaigns they create their own unreality" is pessimistic.

Split infinitives occur when a modifier comes between *to* and the verb form, as in *to loudly cheer*. Some writers avoid them without exception; others accept them occasionally. To avoid objections, do not use this kind of split construction.

18 Parallelism //

Use parallel grammatical forms to express parallel thoughts.

Constructions in a sentence are *parallel* when they are in balance, that is, when a phrase matches up with a phrase, a clause with a clause, a verb with a verb, a noun with a noun, and so forth.

(1) Parallelism in constructions with coordinating conjunctions (*and, but, for*, etc.):

NOT PARALLEL
Sailing ships were *stately* **and** *made* little noise.

PARALLEL
Sailing ships were *stately* **and** *quiet*.

NOT PARALLEL
Young Lincoln read widely for *understanding, knowledge,* **and** *he* just liked books.

PARALLEL
Young Lincoln read widely for *understanding, knowledge,* **and** *pleasure*.

NOTE: Repeat an article *(the, a, an)*, a preposition *(by, in, on,* etc.), the sign of the infinitive *(to)*, or other key words in order to preserve parallelism and clarity:

UNCLEAR
The artist was *a* painter and sculptor of marble.

CLEAR
The artist was *a* painter and *a* sculptor of marble.

UNCLEAR
They passed the evening *by* eating and observing the crowds.

CLEAR
They passed the evening *by* eating and *by* observing the crowds.

(2) Parallelism in constructions with correlatives *(not only . . . but also, either . . . or,* etc.):

NOT PARALLEL   *infinitive*   *preposition*
                        ↓   ↓
Petroleum is used **not only** *to make* fuels **but also** *in* plastics.

NOT PARALLEL
    verb   *preposition*
    ↓   ↓
Not only *is* petroleum used in fuels **but also** *in* plastics.

PARALLEL   *prepositions*
                         ↙   ↘
Petroleum is used **not only** *in* fuels **but also** *in* plastics.

NOT PARALLEL   *adverb*   *pronoun*
                    ↓   ↓
The speeches were **either** *too* long, **or** *they* were not long enough.

NOT PARALLEL

article   *adverb*

Either *the* speeches were too long **or** *too* short.

PARALLEL

adverbs

The speeches were **either** *too* long **or** *too* short.

(3) Parallelism with *and who* and with *and which:*

Avoid *and who* or *and which* unless they are preceded by a matching *who* or *which.*

NOT PARALLEL

The position calls for a person with an open mind *and who* is cool headed.

PARALLEL

The position calls for a person *who* is open-minded and *who* is cool headed.

PARALLEL

The position calls for a person with an open mind and a cool head.

NOT PARALLEL

A new dam was built to control floods *and which* would furnish recreation.

PARALLEL

A new dam was built to control floods and furnish recreation.

PARALLEL

A new dam was built *which* would control floods *and which* would furnish recreation.

■ Exercise 10

Revise sentences with faulty parallelism. Write C by correct sentences.

1. Her children are loving, loyal, and show confidence in her.
   loving, loyal ∧ ~~are loving, loyal, and~~

2. The new sedan is advertised as attractive, inexpensive, and ~~with a new~~ economical.~~motor.~~

3. Adjusting to a large college is difficult for a person who has always attended a small school and ~~being~~ used to individual attention.
   who has been

C 4 Roaming through the great north woods, camping by a lake, and getting away from crowds are good ways to forget the cares of civilization.

5. A good listener must have a genuine interest in people, a strong curiosity, and discipline ~~oneself~~ to keep the mind from wandering.
   enough ∧

6. A young musician must practice long hours, give up pleasures, and ~~one has to~~ be able to take criticism.

7. A good trial lawyer must be shrewd, alert, and ~~a bold speaker.~~
   bold.

8. The delegation found it impossible ~~either~~ to see the governor

   or any other official.

   > **either** (inserted before "to see")

9. Most slow readers could read much faster if they would not

   glance back over lines and mov~~ing~~ their lips.

   > **e** (inserted to make "move")

10. The jaguar is swift, quiet, and ~~moves with~~ grace/

    > **ful.** (inserted to make "graceful.")

---

19   Variety   *var*

Vary sentences in structure and order.

An unbroken series of short sentences may become monotonous and fail to indicate such relationships as cause, condition, concession, time sequence, and purpose. (See **11**.)

The following description of a chimpanzee coming upon a waterfall in a tropical forest is monotonous because of a lack of variety in sentence structure.

> The animal seemed lost in contemplation. He moved slowly closer and began to rock. He began to give a round of characteristic "pant-hoot" calls. He became more excited. He finally began running back and forth, jumping. He called louder and drummed on trees with his fists. He ran back again. The behavior was most reminiscent of that observed by Jane Goodall in groups of chimpanzees. It was at the start of a rainstorm. It has been called the "rain dance." But this one animal was alone. It was not surprised as the animals are by sudden rain. He had not deliberately sought the waterfall. He certainly knew where it was. He also knew when he had come to it.

Study the variety of the sentences in the passage as it was originally written by Melvin Konner:

> The animal seemed lost in contemplation. He moved slowly
> closer and began to rock, while beginning to give a round of charac-
> teristic "pant-hoot" calls. He became more excited, and finally
> began running back and forth, jumping, calling louder, drumming
> on trees with his fists, running back again. The behavior was most
> reminiscent of that observed and described by Jane Goodall in
> groups of chimpanzees at the start of a rainstorm—the "rain
> dance," as it has been called. But this was one animal alone, and not
> surprised as the animals are by sudden rain; even if he had not de-
> liberately sought the waterfall, he certainly knew where it was and
> when he had come to it.
>
> MELVIN KONNER, *The Tangled Wing*

Structure

Do not overuse one kind of sentence structure. Write simple,
compound, and complex patterns. Vary your sentences among
loose, periodic, and balanced forms.

A **loose sentence,** the most common kind, makes its main
point early and then adds refinements.

LOOSE

Boys are wild animals, rich in the treasures of sense, but the New England boy had a wider range of emotions than boys of more equable
climates.

HENRY ADAMS

Uncle Tom's Cabin is a very bad novel, having, in its self-righteous, virtu-
ous sentimentality, much in common with *Little Women*.

JAMES BALDWIN

A **periodic sentence** withholds an element of the main
thought until the end to create suspense and emphasis.

PERIODIC

Under a government which imprisons any unjustly, the true place for a
  just man is also a prison.

HENRY DAVID THOREAU

PERIODIC

There is one thing above all others that the scientist has a duty to teach to
  the public and to governments: it is the duty of heresy.

J. BRONOWSKI

A **balanced sentence** has parallel parts which are similar in
structure, length, and thoughts. Indeed, balance is simply another word for refined parallelism. (See **18.**) The following sentence has perfect symmetry:

Marriage has many pains, but celibacy has no pleasures.

SAMUEL JOHNSON

A sentence can also be balanced if only parts of it are symmetri-
cal:

Thus the Puritan was made up of two different men, the one all self-
  abasement, penitence, gratitude, passion; the other proud, calm, in-
  flexible, sagacious.

THOMAS BABINGTON MACAULAY

Thus
the Puritan
was made up
of two different men,

the one ----- the other
all self-abasement,---proud,
penitence,------calm,
gratitude,-----inflexible,
passion;----- sagacious.

Order

If several sentences follow the order of subject-verb-complement, they can be monotonous. Invert the order occasionally; do not always tack dependent clauses and long phrases on at the end. Study the variations:

NORMAL ORDER

subject *verb* *object* *modifiers* ——›
↓ ↓ ↓
She attributed these *defects* in her son's character to the general weaknesses of mankind

SENTENCE BEGINNING WITH DIRECT OBJECT

These *defects* in her son's character she attributed to the general weaknesses of mankind.

SENTENCE BEGINNING WITH PREPOSITIONAL PHRASE

To the general weaknesses of mankind she attributed the defects in her son's character.

SENTENCE BEGINNING WITH ADVERB

Quickly the swordfish broke the surface of the water.

INVERTED SENTENCE BEGINNING WITH CLAUSE USED AS OBJECT

That the engineer tried to stop the train, none would deny.

SENTENCE BEGINNING WITH PARTICIPIAL PHRASE

Flying low over the water, the plane searched for the reef.

▓ Exercise 11

Rewrite the following sentences and make them periodic. If you consider a sentence already periodic, put a check mark next to it.

1. One machine/ ~~the typewriter~~, revolutionized business prac-

   tices and had a profound influence on the style of many au-
                        : the typewriter.
   thors_∧

                                            N
2. ~~A sense of humor is one quality~~ /no great leader can be with-
        one quality: a sense of humor.
   out_∧

                                                    T
3. ~~Selfishness, some philosophers maintain, is~~ /he reason be-
                    , some philosophers maintain, is selfishness.
   hind every action of any person._∧
           T   **is the blue whale.**
4. ~~The blue whale is~~ /he largest known creature on earth_∧
              W
5. ~~He studied~~ /when all other possible methods of passing the
                        , he studied.
   course proved unworkable/

▓ Exercise 12

Rewrite the following sentences to give them balanced constructions. Put a check mark by a sentence which is already balanced.

1. The rewards of youth are obvious, but ~~much more subtle~~
                        are much more subtle.
   ~~are~~ the rewards of age/

2. A successful advertisement surprises and pleases, but ~~not~~
   an unsuccessful advertisement bores and irritates.
   ~~all advertisements are successful because some are merely~~

   ~~boring and irritating.~~

✓ 3. Realists know their limitations; romantics know only what

   they want.

4. A politician is concerned with successful elections whereas
   a statesman is interested in
   ⋏the future of the people. ~~is foremost in the mind of a~~

   ~~statesman.~~

5. A trained ear hears many separate instruments in an orches-
   untutored hears only the
   tra, but the⋏ melody. ~~is usually all that is heard by the~~

   ~~untutored.~~

■ Exercise 13

Rewrite the following passage so that it is more varied in sentence structure.

Cynicism, despair, and frantic slapstick now run through the

pages of many composition texts. And the same is often true of tests.
                                                                  ,
Grammar examples and test sentences do not exist inert. ~~They are~~

~~not~~ detached from life~~, and they are not~~ in some neutral vacuum.

Most of them, even when disfigured by deliberate mistakes, still re-

          and

flect and reinforce attitudes, ~~They~~ make claims about our world.

Students surely cannot help responding, and we often hand them

melodrama and morbidity. One of my colleagues has even ~~made a~~

         ed that

sugges~~tion. She says~~ this message of despair is a welcome means of

social control. Keep students' anxieties high and they will be more

docile.

Adapted from Ellen Strenski,
"Grammar Sample Sentences and the Power of Suggestion"

Punctuation

20 The Comma ,

Use commas to reflect structure and to clarify the sense of the sentence.

The **comma** is chiefly used (1) to separate equal elements, such as independent clauses and items in a series, and (2) to set off modifiers or parenthetical words, phrases, and clauses.

Elements which are set off within a sentence take a comma both *before* and *after*.

NOT
This novel, a best seller has no real literary merit.

BUT
This novel, a best seller, has no real literary merit.

20a Use a comma to separate independent clauses joined by a coordinating conjunction. (See p. 402.)

Nice is a word with many meanings, and some of them are opposite to others.
Sherlock Holmes had to be prepared, for Watson was full of questions.

NOTE: The comma is sometimes omitted between the clauses when they are so brief that there is no danger of misreading.

The weather was clear and the pilot landed.

20b   Use a comma between words, phrases, or clauses in a series.

The closet contained worn clothes, old shoes, and dusty hats.

The final comma before *and* in a series is sometimes omitted.

The closet contained worn clothes, old shoes and dusty hats.

But the comma must be used when *and* is omitted.

The closet contained worn clothes, old shoes, dusty hats.

And it must be used to avoid misreading.

An old chest in the corner was filled with nails, hammers, a hacksaw and blades, and a brace and bit.

Series of phrases or of dependent or independent clauses are also separated by commas.

PHRASES
We hunted for the letter in the album, in the old trunks, and even under the rug.

DEPENDENT CLAUSES
Finally we concluded that the letter had been burned, that someone had taken it, or that it had never been written.

INDEPENDENT CLAUSES
We left the attic, Father locked the door, and Mother suggested that we never unlock it again.

In a series of independent clauses, the comma is not omitted before the final element.

■ Exercise 1

Insert commas where necessary in the following sentences.

1. Some prominent women authors took masculine pen names in the nineteenth century, for they felt that the public would not read novels written by women.

2. A good speaker should prepare well for a talk, enunciate clearly to be understood, and practice the art of effective timing.

3. The markings on the wall of the cave were not as ancient as others, but none of the experts could interpret them.

4. The hamper was filled with cold cuts, mixed pickles, bread and butter.

5. Some government documents are classified secret, for the safety of the country must be preserved.

6. The sensitive child knew that the earth was round, but she thought that she was on the inside of it.

7. The commissioner stated that taxes are already high, that personal incomes are low, and that rapid transit is expensive.

8. For breakfast the menu offered only bacon and eggs, toast and jelly, and hot coffee.

9. Careless driving includes speeding, stopping suddenly, turning from the wrong lane, going through red lights, and failing to yield the right of way.

10. Driving was easy, for the highway was completed, and traffic was light.

20c Use a comma between coordinate adjectives not joined by *and*. Do not use a comma between cumulative adjectives.

Coordinate adjectives modify the noun independently.

COORDINATE

We entered a forest of tall, slender, straight pines.

Ferocious, alert, loyal dogs were essential to safety in the Middle Ages.

Cumulative adjectives modify the whole cluster of subsequent adjectives and the noun.

CUMULATIVE

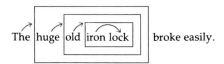

The huge old iron lock broke easily.

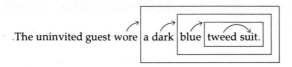

The uninvited guest wore a dark blue tweed suit.

Two tests are helpful.

Test One

And is natural only between coordinate adjectives.

tall *and* slender *and* straight pines
ferocious *and* alert *and* loyal dogs

BUT NOT
dark *and* blue *and* tweed suit
huge *and* old *and* iron lock

Test Two

Coordinate adjectives are easily reversible.

straight, slender, and tall pines
loyal, alert, ferocious dogs

BUT NOT
tweed blue dark suit
iron old huge lock

The distinction is not always clear-cut, however, and the sense of
the cluster must be the deciding factor.

She was wearing a full-skirted, low-cut velvet gown.

(a velvet gown that was full-skirted and low-cut, not a gown that was full-skirted and low-cut and velvet)

■ **Exercise 2**

Punctuate the following. When in doubt, apply the tests described above. Write C by those which require no comma.

1. a graceful, agile cat

C 2. large glass front doors

C 3. a little black recipe book

4. gaudy, shiny earrings

C 5. a wrinkled brown paper bag

6. a hot, sultry, depressing day

7. the gloomy, forbidding night scene

C 8. expensive new electric typewriter

9. a woebegone, ghostly look

C 10. beautiful Persian rugs

20d Use a comma after a long introductory phrase or clause.

LONG PHRASE
With the severe part of the trek behind him, the traveler felt more confident.

LONG CLAUSE
When the severe part of the trek was behind him, the traveler felt more
    confident.

When the introductory element is short and there is no danger of
misreading, the comma is often omitted.

SHORT PHRASE
After the ordeal the traveler felt more confident.

SHORT CLAUSE
When the ordeal was over the traveler felt more confident.

Use of the comma in the above sentences may depend on personal taste. Commas after the introductory elements would be acceptable.
    Introductory verbal phrases are usually set off by commas.

PARTICIPLE
Living for centuries, redwoods often reach great heights.

INFINITIVE
To verify a hypothesis, a scientist performs an experiment.

GERUND
After surviving the ordeal, the traveler felt relieved.

    A phrase or a clause set off by a comma at the beginning of a
sentence may not require a comma if it is moved to the end of the
sentence.

BEGINNING
Because of pity for creatures that must live in cages, some people do not
    go to the zoo.

END

Some people do not go to the zoo because of pity for creatures that must
     live in cages.

20e Use commas to set off nonrestrictive appositives,
phrases, and clauses.

A **nonrestrictive modifier** or **appositive** adds information but
does not point out or identify. When the modifier is omitted, the
sentence loses some meaning but does not change radically.

NONRESTRICTIVE

The painter's latest work, *a landscape,* has achieved wide acclaim.
Salt, *which is plentiful in this country,* is still inexpensive.
Abstract words, *which do not convey images,* are necessary in language.

In these three sentences the italicized elements add information,
but they are not essential to the meaning of the sentence.

NOTE: *That* should never introduce a nonrestrictive clause.

A **restrictive modifier** or appositive points out or identifies
its noun or pronoun. When the modifier is removed, the sentence
radically changes in meaning.

RESTRICTIVE

The Russian ruler *Nicholas* was married to Alexandra.
Huge signs *which are displayed along interstate highways* spoil the beauty
     of the countryside.
Words *which convey images* are important in poetry.

In all these sentences, the italicized expressions identify the
words they modify; to remove the modifiers would be to change
the meaning.

Some modifiers can be either restrictive or nonrestrictive; use or omission of the commas changes the sense.

The coin which gleamed in the sunlight was a Spanish doubloon. (There were several coins.)
The coin which gleamed in the sunlight was a Spanish doubloon. (There was only one coin.)

■ **Exercise 3**

The following pairs of sentences illustrate differences in meaning which result from use or omission of commas with modifiers. Answer the questions about each pair of sentences.

1. A. In Allison Long's novel, *Only Once,* the heroine is a physician.
   B. In Allison Long's novel *Only Once,* the heroine is a physician.

   In which sentence has Allison Long written only one novel? **A**

2. A. The posts which are cut from locust trees will last a long time.
   B. The posts, which are cut from locust trees, will last a long time.

   Which sentence suggests that all the posts are cut from locust trees? **B**

3. A. The plant, which has an elaborately designed pot, is not as pretty as the container.
   B. The plant which has an elaborately designed pot is not as pretty as the container.

   Which sentence makes a false generalization? **B**

4. A. Young drivers, who are not well trained, cause most of our minor automobile accidents.
   B. Young drivers who are not well trained cause most of our minor automobile accidents.

   Which sentence shows a prejudice against young drivers? **A**

5. A. Anthropologists, who respect native ways, are welcome among most tribes.
   B. Anthropologists who respect native ways are welcome among most tribes.

   Which sentence reflects confidence in anthropologists? **A**

■ Exercise 4

Insert commas for nonrestrictive modifiers; circle all unnecessary commas. Write C by correct sentences.

C 1. The name Rover was often associated with dogs which were happy.

2. Barbers who are bald often authoritatively discuss baldness with their customers who are worried about losing their hair.

C 3. The wealthy who keep their expensive jewelry in bank vaults sometimes hire people to wear their pearls for them so that the gems will not lose their luster.

C 4. Americans who have grown up on the prairies may feel shut in when they move to forest regions or to cities with buildings which have more than ten stories.

C 5. Adam's son Abel was a shepherd.

   6. Abel, Adam's son, was a shepherd.

   7. The tree, that stood despite the high winds, was planted by my paternal grandfather, who was born over a hundred years ago.

   8. The most beautiful photograph, a shadowy shot of a white bird against a dark sky, was made on a small island which is about a mile off the eastern coast.

   9. Courses, which are not challenging, usually do not instruct the students who have the best minds.

  10. Shaw's play, *Pygmalion,* was the basis for a musical which was entitled *My Fair Lady.*

20f Use commas to set off sentence modifiers, conjunctive adverbs, and sentence elements out of normal word order.

Modifiers like *on the other hand, for example, in fact, in the first place, I believe, in his opinion, unfortunately,* and *certainly* are set off by commas.

Only a few poets, unfortunately, make a living by writing.
Thomas Hardy's poems, I believe, ask profound questions.

Commas are frequently used with conjunctive adverbs such as *accordingly, anyhow, besides, consequently, furthermore, hence, however, indeed, instead, likewise, meanwhile, moreover, nevertheless, otherwise, still, then, therefore, thus.*

BEFORE CLAUSE

optional

The auditor checked the figures again; therefore, the mistake was discovered.

WITHIN CLAUSE

optional

The auditor checked the figures again; the mistake, therefore, was discovered.

Commas always separate the conjunctive adverb *however* from the rest of the sentence.

The auditor found the error in the figures; however, the books still did not balance.
The auditor found the error in the figures; the books, however, still did not balance.

Commas are not used when *however* is an adverb meaning "no matter how."

However fast the hare ran, he could not catch the tortoise.

Use commas if necessary for clearness or emphasis when part of a sentence is out of normal order.

Confident and informed, the young woman invested her own money.

OR
The young woman, confident and informed, invested her own money.

BUT
The confident and informed young woman invested her own money.

20g Use commas with degrees and titles and with elements in dates, places, and addresses.

DEGREES AND TITLES
Arthur Weiss, M.A., came to the picnic.
Louis Ferranti, Jr., Chief of Police, made the arrest.

DATES
Sunday, May 31, is her birthday.
August 1982 was very warm. (Commas around 1982 are also acceptable.)
July 20, 1969, was the date when a human being first stepped on the moon. (Use commas *before* and *after.*)
He was born 31 December 1970. (Use no commas.)
The year 1980 was a time of change. (Restrictive; use no commas.)

PLACES
Cairo, Illinois, is my home town. (Use commas *before* and *after.*)

ADDRESSES
Write the editor of *The Atlantic*, 8 Arlington Street, Boston, Massachusetts 02116. (Use no comma before the zip code.)

20h Use commas for contrast or emphasis and with short interrogative elements.

The pilot used an auxiliary landing field, not the city airport.
The field was safe enough, wasn't it?

20i Use commas with mild interjections and with words like *yes* and *no.*

Well, no one thought it was possible.
No, it proved to be simple.

20j Use commas with words in direct address and after the salutation of a personal letter.

Driver, stop the bus.
Dear John,
It has been some time since I've written. . . .

20k Use commas with expressions like *he said, she remarked,* and *she replied* when used with quoted matter.

"I am planning to enroll in Latin," she said, "at the beginning of next term."
He replied, "It's all Greek to me."

20L Set off an absolute phrase with commas.

An **absolute phrase** consists of a noun followed by a modifier. It modifies the sentence as a whole, not any single element in it.

┌── *absolute phrase* ──┐
Our day's journey over, we made camp for the night.

┌── *absolute phrase* ──┐
The portrait having dried, the artist hung it on the wall.

20m Use commas to prevent misreading or to mark an omission.

After washing and grooming, the pup looked like a different dog.
When violently angry, elephants trumpet.
Beyond, the open fields sloped gently to the sea.

verb omitted
↓
To err *is* human; to forgive, divine. (Note that *is*, the verb omitted, is the same as the one stated.)

■ Exercise 5

Add necessary commas. If a sentence is correct as it stands, write C by it.

1. Inside, the convention hall resembled a huge, overcrowded barn.

2. A few hours before he was scheduled to leave, the mercenary visited his father, who pleaded with him to change his mind and then finally said quietly, "Good luck."

3. Seeing a nightingale, the American ornithologist recognized its resemblance to other members of the thrush family.

4. Seeing a nightingale for the first time is disappointing; hearing one for the first time, unforgettable.

5. History, one would think, ought to teach people not to make the same mistakes again.

6. Despite the old saying to the contrary, you can sometimes tell a book by its cover.

7. The Vandyke beard, according to authorities, was named after Sir Anthony Van Dyck, a famous Flemish painter.

C 8. Only after reading a book either very carefully or more than once should a critic write a review.

9. While burning, cedar has a distinct and strong odor.

10. The cloverleaf, a road arrangement that looks somewhat like a four-leaf clover, permits traffic to flow easily between two intersecting expressways.

■ Exercise 6

Follow the instructions for Exercise 5.

1. The hippopotamus has a stout hairless body, very short legs, and a large head and muzzle.

2. The tarantula, a large hairy spider, looks frightening; it is not, however, highly venomous.

3. Before students can understand the principles of quantum physics, they must master simple algebra.

4. The ancient urn, labeled "cracked and discolored," stood in the corner of the garden, and the honeysuckle vines almost hid it from view.

5. While the mystery writer was composing his last novel, *The Tiger's Eye*, he received a note warning him not to write about anyone he knew in the Orient.

6. The race being over, the jockey who rode the winning horse turned to the owner and said, "Now, Mrs. Aster, you have the money and the trophy."

7. Gray towers, domes, and skyscrapers looked as colorless as
, (optional)
the low, overhanging clouds.

8. The geographer said that he had spent most of his life living in Taos, New Mexico.

9. The hungry prospector turned from the window, looked into his cabinet, and saw that he still had some tomato ketchup, dried white beans, and beef jerky.

10. Atlanta, Georgia, is lower in latitude than Rome, Italy. Miami,

   furthermore, is not as far south as the equatorial zone, is it?

■ Exercise 7

Add necessary commas.

1. Attempting to save money as well as time, some shoppers go

   to the grocery store only once a month; others, however, go

   almost daily.

2. The menu included beets, carrots, and radishes, for the chef

   was fond of root foods.

3. However the travelers followed the worn, outdated city map,

   they always returned to the same place.

4. The last selection on the program, a waltz by Strauss, brought

   the most applause, I believe.

5. The American frigate *Constitution*, it is true, fought in the War

   of 1812.

6. She wished the warm, sunny day would last forever, but she

   realized that winter was coming.

7. High over the mountain, clouds looked dark, ominous.

8. Edward Friar, Ph.D., was awarded his honorary degree on June 1, 1947, in Fulton, Missouri.

9. With a renewed sense of the importance of his experiment, the chemist continued his work.

10. Yes, friends, the time has come for pausing, not planning.

21 Unnecessary Commas *no ,*

Do not use commas excessively.

Placing commas at all pauses in sentences is not a correct practice.

21a Do not use a comma to separate subject and verb, verb or verbal and complement, or an adjective and the word it modifies.

NOT
The guard with the drooping mustache, snapped to attention.
Some students in the class, admitted, that they had not read, "Mending Wall."
The stubborn, mischievous, child refused to respond.

Two commas may be used to set off a phrase or a word between subject and verb.

The malamute, an Alaskan work dog, can survive extraordinarily cold
   weather.

21b Do not use a comma to separate two compound elements, such as verbs, subjects, complements, or predicates.

compound verb

He *left* the scene of the accident and *tried* to forget that it had happened.

no comma

21c Do not use a comma before a coordinating conjunction joining two dependent clauses.

dependent clauses

The contractor asserted *that the house was completed* and *that the work had*

been done properly.

no comma

21d Do not use a comma before *than* in a comparison or
between compound conjunctions like *as . . . as, so . . . as, so
. . . that.*

no comma

John Holland was more delighted with life on the Continent than he had
   thought he could be.

21e Do not use a comma after *like* and *such as.*

Some languages, such as Latin and Anglo-Saxon, are no longer spoken.

A comma is not used **before** *such as* (as above) when the phrase is restrictive.

21f Do not use a comma with a period, a question mark, an exclamation point, or a dash. These marks stand by themselves.

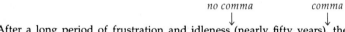

''Did you get the job?'' her roommate asked.

21g A comma may be used after a closing parenthesis, but not before an opening parenthesis.

                                no comma   *comma*
                                  ↓   ↓

After a long period of frustration and idleness (nearly fifty years), the
    poet wrote his best work.

21h A comma is not used to set off coordinating con-junctions. A comma is not required after short introductory adverbial modifiers. (See **20d.**)

NOT
But, some people are excessively tolerant.

OPTIONAL
After a hearty laugh, the class again became quiet.

21i Do not use commas to set off restrictive clauses, phrases, or appositives. (See **20e.**)

NOT
People, who live in glass houses, should not throw stones.

21j Do not use a comma between adjectives which are not coordinate. (See **20c.**)

FAULTY
The tired, old, work horse stopped.

▪ Exercise 8

Circle all unnecessary commas, and be prepared to explain your decisions.

1. Soccer is a popular sport in Great Britain, where it is sometimes called, football.

2. The secretary bird is so named, because, on its crest, it has feathers which resemble quill pens.

3. Restaurants, that serve excellent food at modest prices, are

always popular among local people, though tourists seldom
know about them.

4. Picking vegetables⊙and putting them in crates⊙turned out to
   be more strenuous work⊙than he expected.

5. Picking vegetables⊙(a new job for him), putting them in
   crates, and loading them were strenuous tasks.

   optional
6. That summer he tried many new activities⊙such as⊙riding
   horses, traveling on freight trains, and rowing boats.

7. Communities⊙near large airports⊙have become increasingly
   aware that noise pollution can be just as unpleasant as im-
   purities in the air or in streams.

8. Once, huge movie houses were fashionable, but now most of
   these palaces are like dinosaurs, extinct⊙giants, curious re-
   minders⊙of the past.

9. The Olympic runner was disqualified⊙after he ran out of his
   lane, but he would not have won a gold medal⊙anyway.

10. The accountant vowed that he would never work for the mil-
    lionaire again⊙and that he would go back to his small firm.

22 | The Semicolon   ;

Use a semicolon between independent clauses not joined
by coordinating conjunctions *(and, but, or, nor, for, so, yet)*
and between coordinate elements with internal commas.

Omitting a semicolon between independent clauses may result in
a comma splice or a fused sentence. (See **2**.)

22a   Use a semicolon between independent clauses not
connected by a coordinating conjunction.

WITH NO CONNECTIVE
For fifteen years the painting was stored in the attic; even the artist for-
    got it.

WITH A CONJUNCTIVE ADVERB
A specialist from the museum arrived and asked to examine it; *then* all the
    family became excited.

See **20f** for use of commas with conjunctive adverbs.

WITH A SENTENCE MODIFIER
The painting was valuable; *in fact,* the museum offered ten thousand dol-
    lars for it.

See **20f** for use of commas with sentence modifiers, such as *on the
other hand, for example, in fact, in the first place.*

22b Use a semicolon to separate independent clauses which are long and complex or which have internal punctuation.

In many compound sentences either a semicolon or a comma may be used.

COMMA OR SEMICOLON

Moby-Dick, by Melville, is an adventure story, *(or;)* and it is also one of the world's greatest philosophical novels.

SEMICOLON PREFERRED

Ishmael, the narrator, goes to sea, he says, "whenever it is a damp, drizzly November" in his soul; and Ahab, the captain of the ship, goes to sea because of his obsession to hunt and kill the great albino whale, Moby Dick.

22c Use semicolons in a series between items which have internal punctuation.

The old farmer kept a variety of poultry: chickens, for eggs and Sunday dinners; turkeys, for very special meals; and peacocks, for their beauty.

22d Do not use a semicolon between elements which are not coordinate.

FAULTY

dependent clauses　　　　　　　　　　　　　*independent clause*

After the tugboat had signaled to the barge twice; it turned toward the

↑*use,*

wharf.

■ **Exercise 9**

Circle unnecessary semicolons and commas, and insert necessary ones. Write C by sentences which are correct.

1. The sound of Niagara Falls is deafening it truly demonstrates the power of the cascade.

2. The stipulations of the agreement were that each company would keep its own name that profits would be evenly divided and that no employees would lose their jobs because of the merger.

3. An advanced civilization is guided by enlightened self-interest; however, it is also marked by unselfish good will.

4. The sound of the banjo drifted up from the floor below it blended with the chatter of typewriters and the droning of business conferences.

5. After a prolonged and severe economic depression people are hesitant to spend money freely because they are afraid hard times will recur.

6. The hallway was long and dark; and at the end of it hung a

dim, obscure painting representing a beggar⊙in eighteenth-century London.

7. The mutineers defeated the loyal members of the crew⊙'took command of the ship⊙'and locked the captain and other officers in the brig.

8. Winning is important⊙and rewarding⊙'but sportsmanship is essential in building character.

9. Fortunetelling still appeals to many people ⋏even when they realize it is superstitious nonsense⊙'they continue to patronize charlatans⊙like palm readers.

10. The making of pottery, once a necessary craft as well as an art, has again become popular⊙and hundreds of young people, many of them highly skillful, have discovered the excitement of this art.

23

 The Colon :

Use a colon as a formal mark of introduction.

23a Use a colon before quotations, statements, and series which are introduced formally.

Some of the buildings on the tour are unusual: ante-bellum two-storied homes, built mainly in the 1840's; smaller houses, which have long open hallways; and stores, some of which have two stories with porches.

A colon may be used to introduce a quotation formally.

The warden began with a sharp reminder: "Gentlemen, you are now almost free; but some of you will not remain free long."

23b Use a colon between two independent clauses when the second explains the first

Music communicates: it is an expression of deep feeling.

23c Use a colon before formal appositives, including those introduced by such expressions as *namely* and *that is.*

One factor is often missing from modern labor: pleasure in work.
The author made a difficult decision: he would abandon the manuscript.

NOTE: The colon comes before *namely* and similar expressions, not after.

The author made a difficult decision: namely, that he would abandon the manuscript.

23d Use a colon after the salutation of a formal letter, between figures indicating hours and minutes, and in bibliographical entries.

Dear Dr. Tyndale: 12:15 P.M.   Boston: Houghton, 1929
      PMLA 99(1984): 75

23e Do not use a colon after a linking verb or a preposition.

NOT AFTER LINKING VERB
Some chief noisemakers **are:** automobiles and airplanes.

NOT AFTER PREPOSITION
His friend accused him **of:** wiggling in his seat, talking during the lecture, and not remembering what was said.

24 The Dash   ～

Use a dash to introduce summaries and to indicate interruptions, parenthetical remarks, and special emphasis.

NOTE: In typing, a dash is made by two hyphens (--) with no space before or after it.

FOR SUMMARY
Attic fans, window fans, air conditioners—all were ineffective that summer.

FOR SUDDEN INTERRUPTIONS
She replied, "I will consider the —No, I won't either."

FOR PARENTHETICAL REMARKS
Three horses came from the water—a fourth had disappeared—and
struggled up the bank.

FOR SPECIAL EMPHASIS
Great authors quote one book more than any other—the Bible.

---

25 Parentheses ( )

Use parentheses to enclose a loosely related comment or
explanation, figures which number items in a series, and
references in documentation.

The frisky colt (it was not a thoroughbred) was given away.
The prospector refused to buy the land because (1) the owner had no
clear title, (2) it was too remote, and (3) it was too expensive.

A reference in documentation:

Link does not agree (153). [See **48**.]

A parenthetical sentence within another sentence has no period or capital, as in the first example above. A freestanding parenthetical sentence requires parentheses, a capital, and a period.

capital   *period here*

At the moment all flights are late. (The weather is bad.) Listen for further
announcements.

| 26 | Brackets   [ ] |

Use brackets to enclose interpolations within quotations.

In the opinion of Arthur Miller, "There is no more reason for falling
down in a faint before his [Aristotle's] *Poetics* than before Euclid's
geometry."

Parentheses within parentheses are indicated by brackets ([ ]).
Try to avoid constructions which call for this intricate punctuation.

| 27 | Quotation Marks   " " |

Use quotation marks to enclose the exact words of a
speaker or writer and to set off some titles.

Most American writers and publishers use double quotation
marks (". . .") except for internal quotations, which are set off by
single quotation marks ('. . .').

27a Use quotation marks to enclose direct quotations
and dialogue.

DIRECT QUOTATION
At a high point in *King Lear,* the Duke of Gloucester says, "As flies to
wanton boys are we to the gods."

NOTE: Do not use quotation marks to enclose indirect quotations.

He said that the gods regard us as flies.

In dialogue a new paragraph marks each change of speaker.

DIALOGUE
  "What is fool's gold?" asked the traveler who had never before been prospecting.
  "Well," the geologist told him, "it's pyrite."

In typing, indent ten spaces and single-space prose quotations which are longer than four lines. Do not use quotation marks to enclose these blocked quotations.

Unless your instructor specifies otherwise, poetry of four lines or more should be double spaced and indented ten spaces. Retain the original divisions of the lines.

> If you would keep your soul
> From spotted sight or sound,
> Live like the velvet mole;
> Go burrow underground.

Quotations of three lines of poetry or less may be written like the regular text—not set off. Use a slash (with a space before and after) to separate lines:

Elinor Wylie satirically advises, "Live like the velvet mole; / Go burrow underground."

27b Use single quotation marks to enclose a quotation within a quotation.

The review explained: "Elinor Wylie is ironic when she advises, 'Go burrow underground.' "

27c Use quotation marks to enclose the titles of essays, articles, short stories, short poems, chapters (and other subdivisions of books or periodicals), dissertations (see pp. 332–334), episodes in television programs, and short musical compositions.

D. H. Lawrence's "The Rocking-Horse Winner" is a story about the need for love.
One chapter of *Walden* is entitled "The Beanfield." (For titles of books, see **30a.**)

27d Do not use quotation marks around the title of your own paper.

27e Do not use quotation marks to emphasize or change the usual meanings of words or to justify slang, irony, or attempts at humor.

no

The beggar considered himself a "rich" man.

no

The old politician's opponents were hoping that he would "croak."

27f Follow established conventions in placing other marks of punctuation inside or outside closing quotation marks.

Periods and **commas** in American usage are placed *inside:*

All the students had read "Lycidas."
"Amazing," the professor said.

Semicolons and **colons** are placed *outside:*

The customer wrote that she was "not yet ready to buy the first edition";
it was too expensive.

A **question mark** or an **exclamation point** is placed *inside* quotation marks only when the quotation itself is a direct question or an exclamation. Otherwise, these marks are placed *outside.*

He asked, "Who is she?" (Only the quotation is a question.)
"Who is she?" he asked. (Only the quotation is a question.)
Did he ask, "Who is she?" (The quotation and the entire sentence are questions.)
Did he say, "I know her"? (The entire sentence asks a question; the quotation makes a statement.)
She screamed, "Run!" (Only the quotation is an exclamation.)
Curse the man who whispers, "No"! (The entire statement is an exclamation; the quotation is not.)

After quotations, do not use a period or a comma together with an exclamation point or a question mark.

NOT   BUT
"When?", I asked.   "When?" I asked.

| **28** | End Punctuation | .?! |

Use periods, question marks, or exclamation points to end sentences and to serve special functions.

28a Use a period after a sentence which makes a statement or expresses a command.

Some modern people claim to practice witchcraft.
Water the flowers.
The gardener asked whether the plant should be taken indoors. (This
    sentence is a statement even though it expresses an indirect question.)

28b Use periods after most abbreviations.

Periods follow such abbreviations as Mr., Dr., Pvt., Ave., B.C., A.M., Ph.D., e.g., and many others. In British usage periods are often omitted after titles (Mr).

Abbreviations of governmental and international agencies often are written without periods (FCC, TVA, UNESCO, NATO, and so forth). Usage varies. Consult your dictionary.

A comma or another mark of punctuation may follow the period after an abbreviation, but at the end of a sentence only one period is used.

After she earned her M.A., she began studying for her Ph.D.

But if the sentence is a question or an exclamation, the end punctuation mark follows the period after the abbreviation.

When does she expect to get her Ph.D.?

28c Use three spaced periods (ellipsis dots) to show an omission in a quotation.

Notice the quotation below and how it may be shortened with ellipsis marks.

He [the Indian] had no written record other than pictographs, and his conqueror was not usually interested, at the time, in writing down his thoughts and feelings for him. The stoic calm of his few reported speeches and poems gives only a hint of the rich culture that was so soon forgotten.

ROBERT E. SPILLER

ELLIPSIS

marks not necessary at	*one period to end sentence*
beginning of quotation	*and three for ellipsis*

The Indian "had no written record other than pictographs. . . . The stoic calm of his . . . speeches and poems gives only a

three periods for ellipsis in sentences

hint of the rich culture. . . ."

28d A title has no period, but some titles include a question mark or an exclamation point.

The Sound and the Fury   "What Are Years?"
Westward Ho!   *Ah! Wilderness*

28e Use a question mark after a direct question.

Do teachers file attendance reports?
Teachers do file attendance reports? (a question in declarative form)

Question marks may follow separate questions within an interrogative sentence.

Do you recall the time of the accident? the license numbers of the cars involved? the names of the drivers?

A question mark within parentheses shows that a date or a figure is historically doubtful.

Pythagoras, who died in 497 B.C. (?), was a philosopher.

28f Do not use a question mark or an exclamation point within a sentence to indicate humor or sarcasm.

NOT
The comedy (?) was a miserable failure.

28g Use an exclamation point after a word, a phrase, or a sentence to signal strong exclamatory feeling.

Wait! I forgot my lunch!
What a ridiculous idea!
Stop the bus!

Use exclamation points sparingly. After mild exclamations, use commas or periods.

NOT
Well! I was discouraged!

BUT
Well, I was discouraged.

■ **Exercise 10**

Supply quotation marks as needed in the following passage, and insert the sign ¶ where new paragraphs are necessary.

Alex Tilman, young, vigorous, and alert, walked briskly beside the little stream. As he neared a pond, he thought of Thoreau's essay "Walking" and the calm that pervaded nature. An old man was fishing with a pole on the bank of the pond. Knowing that [¶ (optional)] fishermen dislike noisemakers, Alex strolled quietly up to him and said, "How's your luck today?" ¶ "Oh, about like every other day, except a little worse, maybe." ¶ "Do you mean you haven't caught anything?" ¶ "Well, a couple of bream. But they're small, you know. Before I left home my wife said to me, 'If you don't catch any sizable fish today, you might as well give it up.' And I'm beginning to wonder if she hasn't got something there." ¶ Alex watched the water for a little while, now and then stealing a glance at the unshaved fisherman, who wore baggy breeches and a faded old flannel shirt. Then he dreamily said, "Well, I guess most people don't really fish just for the sake of catching something." ¶ The old gentleman looked up at him a little surprised. His eyes were much brighter and quicker than Alex had expected. "That's right," he said, "but, you know, that's not the kind of wisdom you hear these days. You new around here, son? Yes. My wife and I just bought the old Edgewright place. Oh! Well, maybe you can come fishing with me sometime. I'm usually here about this time dur-ing the day. Alex was not eager to accept the invitation, but he was moved by a sudden sympathy. Yes. Maybe. Say, if you need any work, I might be able to find something for you to do around our place. My wife and I are trying to get things cleaned up. A slight smile came over the man's face, and he said warmly, Much obliged, but I've got more work now than I know what to do with. So I come out here and hum Lazy Bones and fish. On the way back to his house, Alex asked a neighbor who that old tramp was fishing down by the pond. Tramp! his friend repeated. Good heavens, man, that was no tramp. That was Angus Morgan, one of the wealthiest men in the country.

■ **Exercise 11**

Add quotation marks where needed; circle unnecessary ones. Also make all necessary changes in punctuation.

1. "Failure is often necessary for humanity," the speaker said. "Without failure," he continued, "how can we retain our humility and know the full sweetness of success? For, as Emily Dickinson said, 'Success is counted sweetest / By those who ne'er succeed.'"

2. "Madam," said the talent scout, "I know that you think your daughter can sing, but, believe me, her voice makes the strangest sounds I have ever heard." Mrs. Audubon took her daughter (Birdie) by the hand and haughtily left the room wondering (how she could ever have been so stupid as to expose her daughter to such a (common) person).

3. "Your assignment for tomorrow," she said, "is to read the following (to use Poe's own term) tales of ratiocination: 'The Purloined Letter,' 'The Murders in the Rue Morgue,' and 'The Mystery of Marie Roget.' When you have finished these stories you might read some of the next assignment."

4. The boy and his great-uncle were (real) friends, and the youngster listened intently when the old man spoke. "Son," he

would say, "I remember my father's words: 'You can't do better than to follow the advice of Ben Franklin, who said, "One
To-day is worth two To-morrows."'"

5. The expression "population explosion" suggests the extreme
   rapidity with which the world's "population" is increasing.

6. A recent report states the following: "The marked increase in
   common stocks indicated a new sense of national security;"
   however, the report seems to imply "that this is only one of
   many gauges of the country's economic situation."

7. Chapter 4., "The National Mind," develops one of the most
   optimistic views of the country's future to be found in
   "modern" studies of economics.

8. One of Mark Twain's most famous letters, addressed to
   "Andrew Carnegie," reads as follows:

   "You seem to be in prosperity. Could you lend an ad-
   mirer $1.50 to buy a hymn-book with? God will bless you. I
   feel it; I know it. So will I"

"N.B.—If there should be other applications, this one
not to count ."

9. In a ⌢postscript,⌢ Mark Twain added, "Don't send the
hymn-book; send the money; I want to make the selection
myself." He signed the letter simply "Mark."

10. The hermit thought the question ⌢odd,⌢ but he replied,
"You ask me, 'Why do you live here?' I ask you why you do
not live here?"

Mechanics

29 Manuscript and Letter Form *ms*

Follow correct manuscript form in papers and business letters.

29a Papers

Paper

typing: white, 8½ by 11 inches
longhand: ruled
not: onionskin, spiral, legal size

Lines

typing: double-spaced
longhand: skip every other line (or follow your teacher's instructions)

Title

centered with extra space between title and text

Margins

ample and regular at bottom and top—at least one inch on each side

Page numbers

Arabic numerals (2, *not* II) in upper right corner except on first page (omit or center at bottom of page)

Example of correct manuscript form

About 1½ inch margin   Up the Attic ←———— *Center*
                                        ←———— *Triple space*
┌——— *Indent 5 spaces*
↓   It is no topsy-turvy figure of speech to say that the roots of the
                                ⌐*2 spaces after periods*
old American home were in the attic. There beneath the oak or chestnut
                                        ↙*2 hyphens no space for dash*
rafters were stored in endless profusion-–and confusion–-the records of

a family's life, perhaps for a century. On a bright summer day the attic

was unbearably hot and buzzed with flies; in winter it chilled you with

a stale cold. But on rainy days it was a fascinating place to explore by

the hour while the rain made a soft, soothing roar on the roof, and

sounds from the domestic world below came up smothered and unreal. The

roof of the old house where my boyhood was spent was adorned with a

cupola, which in turn was adorned with colored glass windows, a different

color for each point of the compass. Steep stairs led up to it from the

attic, and through the four windows you looked out upon four different

and strange worlds. The total unreality of a world all green, or all

red, or all blue, was never-to-be-too-much savored, but the all-yellow

world was a little terrifying, as if some ominous storm were brewing.

If Emerson's house had been equipped with such a cupola he would not

have had to recommend that clumsier argument for idealism--stooping down

and looking at a familiar landscape between your legs.

    From the foot of the steep stairs to enchantment--or idealism--

there stretched out in all directions until they vanished under the low

eaves every sort of object saved from the long process of living in the

house below. There were, for instance, horsehair trunks lined with old

Leave ample margin at   ↑
bottom of page   │   1 ←——— *Page number for first page*
                          │   *on bottom line (optional)*
                          ↓

29b   The business letter

In writing a business letter follow conventional forms. All essential parts are included in the example on pp. 163–164. Type if possible: single-space, with double-spacing between paragraphs. Paragraphs may begin at the left margin without indentation in block form, or they may be indented.

It is best to determine the title and the name of the addressee. Opinions vary about the best custom when the name, title, or sex of the person is unknown. If the sex of the addressee is known but the name is not, use *Dear Sir* or *Dear Madam.* If the sex is not known, use *Dear Sir or Madam.* Or omit the salutation entirely. When a woman's marital status is unknown or when she prefers it, use *Ms.*

Business letters are usually written on stationery 8½ by 11 inches. Fold horizontally into thirds to fit a standard-sized business envelope. For smaller envelopes fold once horizontally and twice the other way. (See page 164.)

Indented form of letter

141 Oakhurst Drive, Apt. 2A
Singleton, Ohio 54567
March 1, 1986

Mr. Freeman O. Zachary, Manager
Personnel Department
Keeson National Bank
P. O. Box 2387
Chicago, Illinois 34802

Dear Mr. Zachary:

I am writing to ask if you will have an opening this coming summer for someone of my qualifications. I am finishing my sophomore year at Singleton State College, where I intend to major in economics and finance. I have been active in several extracurricular activities, including the Spanish Club and the Singleton Players.

Although I have no previous experience in banking, I am eager to learn, and I am willing to take on any duties you feel appropriate. Chicago is my home town, so I am especially anxious to find summer employment there. I will be in Chicago for spring vacation from March 20 to 26 and available for an interview. In addition, I shall be pleased to furnish you with letters of recommendation from some of my professors here at Singleton State and with a transcript of my college record. I appreciate your consideration, and I look forward to hearing from you.

Sincerely yours,

Audrey DeVeers

Audrey DeVeers

Audrey DeVeers
141 Oakhurst Drive, Apt. 2A
Singleton, OH 54567

```
┌ ─ ─ ┐
|Place |
|stamp |
|here  |
└ ─ ─ ┘
```

Mr. Freeman O. Zachary, Manager
Personnel Department
Keeson National Bank
P. O. Box 2387
Chicago, IL 34802

Blocked form of letter

Address of writer ——————————→ 141 Oakhurst Drive, Apt. 2A
                                       Singleton, Ohio 54567
Date ———————————————————→ March 1, 1986

Mr. Freeman O. Zachary, Manager
Personnel Department   ←———— *Name and title of addressee*
Keeson National Bank
P. O. Box 2387
Chicago, Illinois 34802   ←———— *Full address*

Dear Mr. Zachary:←————————— *Salutation and name. Use a colon.*

I am writing to ask if you will have an opening this coming summer for
someone of my qualifications. I am finishing my sophomore year at
Singleton State College, where I intend to major in economics and
finance. I have been active in several extracurricular activities,
including the Spanish Club and the Singleton Players.

Although I have no previous experience in banking, I am eager to learn,
and I am willing to take on any duties you feel appropriate. Chicago
is my home town, so I am especially anxious to find summer employment
there. I will be in Chicago for spring vacation from March 20 to 26 and
available for an interview. In addition, I shall be pleased to furnish
you with letters of recommendation from some of my professors here at
Singleton State and with a transcript of my college record. I appreciate your consideration, and I look forward to hearing from you.

Sincerely yours,   ←————————— *Complimentary close*

Audrey De Veers ←————————— *Signature, handwritten*

Audrey DeVeers   ←————————— *Name, typed*

Folding the letter

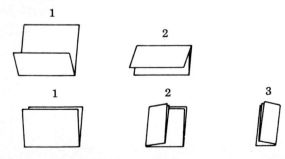

| 30 | Underlining for Italics   *ital* |

Underline titles of independent publications (books, magazines, newspapers), and *occasionally* for emphasis.

Italic type slants *(like this)*. Underline words individually (like this), or underline words and spaces (like this).

30a Underline titles of books (except the Bible and its divisions), periodicals, newspapers, motion pictures, paintings, sculpture, musical compositions, plays, and other works published separately.

Be precise: watch initial articles *(A, An, The)* and any punctuation.

BOOKS
Adventures of Huckleberry Finn *(not* The Adventures . . .)
An American Tragedy *(not* The American Tragedy)

PERIODICALS
The Atlantic Monthly and the American Quarterly

NEWSPAPERS
The New York Times or the New York Times

MOTION PICTURES
Citizen Kane

MUSICAL COMPOSITIONS
Bizet's Carmen
Beethoven's Mount of Olives *(but not* Beethoven's Symphony No. 5)

PLAYS
The Cherry Orchard

30b Underline names of ships and trains.

the Queen Elizabeth II   the U.S.S. Hornet   the Zephyr

30c Underline foreign words used in an English context, except words which have become part of our language.

Consult a dictionary to determine whether a word is still considered foreign or has become part of the English language.

French
↓

He claimed extravagantly to have been au courant since birth.

BUT
Some words which may seem foreign have become a part of the English language.

faux pas, amigo, karate

30d Underline words, letters, and figures being named.

The word puppy usually has delightful connotations.
Don't forget to dot your i's.

NOTE: Occasionally quotation marks are used instead of underlining.

30e   Avoid frequent underlining for emphasis.

Do not sprinkle a page with underlinings, dashes, or exclamation points. Writing is seldom improved by mechanical tricks.

30f   Do not underline the title of your own paper.

■ **Exercise 1**

Underline words as necessary in the following sentences. Put an X over words unnecessarily underlined.

1. The customer was <u>irate</u> ^x when he found no one to help him.

   or **The Los Angeles Times**
2. The Los Angeles <u>Times</u> announced the arrival of the ship

   <u>Tropical Explorer</u>.

3. The author's last novel, <u>The Green Summer</u>, was reviewed in
   or **The Philadelphia Inquirer**
   the Philadelphia <u>Inquirer</u>.

4. The word <u>fabulous</u> is overused.

5. The <u>limousine</u> ^x was used in a motion picture entitled <u>The</u>

   <u>Years of Hope</u>.

6. The <u>Mona Lisa</u> continues to be one of the most popular

   paintings at the Louvre.

7. Jack London's short story "To Build a Fire" is published in the latest edition of the anthology <u>America's</u> <u>Great</u> <u>Tales</u>.

8. The periodical <u>Harper's</u> has an article on the modern opera <u>Streets</u> <u>of</u> <u>the</u> <u>City</u>.

9. He made his i's with little circles over them instead of <u>dots</u>.
   ^x appears above *dots*

9. He made his i's with little circles over them instead of <u>dots</u>.

10. While on the train <u>The</u> <u>Northern</u> <u>Star</u>, she saw a large moose.

---

31 | Spelling *sp*

Spell correctly; use a dictionary to look up words you are unsure of.

Spelling is troublesome in English because many words are not spelled as they sound *(laughter, slaughter)*; because some pairs and triplets sound the same *(capital, capitol; there, they're, their; to, too, two)*; and because many words are pronounced with the vowel sound "uh," which gives no clue to spelling (sens*i*ble, ca-p*a*ble, defi*a*nt).

Many misspellings are due to the omission of syllables in ha-bitual mispronunciations *(accident-ly* for *acciden-tal-ly)*; the addi-tion of syllables *(disas-ter-ous* for *disas-trous)*; or the changing of syllables *(prespiration* for *perspiration)*.

There are no infallible guides to spelling in English, but the following are helpful.

ie or *ei?*

Use *i* before *e*
Except after *c*
Or when sounded as *a*
As in *neighbor* and *weigh.*

WORDS WITH *IE*
believe, chief, field, grief, piece

WORDS WITH *EI* AFTER *C*
receive, receipt, ceiling, deceit, conceive

WORDS WITH *EI* SOUNDED AS *A*
freight, vein, reign

EXCEPTIONS TO MEMORIZE
either, neither, leisure, seize, weird, height

Drop final silent e?

DROP		KEEP	
When suffix begins with a vowel		*When suffix begins with a consonant*	
curse	cursing	live	lively
come	coming	nine	ninety
pursue	pursuing	hope	hopeful
arrange	arranging	love	loveless
dine	dining	arrange	arrangement

TYPICAL EXCEPTIONS
courageous
noticeable
dyeing (compare *dying*)
singeing (compare *singing*)

TYPICAL EXCEPTIONS
awful
ninth
truly
argument

Change y to i?

CHANGE		DO NOT CHANGE	
When y is preceded by a consonant		*When y is preceded by a vowel*	
gully	gullies	valley	valleys
try	tried	attorney	attorneys
fly	flies	convey	conveyed
apply	applied	pay	pays
party	parties	deploy	deploying

When adding -ing

try	trying
fly	flying
apply	applying

Double final consonant?

If the suffix begins with a consonant, do not double the final consonant of the base word (*man, manly*).

If the suffix begins with a vowel:

DOUBLE		DO NOT DOUBLE	
When final consonant is preceded by single vowel		*When final consonant is preceded by two vowels*	
		despair	despairing
Monosyllables		leer	leering
pen	penned		
blot	blotted	*Words ending with two or more consonants preceded by single vowel*	
hop	hopper		
sit	sitting	jump	jumping
		work	working
Polysyllables accented on last syllable		*Polysyllables not accented on last syllable after addition of suffix*	
defér	deferring	defér	déference
begín	beginning	prefér	préference

omít	omitting	devélop	devéloping
occúr	occurring	lábor	lábored

Add s or es?

ADD S		ADD ES	
For plurals of most nouns		*When the plural is pronounced as another syllable*	
girl	girls	church	churches
book	books	fox	foxes
For nouns ending in o preceded by a vowel		*Usually for nouns ending in o preceded by a consonant (consult your dictionary)*	
radio	radios	potatoes	
cameo	cameos	Negroes	
		BUT	
		flamingos *or* flamingoes	

NOTE: The plurals of proper names are generally formed by adding s or es (*Darby,* the *Darbys; Jones,* the *Joneses*).

Words Frequently Misspelled

Following is a list of over two hundred of the most commonly misspelled words in the English language.

absence	amateur	argument
accidentally	among	arithmetic
accommodate	analysis	ascend
accumulate	analyze	athletic
acquaintance	annual	attendance
acquitted	apartment	balance
advice	apparatus	beginning
advise	apparent	believe
all right	appearance	benefited
altar	arctic	boundaries

Britain
business
calendar
candidate
category
cemetery
changeable
changing
choose
chose
coming
commission
committee
comparative
compelled
conceivable
conferred
conscience
conscientious
control
criticize
deferred
definite
description
desperate
dictionary
dining
disappearance
disappoint
disastrous
discipline
dissatisfied
dormitory
eighth
eligible
eliminate
embarrass
eminent
encouraging
environment
equipped
especially
exaggerate

excellence
exhilarate
existence
experience
explanation
familiar
fascinate
February
fiery
foreign
formerly
forty
fourth
frantically
fulfill or fulfil
generally
government
grammar
grandeur
grievous
height
heroes
hindrance
hoping
humorous
hypocrisy
immediately
incidentally
incredible
independence
inevitable
intellectual
intelligence
interesting
irresistible
knowledge
laboratory
laid
led
lightning
loneliness
maintenance
maneuver

manufacture
marriage
mathematics
may
maybe
miniature
mischievous
mysterious
necessary
ninety
noticeable
occasionally
occurred
omitted
opportunity
optimistic
parallel
paralyze
pastime
performance
permissible
perseverance
personnel
perspiration
physical
picnicking
playwright
possibility
practically
precede
precedence
preference
preferred
prejudice
preparation
prevalent
privilege
probably
professor
pronunciation
prophecy
prophesy
quantity

quiet	salary	stationery
quite	schedule	statue
quizzes	secretary	studying
recede	seize	subtly
receive	separate	succeed
recognize	sergeant	successful
recommend	severely	supersede
reference	shining	suppose
referred	siege	surprise
repetition	similar	temperamental
restaurant	sophomore	tendency
rhythm	specifically	their
ridiculous	specimen	thorough
sacrifice	stationary	through

■ Exercise 2

*In each of the following groups of words one, two, or three are mis-
spelled. The others are correct. Put an X over incorrectly spelled
words.*

       x   x
1. lizard, blizard, gizard, wizard, sizzler

                x   x
2. accommodate, acumulate, comming, blooming, ramming

   x   x   x
3. percieve, believe, recieve, achieve, conceive

            x   x   x
4. mountain, villian, protein, maintainance, certian

                    x   x   x
5. credence, precedence, balence, existance, independance

  x   x   x
6. tallys, valleys, bellys, modifys, fancies

  x   x   x
7. defys, relays, conveyes, carries, dirtys

         x   x   x
8. obedience, modifyer, complience, applience, guidance

           x   x
9. incredible, detectable, delectible, dependible, reversible

      x   x   x
10. sensable, receivable, edable, likible, noticeable

32 | Hyphenation and Syllabication ~

Use a hyphen in certain compound words and in words divided at the end of a line.

Two words not listed as an entry in a dictionary are usually written separately *(campaign promise.)*

32a   Consult a dictionary to determine whether a compound is hyphenated or written as one or two words.

HYPHENATED	ONE WORD	TWO WORDS
drop-off	droplight	drop leaf (noun)
white-hot	whitewash	white heat
water-cool	watermelon	water system

32b   Hyphenate a compound of two or more words used as a single modifier before a noun.

HYPHEN	NO HYPHEN AFTER NOUN
She is a *well-known* executive	The executive is *well known.*

A hyphen is not used when the first word of such a group is an adverb ending in *-ly.*

HYPHEN	NO HYPHEN
a *half-finished* task	a *partly finished* task

32c Hyphenate spelled-out compound numbers from *twenty-one* through *ninety-nine.*

32d Divide a word at the end of a line according to conventions.

Monosyllables
Do not divide.

thought   strength   cheese

Single letters
Do not put a one-letter syllable on a separate line:

NOT
a-bout   might-y

Prefixes and suffixes
May be divided.

separ-able   pre-fix

Avoid carrying over a two-letter suffix.

bound-ed   careful-ly

Compounds with hyphen

Avoid dividing and adding another hyphen.

self-satisfied

NOT
self-satis-fied

■ **Exercise 3**

Underline the correct form for the words indicated. Use a dictionary when needed.

1. The (muchdrilled, <u>much-drilled</u>, much drilled) (rescueteam, rescue-team, <u>rescue team</u>) worked fast.
2. (<u>Snowdrifts</u>, snow-drifts, snow drifts) had not yet blocked the (heavilytraveled, heavily-traveled, <u>heavily traveled</u>) roadway.
3. The (<u>foxhound</u>, fox-hound, fox hound) was (welltrained, well-trained, <u>well trained</u>) not to chase rabbits.
4. The (twentyone, <u>twenty-one</u>, twenty one) dancers did not know how to (foxtrot, fox-trot, fox trot).
5. Several words in the paper were hyphenated at the end of lines: a-round, almight-y, <u>al-most</u>, self-in-flicted, marb-le.

33   The Apostrophe   '

Use the apostrophe for the possessive case of many nouns, contractions, omissions, and some plurals.

Use 's for the possessive of nouns not ending in s.

SINGULAR
child's, man's, deer's, lady's, mother-in-law's

PLURAL
Children's, men's

Use 's for the possessive of singular nouns ending in s.

Charles's, Watts's, Dickens's, waitress's, actress's

NOTE: When a singular noun ending in s is followed by a word beginning with s, use only the apostrophe, not 's.

the actress' success, Dickens' stories

Use ' without s to form the possessive of plural nouns ending in s

the Joneses' car, the Dickenses' home, waitresses' tips

Use 's to form the possessive of indefinite pronouns.

anybody's, everyone's, somebody else's, neither's

NOTE: Use no apostrophe with personal pronouns like *his, hers, theirs, ours, its* (meaning "of it"). *It's* means "it is."

Use 's with only the last noun for joint possession in a pair or a series.

the architect and the builder's plan (The two jointly have one plan.)
the architect's and the builder's plans (They have different plans.)

Use ' to show omissions or to form contractions.

the roaring '20's, o'clock, jack-o'-lantern
we'll, don't, can't, it's (meaning "it is")

Use **'s** to form the plural of numerals, letters, and words being named.

three 7**'s** (but *three sevens*), four *a***'s**, six *the***'s**

■ **Exercise 4**

Underline the words that contain correctly used apostrophes.

1. the <u>people's</u> favorite, a persons' favorite, <u>everybody's</u> favorite
2. sheeps' wool, <u>deer's</u> horns, <u>cats'</u> eyes, a <u>cat's</u> eyes
3. the <u>Williams'</u> lawn, the <u>Williamses'</u> lawn, all the neighbor's lawns
4. the <u>youths'</u> organization, the <u>women's</u> club, the womens' club
5. it's food, <u>its food</u>, <u>hers</u>, her's
6. wasnt, <u>wasn't</u>, two ms, <u>three n's</u>
7. three <u>*why's*</u>, four *hows*
8. one <u>o'clock</u>, two oclock, three opossums
9. <u>Mary and Martin's</u> store (together they own one store) <u>Mary's and Martin's</u> stores (each owns a store)
10. our's, ours', its', <u>it's</u>

 Capital Letters   *cap*

Use a capital letter to begin a sentence and to designate a proper noun (the name of a particular person, place, or thing).

Capitalize the first word of a sentence, the pronoun *I,* and the interjection *O.*

How, O ye gods, can I control this joy?

Capitalize first, last, and important words in titles, including the second part of hyphenated words.

Across the River and into the Trees
"The Man Against the Sky"
"After Apple-Picking"

NOTE: Articles *(a, an, the),* short prepositions, and conjunctions are not capitalized unless they begin or end a title.
Capitalize first words of direct quotations.

The instructions warned, "Do not immerse in water."

Capitalize titles preceding a name.

President Truman

Capitalize the title of the head of a nation.

The President is not expected to arrive today.

Capitalize titles used specifically as substitutes for particular names.

Lieutenant Yo pleaded not guilty; the Lieutenant was found innocent.

NOTE: A title not followed by a name is usually not capitalized.

The treasurer gave the financial report.

Titles which are common nouns that name an office are not capitalized.

A college president has more duties than privileges.
A lieutenant deserves a good living allowance.

Capitalize degrees and titles after a name.

Jeffrey E. Tyndale, Ph.D., J.D.
Abraham Lincoln, Attorney at Law

NOTE: Do not capitalize names of occupations used as appositives or as descriptions.

Abraham Lincoln, a young lawyer from Springfield, took the case.

Capitalize words of family relationship used as names when not preceded by a possessive pronoun.

USED AS NAMES
After Father died, Mother carried on the business.

BUT
After my father died, my mother carried on the business.

Capitalize proper nouns but not general terms.

PROPER NOUNS	GENERAL TERMS
Plato, Platonic, Platonism	pasteurize
Venice, Venetian blind	a set of china
the West, a Westerner	west of the river
the Republican Party	a republican government
the Senior Class of Ivy College	a member of the senior class
Clifton Street	my street
the Mississippi River	the Mississippi and Ohio rivers
the Romantic Movement	the twentieth century

Capitalize months, days of the week, and holidays.

April, Friday, the Fourth of July, Labor Day

NOTE: Do not capitalize seasons and numbered days of the month unless they name holidays.

spring, the third of July

Capitalize B.C., A.D., words designating the Deity, religious denominations, and sacred books.

in 273 B.C.
the Messiah, our Maker, the Trinity, Yahweh, Allah, Buddha, Jesus
"Praise God from Whom all blessings flow."
Catholic, Protestant, Presbyterian
the Bible, the Koran

NOTE: Pronouns referring to the Deity are usually capitalized.

From Him all blessings flow.

Capitalize names of specific courses.

I registered for Sociology 101 and Chemistry 445.

NOTE: Do not capitalize studies (other than languages) which do not name specific courses.

I am taking English, sociology, and chemistry.

35 Abbreviations *ab*

Avoid most abbreviations in formal writing.

Spell out names of days, months, units of measurement, and (except in addresses) states and countries.

Friday (*not* Fri.)	pounds (*not* lbs.)
February (*not* Feb.)	Sauk Centre, Minnesota (*not* Minn.)

Do not use note-taking or shortcut signs such as *w/* for *with* and *&* for *and* in formal writing.

ABBREVIATIONS ACCEPTABLE IN ANY CONTEXT
Washington, D.C.

ABBREVIATIONS BEFORE NAMES
Mr., Mrs., Ms., Messrs., Mmes., Dr., St. *or* Ste. (for *Saint,* not *Street*), Mt.,
    Rev. (but only with a first name: *the Rev. Ernest Jones,* not *Rev. Jones*)

ABBREVIATIONS AFTER NAMES
M.D. (and other degrees), Jr., Sr., Esq.

ABBREVIATIONS WITHOUT PERIODS FOR MANY AGENCIES AND
ORGANIZATIONS
TVA, NAACP, FBI

ABBREVIATIONS WITH DATES AND TIME
B.C. and A.D. (with dates expressed in numerals, as *500 B.C.*) A.M. and P.M.
    or a.m. and p.m. (with hours expressed in numerals, as *4:00 A.M.*)

36 | Numbers   *num*

Spell out numbers that can be written in one or two words.

twenty-three, one thousand

Use figures for other numbers.

123   1¹³⁄₁₆ $1,001.00

NOTE: Newspapers and government publications generally use figures for numbers above ten.

EXCEPTIONS: Never use figures at the beginning of a sentence. Spell out the number or recast the sentence.

Use numerals for figures in sequences.

One polar bear weighed 200 pounds; another, 526; the third, 534.

Use figures for dates, street numbers, page references, percentages, and hours of the day used with A.M. or P.M.

USE FIGURES	SPELL OUT
July 3, 1776 (*not* 3rd)	the third of July
1010 State Street	Fifth Avenue
See page 50.	The book has fifty pages.
He paid 15 percent interest.	
The concert begins at 6 P.M.	The concert begins at
(or 6:00 P.M.)	six o'clock.

■ Exercise 5

Supply capitals as needed below. Change capital letters to lower case as necessary.

                          T   **L**   **R**   **W**   **S**
1. The book was entitled *the long road to wealth and the short*
   R   **P**
   road to poverty.

            C   C W

2. The small Country appeared to be headed for a Civil War,
        f

   but the Factions arrived at a peaceful settlement.
                          U   A   W

3. Captain Kaplan, united States Army, arrived on Wednesday
                                      B

   to find that he was late for the tour of buddhist temples.
                         C   M

4. When she registered for Chemistry, martha was told that she

   would need to take Algebra 101.
                    M D

5. Alfred Curall, m.d., attended the meeting of the American
                   A   T

   Medical Association and returned home before thanksgiving
   D

   day.
        W   C   n   c

6. Out West, Cowboys were numerous in the Nineteenth Cen-

   tury.
        w   s

7. In the Winter we sat around the fire, thinking of the Spring
                                                           R

   thaw and the pleasure of swimming again in the Ohio river.
                                                   A

8. Though the printer lived for a while on Magoni Avenue, he
                    D

   moved to detroit last August.
        v   p

9. The Salk Vaccine has all but eliminated the dangers of Polio,
                             m   j

   according to an article in a Medical Journal.
                               l

10. She wanted to become a Lawyer, she explained, because she
                                    l   m

   saw a direct connection between the Law and Morals.

■ **Exercise 6**

Place an X by the following which are not acceptable in formal writing, a ✔ by those which are acceptable.

✔ 1. May thirteenth
x 2. Twelve thirteen Jefferson Street
x 3. Jefferson Ave.
x 4. Mister and Mrs. Smidt
x 5. the biography of the ste.
x 6. Minneapolis, Minn., on 3 June 1940
x 7. Eng. 199 in the Dept. of English
x 8. the Cumberland and Tennessee Rivers
✔ 9. Page 10 in Chapter 11
x 10. Geo. Smith
x 11. William Adams, Junior
✔ 12. 300 B.C.
x 13. etc.
✔ 14. five hundred dollars
x 15. five hundred and ten bushels
x 16. December 24th, 1985
x 17. Interstate Seventy-Five
✔ 18. five million dollars
✔ 19. Friday, June 13
x 20. 103 lbs.

Diction and Style

37	Standard English
	and Style *d*

Use Standard English. Conform to established usage in writing and speech.

Standard English is the generally accepted language in English-speaking countries. It is the language of educated persons. Though it varies in usage and in pronunciation from one country or region to another (indicated by labels such as *U.S.* or *Brit.* in dictionaries), it is the standard which is taught in schools and colleges.

    Nonstandard English consists of usages, spellings, and pronunciations not usually found in the speech or writing of educated persons. Read the entry labels in a dictionary to determine whether a word is standard or nonstandard. The presence of a word in a dictionary does not make it always appropriate and correct.

    Diction is the choice and use of words. Consult your dictionary for definitions of the labels it employs (for example, *Slang, Dialect, Vulgar, Poetic, Informal, Obsolete*).

    Informal or **colloquial** language (terms used almost interchangeably) is appropriate in certain situations though not usually in college papers. Contractions—*don't, isn't,* and so forth—are informal. **Colloquial** does not mean **dialect.**

37a Using the Dictionary

Dictionaries, which record current and past usage, are good sources of information about language. In minor matters dictionaries do not always agree. In current dictionaries, for example, you will find disagreement about *cooperate, co-operate,* and *coöperate.*

Particularly useful at the college level are the following desk dictionaries:

The American Heritage Dictionary. Boston: Houghton Mifflin Company.
The Random House College Dictionary. New York: Random House.
Webster's New Collegiate Dictionary. Springfield, Mass.: G. & C. Merriam
   Company.
Webster's New World Dictionary of the American Language. Cleveland: Wil-
   liam Collins Publishers, Inc.

You should know how to look up a word, a word group, and many kinds of information in your dictionary. It is not necessary to know all the different methods used by different dictionaries. Instead, select one and study carefully its explanations and systems. Read the entry on pp. 190–191 for the word *double* as given in *The American Heritage Dictionary* and study the explanatory material in red. Use this example as a guide. (A similar chart is included in the prefatory material of *Webster's New Collegiate Dictionary.*)

Style is the way writers express their thoughts in language. Effective writing always involves the choice of words and expressions, the arrangement of words, and variety in the patterns of sentences. The ways in which similar ideas are expressed may have vastly different effects, and many of the distinctions are a matter of style. Writing may be whimsical, poetic, terse, flippant, imaginative, literal, and so on. Develop the habit of noticing the personality of what you read and what you write. Your style should be appropriate to your subject and to your own character.

37b Generally, avoid slang.

Too often slang is a popular rubber stamp which only approximates exact thought. The expression "He's a jerk" does not com-

Dictionary Entry

Dictionaries provide the kinds of information indicated here in several ways. Other information (synonyms, variants, capitalization, and so on) appears in many entries. Find the explanations you need in any dictionary.

① Boldfaced main entry   ② Dot indicating division between syllables   ③ Phonetic spelling for pronunciation (see key at bottom of page)   ④ Accented syllable   ⑤ Abbreviation for part of speech—adjective   ⑥ Illustrative example (see all the words in red ovals in the entry)   ⑦ Words in red blocks indicate abbreviations for terms which label specialized or technical meanings   ⑧ Part of speech—noun. Note that the numbers start over when the part of speech changes.   ⑨ Part of speech—verb   ⑩ Forms of the verb—past tense and past participle, present participle, third-person singular   ⑪ Kind of verb—transitive (see **5** in this book)   ⑫ Kind of verb—intransitive (see **5** in this book)   ⑬ Phrasal verb (used in *AHD* to mean verb plus adverb *or* preposition)   ⑭ Part of speech—adverb   ⑮ Idioms (see **37f** in this book)   ⑯ Usage label (see **37, 37b-d** in this book)   ⑰ Etymologies are given in square brackets. Some dictionaries give the etymology early in the entry.   ⑱ A noun derived from the main entry.

① ②   ③ ④ ⑤   ⑥

dou·ble (dŭb′əl) *adj.* **1.** Twice as much in size, strength, number, or amount: *a double dose.* **2.** Composed of two like parts: *double doors.* **3.** Composed of two unlike parts; dual: *a double meaning.* **4.** Accommodating or designed for two: *a double sleeping bag.* **5. a.** Acting two parts: *a double role.* **b.** Characterized by duplicity; deceitful: *speak with a double tongue.* **6.** *Bot.* Having many more than the usual number of petals, usually in a crowded or overlapping arrangement: *a double chrysanthemum.* —*n.* **1.** Something increased twofold. **2. a.** A duplicate of another; counterpart. **b.** An apparition; wraith. **3.** An actor's understudy. **4. a.** A sharp turn in running; reversal. **b.** An evasive reversal or shift in argument. **5. doubles.** A game, such as tennis or handball, having two players on each side. **6.** *Baseball.* A two-base hit. **7. a.** A bid in bridge indicating strength to one's partner; request for a bid. **b.** A bid doubling one's opponent's bid in bridge thus increasing the penalty for failure to fulfill the contract. **c.** A hand justifying such a bid. —*v.* **-bled, -bling, -bles.** —*tr.* **1.** To make twice as great. **2.** To be twice as much as. **3.** To fold in two. **4.** To duplicate; repeat. **5.** *Baseball.* **a.** To cause the scoring of (a run) by hitting a double. **b.** To advance or score (a runner) by hitting a double. **6.** *Baseball.* To put out (a runner) as the second part of a double play. **7.** To challenge (an opponent's bid) with a double in bridge. **8.** *Mus.* To duplicate (another part or voice) an octave higher or lower or in unison. **9.** *Naut.* To sail around: *double a cape.* —*intr.* **1.** To be increased twofold. **2.** To turn sharply backward; reverse: *double back on one's trail.* **3.** To serve in an additional capacity. **4.** To replace an actor in the execution of a given action or in the actor's absence. **5.** *Baseball.* To hit a double. **6.** To announce a double in bridge. —*phrasal verb.* **double up. 1.** To bend suddenly, as in pain or laughter. **2.** To share accommodations meant for one person. —*adv.* **1. a.** To twice the extent; doubly. **b.** To twice the amount: *double your money back.* **2.** Two together: *sleeping double.* **3.** In two: *bent double.* —*idioms.* **on (or at) the double.** *Informal.* **1.** In double time. **2.** Immediately. **see double.** To see two images of a single object, usually as a result of visual aberration. [ME < OFr. < Lat. *duplus.*] —**dou′ble·ness** *n.* ⑱

municate exactly. What precisely does it mean—except that he is in some vague way unattractive?

Slang expressions in student papers are usually out of place. They are particularly inappropriate in a context that is otherwise dignified.

In the opinion of some students, the dean's commencement address *stunk.*

When Macbeth recoiled at the thought of murder, Lady Macbeth urged him not to *chicken out.*

Although slang can be offensive, it is sometimes colorful. Some words that once were slang are now considered Standard English. "Jazz" in its original meaning and "dropout" were once slang; and because no other word was found to convey quite the same social meanings as "date," it is no longer slang. As a rule, however, you should avoid words still considered slang, not because they are too modern for conservative ears and eyes or because they are offensive to stuffy people, but because they are generally not as precise or as widely known as Standard English.

37c Avoid illiteracies and dialect (substandard English).

Illiteracies, which are found in the language of uneducated people, should be avoided in speech or writing.

NOT
The dentist ain't ready yet. Would you care to set down?

Dialect—Regional, occupational, or ethnic words and usages should be avoided except when they are consciously used to give a provincial flavor to language.

There is no reason to erase all dialectal characteristics from talk and writing. They may be a cultural heritage and a source of richness and variety, but in general communication avoid expressions which are local or substandard.

37d   Avoid archaic words.

Archaisms (*oft* for "frequent" and *yond* for "yonder" are examples) are out-of-date words and therefore inappropriate in modern speech and writing.

■ Exercise 1

In class, discuss usage in the following sentences.

1. Teen-agers is just as hip as they ever was, but a lot of them keep their doings quiet.
2. The speedsters heard on their ears that smokey was only three miles away on the blacktop.
3. The hairdresser was shook up because the shoppe had been sold.
4. The teller was instructed to tote the bread back to the vault and to follow the boss to his office.
5. Late payments always gross out sourpuss bill collectors.
6. What cleared him was that the pigs discovered the loot in his friend's suitcase.
7. Ere the rain ceased, the group of tourists were besprinkled, but their enthusiasm was not dampened.
8. He couldn't do nothing without the supervisor's giving him the eyeball and coming down hard on him.
9. The dispatcher reckoned that the plane'd arrive betimes, provided of course that the runways was not congested.
10. The award went to a little-known actress who played good the part of an erstwhile beauty.

37e Do not use a word as one part of speech when it should be another.

Generally any improper use of a word is called an **impropriety.** More narrowly, the term is used to apply to words which are used as the wrong part of speech. Many nouns, for example, cannot also be used as verbs and vice versa. When in doubt, check the part of speech of a word in a dictionary.

NOUN FOR ADJECTIVE   VERB DERIVED FROM NOUN FORM
psychology approach   *suspicioned*

VERB FOR NOUN   VERB FOR ADJECTIVE
good *eats*   *militate* leader

ADJECTIVE FOR ADVERB
surprising large number

Words that are used inexactly in meaning are also improprieties. See **37i.**

37f Use correct idioms.

An **idiom** is a construction with its own distinct meaning. Taken literally, the individual words may seem to mean something entirely different from their meaning in the complete expression. Expressions such as "catch the eye" and "by and large" are strange and puzzling unless their idiomatic meanings are known. Idioms come automatically to one who knows the language well, but they may cause serious difficulties to others.

Be sure that you are using all the words correctly in an idiomatic expression, for one wrong word will make the whole expression a glaring error.

Most errors in idioms result from using a preposition and a verb which do not ordinarily belong together.

UNIDIOMATIC	IDIOMATIC
according with	according to
capable to	capable of
conform in	conform to (*or* with)
die from	die of
ever now and then	every now and then
excepting for	except for
identical to	identical with
in accordance to	in accordance with
incapable to do	incapable of doing
in search for	in search of
intend on doing	intend to do
in the year of 1976	in the year 1976
lavish with gifts	lavish gifts on
off of	off
on a whole	on the whole
outlook of life	outlook on life
plan on	plan to
prior than	prior to
similar with	similar to
superior than	superior to
try and see	try to see
type of a	type of

See **49** or a dictionary for help with other idioms.

■ **Exercise 2**

Select a verb that is the common denominator in several idioms, such as carry *(carry out, carry over, carry through, and so forth). Look it up in a dictionary. Study the idioms and be prepared to discuss them in class. Does the change of a preposition result in an opposite meaning? A slight change in meaning? No change?*

■ **Exercise 3**

Point out the incorrect prepositions and supply the correct ones in the following sentences.

                                            to

1. All delegates to the meeting were committed <u>for</u> a plan for

    peace.

                          of

2. The jury acquitted him <u>by</u> the charge of loitering.

                                              with

3. The candidate maintained that he had complied <u>to</u> every one

    of the laws.

                                    of

4. The hiker said that he was incapable <u>to</u> going on.

5. The professor stated that his good students would conform
   to
   <u>with</u> any requirement.

                               to

6. The employees complained <u>with</u> the manager because of

    their long hours.

                              in

7. Many vitamins are helpful <u>to</u> preventing diseases.

                             to

8. The lecturer took exception <u>about</u> the questioner's final

    point.
   On

9. <u>Upon</u> the whole, matters could be much worse.

                      in

10. Let us rejoice <u>for</u> the knowledge that we are free.

37g Avoid specialized vocabulary in writing for the general reader.

All specialists, whether engineers, chefs, or philosophers, have their own vocabularies. Some technical words find their way into general use; most do not. The plant red clover is well known, but not by its botanical name, *Trifolium pratense.*

Specialists should use the language of nonspecialists when they hope to communicate with general readers. The following passage, for instance, would not be comprehensible to a wide audience.

> The neonate's environment consists in primitively contrasted perceptual fields weak and strong: loud noises, bright lights, smooth surfaces, compared with silence, darkness and roughness. The behavior of the neonate has to be accounted for chiefly by inherited motor connections between receptors and effectors. There is at this stage, in addition to the autonomic nervous system, only the sensori motor system to call on. And so the ability of the infant to discriminate is exceedingly low. But by receiving and sorting random data through the identification of recurrent regularity, he does begin to improve reception. Hence he can surrender the more easily to single motivations, ego-involvement in satisfactions.
>
> JAMES K. FEIBLEMAN,
> *The Stages of Human Life: A Biography of Entire Man*

Contrast the above passage with the following, which is on the same general subject but which is written so that the general reader—not just a specialized few—can understand it.

> Research clearly indicates that an infant's senses are functional at birth. He experiences the whack from the doctor. He is sensitive to pressure, to changes in temperature, and to pain, and he responds specifically to these stimuli. . . . How about sight? Research on infants 4–8 weeks of age shows that they can see about as well as adults. . . . The difference is that the infant cannot make sense out of what he sees. Nevertheless, what he sees does register, and he begins to take in visual information at birth. . . . In summary, the neonate (an infant less than a month old) is sensitive not only to inter-

nal but also to external stimuli. Although he cannot respond adequately, he does take in and process information.

IRA J. GORDON,
Human Development: From Birth through Adolescence

The only technical term in the passage is *neonate;* unlike the writer of the first passage, who also uses the word, the second author defines it for the general reader. Special vocabularies may obscure meaning. Moreover, they tempt the writer into the use of inflated words instead of plain ones—a style sometimes known as *gobbledygook* or *governmentese* because it flourishes in bureaucratic writing. Harry S Truman made a famous statement about the presidency: "The buck stops here." This straightforward assertion might be written by some bureaucrats as follows: "It is incumbent upon the President of the United States of America to uphold the responsibility placed upon him by his constituents to exercise the final decision-making power."

37h   Avoid triteness and clichés. Strive for fresh and original expressions.

Clichés are phrases and figures of speech that were once fresh and original but have been used so much that they have lost their effectiveness. Avoid extravagance, but be original enough so that your words have the freshness of a newly typed page rather than the faint tracings of a carbon copy.

Study the following twenty phrases as examples of triteness. Avoid pat expressions like these.

words cannot express	method in their madness
each and every	straight from the shoulder
Mother Nature	first and foremost
sober as a judge	hard as a rock

other side of the coin	in the final analysis
slowly but surely	sweet as sugar
in this day and age	the bottom line
few and far between	all walks of life
last but not least	easier said than done
interesting to note	better late than never

37i Be exact. Use words in their precise meanings.

Misuse of a word so that it does not convey exactly the intended meaning produces confusion. Preciseness requires knowledge of idiom and a good vocabulary. Check a dictionary whenever you have the slightest question. Misuse of *preservation*, for example, for *conservation* would cause misunderstanding. The italicized words in the following sentences are used inexactly.

The new rocket was *literally* as fast as lightning. (*Figuratively* is intended. Use *seems to be.*)
The captain of the team was *overtaken* by the heat. (The proper word is *overcome.*)

Words that are similar in sound but different in meaning can cause the writer embarrassment and the reader confusion.

A wrongful act usually results in a guilty *conscious. (conscience)*
The heroine of the novel was not embarrassed by her *congenial* infirmity. *(congenital)*
As the sun beams down, the swamp looks gray; it has only the unreal color of dead *vegetarian. (vegetation)*

Other words sometimes confused because they sound alike are *climatic* for *climactic, statue* for *stature* (or vice versa), *incidences* for *incidents,* and *course* for *coarse.* Nonwords should never be used: *interpretate* for *interpret,* and *tutorer* for *tutor.*

■ **Exercise 4**

Point out clichés and inexact words and expressions in the following sentences.

1. It goes without saying that the value of a college education cannot be measured in money, but tuition is high as a kite.
2. The meal was fabulous, and the service was fantastic.
3. Although the model claimed she wanted to marry a strong, silent type, she tied the knot with a man who could talk the horns off a billygoat.
4. Holidays always repress some people.
5. On the outskirts of the small town a sign was erected that renounced that this was the home of the one and only Fitz Fritzsimmons.
6. The survivor was weak as a kitten after eight days on the ocean, but his overall condition was unbelievable.
7. The brothers were as different as night and day, but each drank like a fish.
8. The eager young attorney jumped to her feet and cried, "That is irrelavent and immaterial."
9. At the retirement dinner the corporation president toasted the old engineer and told him that his daily presents in the building would be soarly missed.
10. As he looked back, the farmer thought of those mornings as cold as ice when the ground was hard as a rock and when he shook like a leaf as he rose at the crack of dawn.

37j   Add new words to your vocabulary.

Good writers know many words, and they can select the precise ones they need to express their meanings. A good vocabulary displays your mentality, your education, and your talents as a writer.

In reading, pay careful attention to words you have not seen before. Look them up in a dictionary. Remember them. Recognize them the next time you see them. Learn to use them.

■ **Exercise 5**

Underline the letter identifying the best definition.

1. *contingency:* (a) series (b) important point (c) possible condition (d) rapidly
2. *aegis:* (a) sponsorship (b) eagerness (c) foreign (d) overly proper
3. *summit:* (a) highest point (b) total amount (c) heir (d) exhibition
4. *magnanimity:* (a) state of wealth (b) excellent health (c) strong attraction (d) generosity
5. *credibility:* (a) debt (b) kindness (c) knowledge (d) believability
6. *gullible:* (a) capable of flight (b) flexible (c) easily tricked (d) intelligent
7. *patent:* (a) obvious (b) long-suffering (c) omen (d) victim
8. *audible:* (a) capable of being heard (b) overly idealistic (c) easily read (d) tasty
9. *adamant:* (a) without measure (b) unyielding (c) fragrant (d) judicial decision
10. *travesty:* (a) long journey (b) congested traffic (c) scaffolding (d) mockery
11. *innate:* (a) void of sense (b) inborn (c) applied (d) digestible
12. *acrimonious:* (a) bitter (b) ritualistic (c) hypocritical (d) massive
13. *insurgents:* (a) deep cuts (b) rebels (c) music makers (d) physicians
14. *duress:* (a) fancy dress (b) with quickness (c) stress (d) penalty
15. *flagrant:* (a) odorous (b) conspicuously bad (c) beaten (d) delicious

16. *substantive:* (a) substantial (b) in place of (c) religious (d) hardheaded
17. *imprudent:* (a) unwise (b) lacking modesty (c) ugly (d) incapable of proof
18. *solicitous:* (a) seeking sales (b) without energy (c) heroic (d) concerned
19. *valid:* (a) butler (b) favorable (c) desirable (d) founded on truth
20. *charlatan:* (a) robe (b) quack (c) high official (d) strong wind

■ **Exercise 6**

Underline the letter identifying the best definition.

1. *impetus:* (a) egomaniac (b) incentive (c) ghost (d) perfectionist
2. *dire:* (a) terrible (b) bare (c) final (d) dishonest
3. *subpoena:* (a) below ground (b) in disguise (c) legal summons (d) unspoken
4. *commentary:* (a) explanations (b) military store (c) grouch (d) headland
5. *prodigy:* (a) extraordinary person (b) wasteful person (c) lover of children (d) musician
6. *vacillate:* (a) oil (b) repair (c) waver (d) empty
7. *peer:* (a) an equal (b) an ideal (c) an emotion (d) intense
8. *poignant:* (a) housecoat (b) fruitful (c) hostile (d) piercingly effective
9. *spurious:* (a) brimming over (b) pricking (c) not genuine (d) affectionate
10. *perennial:* (a) continuing (b) circus show (c) circular (d) filial
11. *contend:* (a) incantate (b) appease (c) compete (d) look after
12. *scapegoat:* (a) one being sought (b) one taking blame for others (c) one who looks stupid (d) one guilty of crime
13. *pomposity:* (a) heaviness (b) splendor (c) scarcity (d) arrogance
14. *banal:* (a) commonplace (b) fatal (c) aggressive (d) tropical
15. *parameter:* (a) restatement (b) expansion (c) limit (d) device for measuring sound

16. *acute:* (a) appealing (b) critical (c) average (d) unorthodox
17. *vibrant:* (a) blunted (b) double (c) irritating (d) energetic
18. *presume:* (a) guess (b) judge (c) know (d) take for granted
19. *gesture:* (a) demonstration (b) internal disorder (c) joke (d) court clown
20. *veracity:* (a) boldness (b) speed (c) great anger (d) truthfulness

■ **Exercise 7**

Place the number on the left by the appropriate letter on the right.

1. heady	12	a.	exaggeration
2. reciprocate	13	b.	customary
3. dispiriting	2	c.	repay
4. literally	17	d.	a ranking
5. consecrate	15	e.	imitation
6. bolster	16	f.	basic
7. ideology	4	g.	in actuality
8. anticipate	10	h.	unreal
9. incorrigible	11	i.	opposition
10. fantastic	1	j.	impetuous
11. antagonism	14	k.	a showing forth
12. hyperbole	18	l.	one who comes before
13. conventional	19	m.	twist
14. manifestation	9	n.	not reformable
15. mimicry	3	o.	disheartening
16. seminal	8	p.	foresee
17. hierarchy	5	q.	make sacred
18. predecessor	7	r.	set of beliefs
19. distort	20	s.	maze
20. labyrinth	6	t.	support

■ **Exercise 8**

Select the word or phrase that most exactly defines the italicized word in each sentence.

1. An *obdurate* attitude seldom leads to prosperity. (egotistical, hard-hearted, wasteful, false)
2. He felt it his *prerogative* to speak out. (turn, responsibility, right, nature)
3. The speech was marked by *vapid* expressions. (inspiring, dull, vigorous, sad)
4. The *renowned* singer performed in the small town. (famous, unknown, opera, talented)
5. *Gluttony*, explained the slim traveler, was not one of his faults. (hitchhiking, stagnation, overeating, speeding)
6. The banker's *salient* traits were frugality and kindness. (prominent, best, hidden, lacking)
7. Imagining himself a great statesman, he was the prime minister's *lackey*. (assistant, servile follower, hair groomer, moral superior)
8. The *laconic* old woman stood out among the group of excited young men. (untalkative, diseased, depressed, evil)
9. Not all those who took part in the robbery were *depraved*. (needy, evil, prepared, punished)
10. The gem was pronounced an *authentic* emerald. (genuine, artificial, rare, expensive)

■ **Exercise 9**

Follow the instructions for Exercise 7.

1. The judge found the defendant's answer *incredible*. (highly impressive, wonderful, not believable, awful)
2. A *transcript* was made of the tapes. (recording, written copy, mockery, extension)
3. To discuss the matter further would be to *obfuscate* it. (avoid, obscure, criticize, clarify)
4. I *deplore* the method used to recover the gems. (praise, understand, regret, follow)

5. The poem was composed by an *anonymous* author. (dead, foreign, excellent, <u>unknown</u>)
6. Finding the essay *provocative,* she discussed it with her tutor. (<u>stimulating</u>, disgusting, prolonged, offensive)
7. The child *reluctantly* joined her brother in the swimming pool. (rapidly, <u>hesitantly</u>, joyfully, playfully)
8. *Platitudes* can quickly destroy the effectiveness of a lecture. (catcalls, stutterings, <u>stale truisms</u>, bad jokes)
9. A *sorcerer* was said to be the king's only companion. (healer, valiant warrior, jester, <u>wizard</u>)
10. Make the report as *succinct* as possible. (colorful, <u>concise</u>, long, accurate)

■ **Exercise 10**

Dictionaries disagree about the levels of particular words. Read the preliminary pages in your dictionary, and study the labels which it applies to particular words. Webster's New Collegiate Dictionary *uses fewer and less restrictive labels than other college dictionaries. Without your dictionary, put by ten of the following words the labels which you believe they should have. Then look each word up and determine which label it has in your dictionary.*

If a word is not labeled, it is considered formal.

1. corny
2. flicks (motion pictures)
3. flickers (motion pictures)
4. ain't
5. tram (a streetcar)
6. cram (concentrated study)
7. the tube (television)
8. the telly (television)
9. TV
10. goof (bungle)
11. bomb (to fail)
12. bull (nonsense)
13. phony
14. kook
15. wimp
16. hi-fi
17. freak (an enthusiast)
18. freakish
19. squeal (to betray)
20. bummer (a failure)

38 | Wordiness   *w*

Do not use needless words and irrelevant ideas.

Conciseness increases the force of writing. Do not pad your paper merely to obtain a desired length or number of words.

USE ONE WORD FOR MANY

The love letter was written by somebody who did not sign a name. (13 words)

The love letter was anonymous (*or* not signed). (5 or 6 words)

USE THE ACTIVE VOICE FOR CONCISENESS (SEE **5**)

The truck was overloaded by the workmen. (7 words)

The workmen overloaded the truck. (5 words)

REVISE SENTENCES FOR CONCISENESS

Another element which adds to the effectiveness of a speech is its emotional appeal. (14 words)

Emotional appeal also makes a speech more effective. (8 words)

AVOID CONSTRUCTIONS WITH *IT IS . . .* AND *THERE ARE . . . .*

There are some conditions *that* are satisfactory. (7 words)

Some conditions are satisfactory. (4 words)

It is truth *which* will prevail. (6 words)

Truth will prevail. (3 words)

DO NOT USE TWO WORDS WITH THE SAME MEANING (TAUTOLOGY)

basic and fundamental principles (4 words)

basic principles (2 words)

Study your sentences carefully and make them concise by using all the preceding methods. Do not, however, sacrifice concreteness and vividness for conciseness and brevity.

CONCRETE AND VIVID
At each end of the sunken garden, worn granite steps, flanked by large
magnolia trees, lead to formal paths.

EXCESSIVELY CONCISE
The garden has steps at both ends.

■ Exercise 11

Express the following sentences succinctly. Do not omit important ideas.

1. The kudzu plant is a plant which was introduced into America from Japan in order to prevent erosion and the washing away of the land and which has become a nuisance and a pest in some areas because it chokes out trees and other vegetation.
   Kudzu, which was introduced into America from Japan in order to prevent erosion, has become a nuisance in some areas because it chokes out other plants.

2. The cry of a peacock is audible to the ear for miles.
   The cry of a peacock is audible for miles.

3. The custom which once was so popular of speaking to fellow students while passing by them on the campus has almost disappeared from college manners and habits.
   The once-popular custom of speaking to fellow students on the campus has almost disappeared.

4. There are several reasons why officers of the law ought to be trained in the law of the land, and two of these are as follows. The first of these reasons is that policemen can enforce the law better if they are familiar with it. And second, they will be less likely to violate the rights of private citizens if they know exactly and accurately what these rights are.
   Officers should know the law so that they can enforce it better and avoid violating the rights of citizens.

5. Although the Kentucky rifle played an important and significant part in getting food for the frontiersmen who settled the American West, its function as a means of protection was in no degree any less significant in their lives.

   Although the Kentucky rifle played an important part in getting food for the frontiersmen, its protective function was just as significant.

6. Some television programs, especially public television programs, assume a high level of public intelligence and present their shows to the public in an intelligent way.

   Some public television programs assume a high level of public mentality and present intelligent shows.

7. It is not possible that any large American chestnut trees survived the terrible blight of the trees in the year of 1925.

   No large American chestnut trees survived the terrible blight of 1925.

8. The pilot who will fly the plane is a cautious man, and he foresees unusual flying conditions.

   The pilot is a cautious flyer.

9. It is a pleasure for some to indulge in eating large quantities of food at meals, but medical doctors of medicine tell us that such pleasures can only bring with them unpleasant results in the long run of things.

   The joys of overeating, doctors say, can have only unpleasant results.

10. The essay consists of facts which describe vividly many of the events in the life of a typical juggler. In this description the author uses a vocabulary which is easy to understand. This vocabulary is on neither too high a level nor too low a level, but on one which can be understood by any high school graduate.

    In simple language the essay describes vividly many events in the life of a typical juggler.

39 | Repetition   *rep*

Avoid redundancy—excessive repetition of words and sounds. Repeat for emphasis rarely and carefully.

Unintentional repetition is seldom effective. Avoid by using synonyms and pronouns and by omitting words.

39a Do not needlessly repeat words.

REPETITIOUS
The history of human flight is full of histories of failures on the part of those who have tried flight and were failures.

IMPROVED
The history of human flight recounts many failures.

Do not revise by excessively substituting synonyms for repeated words.

WORDY SYNONYMS
The history of human flight is full of stories of failures on the part of those who have tried to glide through the air and met with no success.

39b Do not needlessly repeat sounds.

REPEATED SOUNDS
The biologist again *checked* the *charts* to determine the *effect* of the poison on the *insect.*

IMPROVED

The biologist again studied the charts to determine the effect of the poison on the moth.

39c Repeat only for emphasis or for clarity.

Effective repetition of a word or a phrase may unify, clarify, or create emphasis, especially in aphorisms or poetry.

Searching without knowledge is like *searching* in the dark.

"Beauty is truth, truth beauty."

JOHN KEATS

■ **Exercise 12**

Rewrite the following passage. Avoid wordiness and undesirable repetition.

~~One of the pleasing things that all~~ **P**eoples of all lands **and ages** have

enjoyed ~~since the earliest dawning of civilizations is the pleasure~~

~~of listening to~~ the melodious strands of music. **, which some great** ~~Music, wrote some~~

poet has said **it**
~~great poet,~~ can soothe the savage breast and make ~~him or her~~

Possibly, however, some younger people may be listening
calm. ~~A question may arise in the minds of many, however, as to~~

too frequently to their favorite music.
~~whether some of our members of the younger generation may~~

~~not be exposing themselves too frequently to music they like and~~

~~listen to almost constantly.~~

Nearly every day one meets a young person, for example, with a
~~To me, the answer to the above question is just possibly in~~
radio who listens to music
~~the affirmative, and the evidence that I would give would be in~~

~~the form of a figure that we see nearly every day. This is the fig-~~

~~ure, usually a young person but not always, of a person with a~~

~~radio or stereo headset who is listening to music~~ while doing
should   the full
some ~~such~~ activity that ~~used to~~ occupy ~~all of one's~~ attention and
Sometimes a person in the library looks through books while
time. ~~In the library of a college such a figure is now sometimes to~~
wearing a headset.
~~be seen looking through books with a headset on his or her head.~~
of this sort
Some ~~of these~~ music lovers seem incapable of ~~even~~ taking a walk
and enjoying
~~to enjoy~~ the beauty of nature.~~without their headsets.~~

If we enjoy good music,
~~If music is good and if we enjoy it, the reader may now ask,~~

It so   as modern
what is wrong with listening to ~~music more~~ frequently ~~than we~~
~~electronics enable us to do? It is not old-fashioned to believe that those~~
~~used to be able to listen to music thanks to the present modern~~
who spend much of their time with headsets on are missing some-
~~improvements and developments in the electronic medium? It~~
thing, other important and pleasurable sensory experiences—the
~~may seem old-fashioned and out-of-date to object to headsets~~
sounds of birds and even just the quiet of the morning. Further, it is
~~just because we did not used to have them and they are relatively~~
hard to think while the ear is piped full of music. Time that should be
~~new on the scene. What is important, here, however, is the point~~
used for thinking is also lost, time when we develop and mature intel-
~~that those who spend so much of their time with headsets on are~~

lectually. All kinds of music, even rock, have an important place, but
~~missing something. They may be getting a lot of music, but they~~
music should not be allowed to exclude too many other valuable expe-
~~are missing something. What they are missing can be classified~~
riences.
~~under the general heading of other important and pleasurable~~

~~sensory experiences that they could be experiencing, such as~~

~~hearing the sounds that birds make and just enjoying the quiet~~

~~that morning sometimes brings. In addition to this, it is hard to~~

~~think while music is being piped into the ear of the listener. We~~

~~lose time, therefore, that should by all rights be reserved for~~

~~thinking and contemplation, which is to say, that time when we all~~

~~develop and mature intellectually. Music, all kinds of music, even~~

~~rock music, has an important place in the lives of humankind, but~~

~~let us not so fall in love with its seductive appeal that beckons us~~

~~that we let it intrude upon the territory of other valuable and es-~~

~~sential experiences.~~

40 Abstract and General Words   *abst*

Do not write abstractly or vaguely. Choose specific and
concrete words.

Abstract writing may communicate little information or even cause misunderstanding.

Words which pinpoint meaning form the basis of the most exact and the best writing. To describe a sofa as **pleasing** is to be less precise than to say it is **comfortable.** Specific words say what you think. They do not permit disputable or ambiguous meanings.

NOT SPECIFIC
She complained that *things* prevented her from studying.

SPECIFIC
She complained that *conversations with her friends* prevented her from studying.

Concreteness is relevant in all kinds of writing: a college catalogue; a business letter; instructions on how to put together a gas grill; a speech; a paper; art, fiction, or poetry.

■ Exercise 13

The following ten words or phrases are general. For any five of them substitute four specific and concrete words. Do not let your substitutions be synonymous with each other.

EXAMPLE
tools   claw hammer, screwdriver, monkey wrench, saw

1. decorations
2. buildings
3. leaders
4. plants
5. food
6. electric machines
7. communications

8. workers
9. emotions
10. hobbies

■ **Exercise 14**

Write your personal definition of one of the following abstract terms in a paragraph of about two hundred words. Give concrete instances from your experience.

wisdom   love   progress   peace of mind   integrity

41 Connotation   *con*

Choose words with connotations appropriate to tone and content.

Many words carry special associations, suggestions, or emotional overtones—**connotations.** What *dog* suggests besides the literal *four-legged carnivore* is connotation, which can be pleasant or unpleasant. To one person *dog* may suggest friendship; to another once attacked by a dog, the word may connote terror.

A good writer uses connotations to evoke planned emotional reactions. To suggest sophistication, the writer may mention a *lap dog;* to evoke the amusing or the rural, *hound dog.* To connote a social or moral distinction, the writer may call someone a *cur.* Even this word may have different connotations: a social worker may react sympathetically to it; a snob, contemptuously. Consider the associations aroused by *canine, pooch, mutt, mongrel, puppy,* and *watchdog.* Even some breeds arouse different responses: *bloodhound, shepherd, St. Bernard, poodle.*

Denotations of words are precise meanings, the exact definitions given in dictionaries. Words that are denotative synonyms may have very different connotative overtones. Consider the following:

drummer—salesperson—field representative
slender—thin—skinny

Be sure that your words give the suggestions you wish to convey. A single word with the wrong connotation can easily spoil a passage. Only one word has been changed in the following quotation:

Let us never bargain out of fear. But let us never fear to bargain.

President Kennedy actually wrote:

Let us never negotiate out of fear. But let us never fear to negotiate.

Because it is too informal, the word *bargain* ruins the tone of the statement even though it is a close synonym for *negotiate.*

▨ Exercise 15

The ten words or phrases in the left column below name a subject. The right column gives a word referring to that subject. For each word in the right column, list a close synonym that is much more favorable in connotation and another that is much more unfavorable.

Subject matter

1. weight	**stout**
2. intelligence	**sense**
3. writing style	**intelligible**

4. food	**edible**
5. degree of value	**economical**
6. personality	**fairly agreeable**
7. physical skill	**coordinated**
8. exactness of measurement	**close enough**
9. efficiency	**competent**
10. beauty	**attractive**

Figurative Language   *fig*

Avoid mixed and inappropriate figures of speech. Use fresh figures.

Figures of speech compare one thing (usually abstract) with another (usually literal or concrete).

Mixed figures associate things which are not logically consistent.

MIXED

These corporations lashed out with legal loopholes.
(You cannot *strike* with a *hole.*)

Inappropriate figures of speech compare one thing with another in a way that violates the mood or the intention.

INAPPROPRIATE

Shakespeare is the most famous brave in our tribe of English writers. (It is inappropriate and puzzling to compare Shakespeare to an Indian brave and a group of writers to an Indian tribe.)

Use figurative comparisons (of things not literally similar) for vivid explanation and for originality. A simile, a metaphor, or a personification gives you a chance to compare or to explain what you are saying in a different way from the sometimes prosaic method of pure statement, argument, or logic.

METAPHORS (IMPLIED COMPARISONS)
Though calm without, the young senator was a volcano within.
Old courthouse records are rotting leaves of the past.

SIMILES (COMPARISONS STATED WITH *LIKE* OR *AS*)
Though calm without, the young senator was like a volcano within.
Old courthouse records are like rotting leaves of the past.

■ **Exercise 16**

Explain the flaws in these figures of speech.

1. The new racer flew once around the track and then limped into the pit like a sick horse into its stable.
   Comparing a machine first to a bird and then to a horse is a flawed mixture.
2. The speaker's flamboyant oration began with all the beauty of the song of a canary.
   The volume, pitch, and rhythm of an oration are not embodied well in a sound like the song of a canary.
3. The faucet was leaking with the steadiness of the tread of a marching army.
   The pounding of a marching army does not figure a faucet well.
4. The warm greetings of the students sounded like a horde of apes rushing through a jungle.
   Mannerly human responses are not well expressed in the simile of rushing apes.
5. He nipped the plan in the bud by pouring cold water on all suggestions.
   Nipping (cutting) is not similar to pouring a cold liquid.

■ **Exercise 17**

Compose and bring to class two fresh and appropriate figures of speech.

■ **Exercise 18**

Find two figures of speech in your reading and show how they are mixed or especially appropriate or inappropriate.

 Flowery Language   *fl*

Avoid ornate and pretentious language.

Flowery language is wordy, overwrought, and artificial. Often falsely elegant, it calls attention to itself. In the hope that such language will sound deep and wise, some inexperienced writers substitute it for naturalness and simplicity.

PLAIN LANGUAGE	FLOWERY LANGUAGE
The year 1981	The year of 1981
Now	At this point in time
Lawn	Verdant sward
Shovel	Simple instrument for delving into Mother Earth
A teacher	My fellow toiler in the arduous labors of pedagogy
Reading a textbook	Following the lamp of knowledge in a textual tome
Eating	Partaking of the dietary sustenance of life
Going overseas	Traversing the ever-palpitating deep

Writing Logically and Accurately

44 | Clear and Logical Thinking *log*

The two most common kinds of logic or reasoning are **inductive** and **deductive.**

Inductive reasoning is mainly scientific and factual. It begins with collected data, experiments, and examples. When enough information has been collected, a statement of a principle is taken from the examples.

Deductive reasoning begins with a general principle and applies it to a specific instance or specific instances. The conclusions of deductive thinkers are more tentative than the conclusions of inductive thinkers, who arrive at a principle instead of starting from one. Deductive thinkers are accurate only to the extent that their principle is correct and only to the extent that they have applied it truly.

Both inductive and deductive thinking are tested and questioned by those to whom the conclusions are presented. Of an inductive thinker, one asks whether the facts are true, whether the exceptions have been noted, whether the selection of materials is representative, whether the conclusions are truly and accurately drawn from the data, whether the conclusions are stated precisely or exaggerated. Of a deductive thinker, one asks whether the given principle is impartial truth or mere personal opinion, whether it is applied to materials relevantly, whether the conclusion is accurate according to the principle, and whether exceptions have been noted.

With good motives and bad, with honesty and with deceit, different thinkers reach different conclusions derived from the same data or from the same principles. Learn to discriminate between sound and illogical reasoning in everything you read or hear. Indeed, when you write, you must constantly question your own reasoning. Watch for errors in thinking, which are called **logical fallacies.**

44a Use only accurate and verified data.

Facts can be demonstrated. They form the bases of judgments. A writer should distinguish carefully between the facts and the judgments derived from them and then explain how one comes from the other.

Errors, whether of fact, ignorance, or dishonesty, make the reader suspicious and lead to distrust. An otherwise compelling argument crumbles when just one or two facts are wrong. The following statements contain factual errors.

The traveler testified that he had entered the country on June 31, 1976. ("Thirty days hath June.")
Only wealthy people buy original oil paintings. (The facts do not bear out this contention.)

44b Use reliable authorities.

For various reasons, not all so-called specialists are reliable. Do not accept everything in print as equally authoritative. In evaluating an authority you may use some of the following criteria and perhaps additional methods.

1. When was the work published? An old publication may contain superseded information.
2. Who published the work? University presses and well-established publishing houses employ informed consultants whereas others may not.
3. Does the work have a reputation for reliability? For example, how has it been evaluated by other authorities in annotated bibliographies and reviews?
4. Is the presumed authority writing about his or her own field? (An atomic scientist may not be an expert on the life and writings of Shakespeare.)

5. Are the language and the tone reasonable, or does the authority attempt to persuade by using ornate rhetoric or slanted words and terms? If so, beware.
6. Does the authority show objectivity by admitting the existence of facts that seem contradictory?
7. Does the authority distinguish fact from opinion?

44c   Avoid sweeping generalizations.

Generalize with great care. If you know that three of your friends oppose capital punishment, you should not assert that "everyone wishes to have capital punishment abolished" or even that "most people wish to have capital punishment abolished." These statements are too broad for the evidence on which they are based. Sweeping generalizations like the following may contain an element of truth which is lost in exaggeration.

A poor person cannot get a fair trial in America.
Russian athletes are the best in the world.

Sweeping generalizations about nationalities and races are among the most pernicious. If you have not done extensive and conclusive research on your subject, qualify your opinions.

Some poor people feel that they cannot get a fair trial in America.
Many Russian athletes are among the best in the world.

CAUTION: You cannot get around objections to sweeping generalizations merely by adding "in my opinion."

Resist the temptation to claim too much. Remember that a sweeping generalization is often a falsification.

44d   Use specific and accurate evidence to support your argument.

Truth and accuracy depend on an adequate number of examples. Statistics and samplings of opinions, polls, and other kinds of data should be not only sufficiently extensive but also fairly and representatively chosen. Sometimes it is not enough for the data to be picked at random. A public opinion poll taken from only one social, educational, or occupational group, for example, would probably be misleading.

44e   Stick to the point.

Be sure you have a point and then do not wander off the subject. Test every sentence to be sure that it has a place in your discussion and that it is not simply an interesting digression or extraneous comment. First or last paragraphs of papers may be especially irrelevant because they begin or end at a point too far removed from the subject. Failure to focus attention continually on the announced topic results in loss of power to convince your reader.

44f   Do not ignore conflicting facts or evidence.

Be aware of facts and instances which seem to refute or qualify your views and conclusions. Deal with them fully and honestly. You can actually strengthen your case by taking opposing evidence into consideration.

44g   Do not reason in a circle or beg the question.

A writer who **reasons in a circle** simply states the assumption in two different ways.

CIRCULAR REASONING
This particular fish is inedible because it is not fit for human consumption.

A writer **begs the question** by assuming that a questionable premise has already been proven.

BEGGING THE QUESTION
Modern art is more profound than earlier painting because it is less realistic. (The writer has not proved that shallowness results from realism or that depth is necessarily to be associated with the unrealistic.)

44h Do not draw conclusions from faulty assumptions.

Make sure that one idea follows logically from another. The argument that "he cannot be elected to Phi Beta Kappa because he is a football player" is based on a false assumption: that no football player ever makes good grades, or that Phi Beta Kappa will refuse to elect someone who plays football. Similar errors in thought occur in the following sentences. What are the unstated assumptions, and why are the conclusions false?

Since she made good grades in high school, she will undoubtedly be a good student in college.
She will not make a good judge because she was once fined for speeding.
He has a wonderful personality and will certainly be a successful salesman.

44i Do not substitute an appeal to emotions for an appeal to reason.

Name-calling attempts to appeal to prejudice. Calling someone who does not share your views an idiot will not advance your own argument but will probably have the opposite effect. This is argument against a person rather than against a principle or a point of view.

Loaded words and **labels** similarly attempt to shape an attitude through prejudice instead of reason. In loaded terms a government subsidy plan might be described as a "hand-out scheme that a bunch of radical do-gooders are trying to fasten on the taxpayers."

Flattery attempts to persuade through excessive praise. The political candidate who tells the people that he knows they will vote for him because of their high intelligence is attempting to convince by flattering.

Snob appeal asserts that one should adopt a certain view because all the better people do. The use of athletes, beauty queens, or motion picture stars in advertising is a form of snob appeal.

Mass appeal attempts to persuade by asserting that everyone follows a certain pattern. It suggests that one who does not follow the herd is in error (*everyone ought* to go to college; *everyone ought* to own a home).

44j Do not draw false conclusions about cause and effect.

When two things happen in sequence, the second is not necessarily caused by the first. If a man walks under a ladder and shortly thereafter loses his wallet, he should not assume that he lost his wallet *because* he walked under the ladder. Showing a cause-and-effect relationship between two events requires evidence of real causation. The root of this fallacy is frequently superstition.

44k Be moderate.

Be temperate in your judgments and in your choice of words. Overstatement and overemphasis to make a point not only irritate readers but arouse doubt or even disbelief. The temptation to exaggerate is natural, but most seasoned writers know that moderation and even understatement convince where brashness and arrogance alienate.

44L Allow for adequate options.

On some questions it is illogical to assume that there are *two and only two* alternatives. Often other possibilities exist. If, for example, a father tells his son that he must go to college or fail in life, he has not recognized that his son may succeed without a college education. This kind of error in thinking is called an **either/or fallacy** or a **false dilemma.**

■ **Exercise 1**

Describe the errors in content and thought in each of the following. Some sentences contain more than one kind of error.

1. Do not take an umbrella to the picnic; every time you bring an umbrella, it rains.
   44j—cause and effect
2. Boys are good in mathematics and science; girls are good in English and the fine arts.
   44a—data not verified
3. I love to attend the ballet because I enjoy it so much.
   44g—reasoning in a circle

4. American medicine is far behind that in Russia because our doctors are interested only in money.
   44a & 44h—unverified data & faulty assumption

5. Percy Luciat's new novel has to be a failure; everything else he has written has been.
   44h—faulty assumption

6. Anyone who reaches the age of eighteen is old enough to make decisions without advice from other people.
   44a & 44c—dogmatic assertion & sweeping generalization

7. John Quincy Adams, the second President of the United States, was respected for his idealism and great knowledge.
   44a—wrong data. John Quincy Adams was the sixth President.

8. Nearly all the great monuments of this world are made of marble.
   44a—inaccurate data. Many are made of granite or other materials.

9. All college graduates are unusually intelligent; otherwise, they could not have passed the courses and completed their education.
   44c & 44d—sweeping generalizations & not enough evidence

10. The fact that you could vote as you did on this issue shows me that you are a dirty coward and a shameless hypocrite.
    44i—name-calling

11. After only one week at Reduso Spa, Mrs. Wentworth lost sixteen pounds; the program works for everyone.
    44h—faulty assumption

12. My professor must be a good scholar; he is a member of the Modern Language Association.
    44i—snob appeal

13. All students should go to trade school before going to college because it is extremely difficult for college graduates to get good jobs unless they can do something with their hands.
    44c & 44d—sweeping generalization & insufficient evidence

14. Order our new device for restoring hair in your bald spots, and new hair will begin to grow within two weeks.
    44d—insufficient evidence

15. Not much rain falls in the Sahara Desert because it is so dry.

    44g—reasoning in a circle

16. Her parents deserted her when she was an infant. No wonder she has spent much of her life in prison.

    44j—cause and effect

17. The welfare system in this country makes the people who have earned their money give it away to lazy good-for-nothings who are not willing to work for themselves.

    44a and 44i—unverified data and name calling

18. Joseph Conrad was the greatest novelist who ever lived.

    44c—sweeping generalization

19. Those who follow the Golden Rule will have no serious problems in life.

    44h—faulty assumption

20. A great many people have already purchased home computers, everyone should own one.

    44h—faulty assumption

21. According to an editorial in the high school paper, Einstein's theory of relativity is all wrong.

    44b—unreliable authority

22. Subscribe to *Now*, the intellectual's magazine, and join the most enlightened readers of the day.

    44i—snob appeal

23. I know that a professor as brilliant and as distinguished as you will see the validity of my point.

    44i—flattery

24. Fortunetellers are not fakes. The palmist said that I was going on a trip within three months, and I did.

    44h—faulty assumption

25. All the weird ideas in this country initiate in California.

    44a and 44h—unverified data and faulty assumption

Paragraphs

45 | Writing Paragraphs   ℍ

A unified group of sentences with the first line indented is a paragraph. Effective paragraphs are distinct units of thought. A sentence should have its own place within the paragraph. State the purpose of a paragraph or at least imply it. Keep the purpose in mind throughout.

Each new paragraph should mark a shift in thought or emphasis and therefore should play its part in directing the reader's attention progressively from point to point through the entire body of writing. In the process of composition, nothing is more important than learning to organize the ideas that make up an essay or chapter into distinctive blocks, each one clearly carrying its own main thought but also closely related to all the others.

45a State the main idea of a paragraph in a topic sentence.

The **topic sentence** is the crucial part which attaches the paragraph to the whole and also defines the function of the sentences it controls and manages. Topic sentences supply the direction. Other sentences add evidence, make refinements, develop the main idea; but as a rule they do not control the purpose of the paragraph. Consequently, taken together, the topic sentences of a paper are a sort of skeleton of the whole. Reading only the topic sentences may show a writer whether the lines of thought are clear. The topic sentences also may enable a reader to scan a piece of writing and to see generally its major points.

Test your own papers by examining the topic sentences. If they move logically and clearly through the main outlines of your work, that is a good sign. If not, you may have omitted ideas, arranged thoughts in the wrong sequence, or neglected to state purpose and direction. Then you may need to replan your paper, to rewrite topic sentences, or to formulate ideas which you have previously just assumed.

Topic sentences do not have to come at the beginning of a paragraph. They may appear almost anywhere. It is not uncommon to find them at the end or, occasionally, in the middle. Most of them, however, come at the beginning.

A topic sentence at the beginning of a paragraph usually states a general thought, and then the following sentences exemplify, modify, qualify, add to, or develop it in a variety of ways.

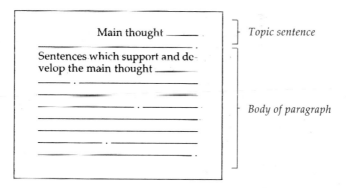

The following paragraph illustrates this diagram. It has a clear and pointed topic sentence, which is explained and supported by the subsequent sentences.

Topic sentence Today, Japanese leaders have a new purpose and a new strategy. They have made the achievement of world technological supremacy a national priority. And they intend to achieve it, not just *Body of paragraph* by adaptation, but by generating a burst of original technological breakthroughs. They are creating a massive research apparatus with a double mission: to spawn path-breaking, profit-making inventions while also plumbing the fundamental puzzles of science and nature. "There's no doubt," says Justin Bloom, former science attaché for

the American Embassy in Tokyo, "that Japan is shifting to a basic research phase."

STEVE LOHR,
"The Japanese Challenge: Can They Achieve Technological Supremacy?"

A topic sentence may come at the end of a paragraph. Here
the writer collects a series of facts or examples or pieces of information. The paragraph then concludes with a topic sentence
which not only sums up and brings together all the previous sentences but also shows their connection to the central thought and
the rest of the paper. This kind of paragraph is usually based on
inductive thinking (see pp. 220–221).

Sentences which carry
the load of information.

——————————————
————————— · —————
—————————————
——— Topic sentence which
sums up paragraph and con-
nects it to entire paper.

In a well-structured paper, every part looks back to what has
gone before and forward to what will come later. Leaving out any
necessary part of a paper is a failure as serious as the omission of
an essential structural element of a building. Omit the floors or
the beams, and the thought collapses.

Notice how the following paragraph is constructed in three
separate parts.

*A topic sentence states what the writer believes about the position of some
urban universities in regard to urban issues.*

↓

Some urban universities fail to communicate their vision of the
city to faculty, students, and constituents. They remain silent on the
important issues of the day for fear of alienating one faction or an-

other. They justify their silence on the grounds that universities are neutral and should not become involved. The unwillingness to participate in dialogue turns off many students and members of the community who look to universities for wise, temperate, and moral leadership. Campuses should serve as marketplaces for ideas. If universities participate in their communities and follow rigorous professional principles, reactions will almost surely be positive. By participating they will provide a genuine service, even to many who believe that universities are academic in the worst sense of the term.

ADAPTED FROM MARSHALL KAPLAN,
"Point of View,"*Chronicle of Higher Education,* October 31, 1984, p. 80.

The body of the paragraph analyzes the stand of the universities and proposes a change.

The last sentence draws a conclusion about predicted results of the suggested change.

The following selection about news illustrates a skillful method of writing good paragraphs. Notice particularly the key function of the topic sentences (printed in red).

News is the consciousness of Society. It is the means whereby events in the body politic are brought into awareness. And it is curious that regimes which we call *repressive* tend to exhibit the same characteristic of repressed personalities; they are unable, or unwilling, to allow conflictive material into awareness. The disability stems from deep insecurities. The censoring of the repressed material does not eliminate it, but forces it to fester without anyone's rationality coming to grips with it.

Inevitably news comes to be controlled by the dominant political forces of a society. In a totalitarian regime the government attempts to create the image of a world, and of events, that reflects most favorably on those in power. The democratization of news, which goes hand in hand with the diffusion of political power among those governed, is a relatively recent development whose permanence cannot be assured. Democracies are far better able to cope with the reality of events than are totalitarian regimes. Such regimes promulgate a myth of their omnipotence, and are threatened even by events outside the control of the political process. Thus, typically, the Soviet press does not report air crashes, and even natural disasters such as earthquakes are suppressed, out of the notion—rooted in political insecurity—that the event in some manner reflects badly on the regime.

The question for any society is not whether there shall be news, but rather who shall have access to it. Every political system may be characterized by the proportion of information it has which is shared with the people and the proportion withheld. That is why the growth of secret news-gathering agencies, such as the C.I.A., is a troubling one for a democracy. It appears our government wants to keep some news to itself.

At a deeper historical level we can see that news in its present form is closely tied to the rise of the economy, and specifically to the exploitative and risk elements of capitalism. For the nineteenth-century merchant, news meant reports of his ship, of resources to exploit, and the means of minimizing the risk element inherent in entrepreneurship by gaining as much information as possible before his competitors. News services, such as Reuters, developed to serve business and investment interests, who discovered that getting the news quickly was the first step to financial gain.

In a civilization in which all activities tend toward commercial expression—for example, our own—news becomes a product to manufacture and dispense to the consumer. Thus a large-scale industry for the production and consumption of news has evolved. We ingest it with the same insatiable appetite that moves us to purchase the manifold products of our commercial civilization.

News under such circumstances tends toward decadent use. It no longer serves first the classic function of giving us information on which to act, or even to help us construct a mental model of the larger world. It serves mainly as entertainment. The tales of earthquakes, political assassinations, and bitterly fought elections are the heady stuff of which drama or melodrama is made. Happily, we are able to indulge our taste for thriller, romance, or murder mystery under the guise of a patently respectable pursuit. All enlightened people are supposed to know what is going on in the world. If what is going on also happens to be thrilling and exciting, so much the better.

Another feature of the decadent use of news is its increasing ritualization. The information becomes subservient to the form in which it is delivered. News is broadcast every evening, whether or not there is vital information to be conveyed. Indeed, the problem for the news networks is to generate sufficient news to fill a given time period. The time period becomes the fundamental fact, the framework into which events must be fitted. As in any ritual, the form persists even when a meaningful content is missing.

STANLEY MILGRAM,
"Reflections on News"

Each topic sentence in these paragraphs lends a sense of direction to the passage. Each paragraph deals clearly with a single idea related to news.

45b Write unified paragraphs. Relate each sentence clearly to the central idea expressed in the topic sentence.

Every sentence in a good paragraph should bear on the main point. An irrelevant sentence which digresses from the main point puzzles the reader about its connection to other sentences and the purpose of the paragraph.

The following paragraph attempts to develop the central idea of preserving our forests, but about halfway through, the writer abruptly changes to the topic of beauty and thus destroys the unity of what would otherwise have been an effective paragraph.

> An encouraging sign in modern management of national resources is the planting of trees systematically to replace those harvested. Large lumber companies have learned that it is in their best interests to look to the future and not merely to get what they can at the moment from the land. *Besides that, trees are beautiful and add much to the pleasure of being in nature. Only God, as the poet so aptly put it, can make a tree.* With modern tools and methods, whole forests can be destroyed in a fraction of the time that lumberjacks with their axes and handsaws attacked the woods. It is more necessary than ever, therefore, that conservation be a primary concern not only of the general citizenry but also of industry.

If the two digressive sentences above, printed in red, were deleted, the paragraph would be coherent and would communicate, as it should, a single well-argued point. Often it is not so easy to make a good paragraph from a flawed one. Without planning and care, a paragraph may be merely a random collection of thoughts with only a vague central idea. The writer of the following paragraph seems not to have thought through what he or she wanted to say before writing.

> It is not an easy matter to be an only child. Children have differing characteristics, and some people say that infants have traits that will remain throughout their lives. As people grow up, they find that their views change, especially when they reach college. In order to understand children, we need to treat them as individuals, not as playthings. There is much truth in the saying that the child is the parent of the adult. Some writers believe that children are more mature in important ways than adults. At any rate, children do feel things keenly.

The sentences that make up this paragraph are not closely related and do not work toward the development of a thesis. Though it is on the general subject of children, it is so fragmented that it conveys disorder and confusion.

■ **Exercise 2**

By deleting extraneous material, improve the paragraphs below that are not unified (as many as three sentences may be extraneous). Put a check next to paragraphs that are acceptable. Underline all topic sentences.

1. The motion picture *All Quiet on the Western Front* was actually created as an antiwar protest. It deals with World War I from a German perspective. ~~The hero has a professor he first admires but comes to distrust.~~ Even though it is about the Germans, it does not glorify the German cause. It depicts the plight of the sensitive human spirit caught in the terrible grip of war. ~~World War I started when Archduke Ferdinand was assassinated. Probably no one would have guessed that this~~

~~incident would grow quickly into the greatest war the world had ever known.~~ The theme of the picture is expressed in the ending, where the hero is killed while reaching for a flower he sees on the battlefield.

The last sentence has some of the qualities of a topic sentence.

✓ 2. Sensible business people who deal in realities every day will often go out of their way on the street to avoid walking under a ladder. Diners in restaurants throw salt over their shoulders to ward off bad luck when they spill a little. It is not at all unusual to see a perfectly sane adult knock on wood to insure continued good fortune. Many people moan over broken mirrors not because the accident will cost them the money to buy new mirrors but because they are worried that they may be in for seven years of bad luck. Superstitions, then, are many and various and still manifest themselves in the actions of a great many normal people.

This paragraph is unusual because its topic sentence comes at the end.

3. As the basic social unit the family is as important today in America as it ever was, though perhaps in a different way. Family coherence was essential in the early days of the country to insure the survival of the individual members. They helped each other and protected each other. Today people need their families not so much to insure physical survival as to help them through the perils of modern times, especially through such psychological perils as loss of identity. ~~America is not all bad, however. It offers the greatest freedom of all countries for individual development. America is still the land of opportunity.~~ The family gives one a sense of belonging, a sense of the past. When all else seems severed, the family can be the anchor to sanity.

✓ 4. A Saturday visit to the barber shop was once an exciting and meaningful experience for a boy. It offered an almost unique opportunity for a youngster to enter for a while the adult masculine world. At school a boy had no opportunity to see this world. At home he was often with his father and perhaps his brothers, but that was not the same as sitting among men and listening to their jokes—often slightly off-color—and their strong opinions on people and politics and their stories, sometimes of violence and courage. If he was wise, the lad sat in the barber chair and listened carefully with silent respect, for he sensed that he was being given the rare opportunity of visiting a world he would someday enter.

45c   Avoid skimpy paragraphs. Develop your paragraphs adequately.

In most expository writing, a series of short, skimpy paragraphs suggests that a writer does not know much to write about each point, has not grouped thoughts well, has not developed each thought fully, or has not been careful about paragraph divisions.

Do not omit the examples, the proof, the explanations, the exceptions—in short, the finer and the fuller details that make good paragraphs. Instead of merely mentioning points, you should develop and clarify them for the reader. Details flesh out your ideas.

The following three topic sentences alone lack the fullness of good writing. The basic principles are introduced, but nothing is developed.

Most of American history and much of American literature have been conditioned or influenced by the existence of a changing frontier.
Until recently, a politician who had not been born in a log cabin was handicapped in any election.
For Americans, the frontier has always been an ambivalent symbol.

In the paragraphs as they were originally written, the subject—the frontier—comes alive:

> Most of American history and much of American literature have been conditioned or influenced by the existence of a changing frontier. In our homes and in our schools many of our greatest stories and legends are about men like Captain John Smith, Lewis and Clark, Daniel Boone, Davy Crockett, and Kit Carson. We celebrate not only Washington's achievements as our Revolutionary leader and first President, but also his exploits as an Indian fighter and surveyor of the wilderness. We remember Andrew Jackson as Old Hickory, a frontier figure. We honor Abraham Lincoln as a son of the prairie woodland, a rail-splitter who read the Bible by light from a fireplace.
>
> Until recently, a politician who had not been born in a log cabin was handicapped in any election. Theodore Roosevelt gained glamor from his career as a cattleman and his fame as the organizer of the Rough Riders. Even a New Englander like Calvin Coolidge found it wise to visit the Black Hills of South Dakota and wear an Indian headdress for newspaper photographers. And in 1960 we elected as President another New Englander who promised us a "New Frontier."
>
> For Americans, the frontier has always been an ambivalent symbol. It has been considered a source of freedom and a place of danger; an exciting challenge, but also a cause of hardship and exhaustion; a place for heroism, but also an excuse for racism, sadism, and brutality; an inexhaustible mine of humor, but humor too often tinged with cruelty or false sentimentality. It has been idealized as a source of health, vitality, and nobility; but it has been condemned as rude, ugly, and barbaric.
>
> PHILLIP DURHAM AND EVERETT L. JONES,
> *The Frontier in American Literature*

In the first two paragraphs, the topic sentences are developed by references to typical and famous Americans related in some way to the frontier. In the last paragraph, interpretation is more significant, and the qualities in the people and the meaning of the frontier are the basis of development.

In some kinds of writing, short paragraphs are acceptable and expected. Newspapers, for example, generally use short paragraphs. They allow a reader to skim a story, to select the most interesting points and skip the others. It can be effective to use a short paragraph amid longer ones to put special stress on a point. To some extent the length of a writing assignment will influence the length of paragraphs. The paper of a thousand words may allow more room to develop full paragraphs than a short assignment.

■ **Exercise 3**

Five subjects for paragraphs are listed below. Choose from them the two which you like best. On each, first write a short, skimpy paragraph. Then write a paragraph of 125 to 175 words with a fuller development on the same subject.

Ways to mediate
Working for pleasure
Daydreaming
Reading while listening to music
Your favorite hobby

45d   Avoid excessively long paragraphs.

Very long paragraphs make it difficult for a reader to digest meaning easily. To reduce excessive length you may find it necessary to reduce the scope of the controlling idea—to limit purpose. But sometimes a paragraph can be trimmed by simply discarding material. You may not need ten examples to prove or illustrate a point. Four or five may do it more effectively.

■ **Exercise 4**

The passage below was published as seven paragraphs rather than as one. Decide where the breaks should come and underline the topic sentence for each paragraph. Be prepared to discuss the topic sentences and the organization which is reflected in them. The subject of the sentence and of the paragraph should be almost identical. What does each paragraph say about New York? Is each based on kinds of persons, a kind of persons and their similar activities, a general idea about the entire city, the condition of the city at a certain time, a collection of strange bits of information about the city which amount to a paragraph without a central topic sentence, or some other principle? Would the passage be less effective if there were no divisions, no topic sentences? Does it need stronger topic sentences which are less concrete and which state more general truths? These topic sentences resemble each other. How? How are they different from the topic sentences which might be written about a subject like, say, New York's social or economic conditions? Make brief notes about the passage so that you will be prepared to discuss it in class or in an extemporary written paragraph.

¶

New York is a city of things unnoticed. It is a city with cats sleeping under parked cars, two stone armadillos crawling up St. Patrick's Cathedral, and thousands of ants creeping on top of the Empire State Building. The ants probably were carried up there by wind or birds, but nobody is sure; nobody in New York knows any more about the ants than they do about the panhandler who takes taxis to the Bowery; or the dapper man who picks trash out of Sixth Avenue trash cans; or the medium in the West Seventies who claims, "I am clairvoyant, clairaudient and clairsensuous."

¶
New York is a city for eccentrics and a center for odd bits of infor-

mation. New Yorkers blink twenty-eight times a minute, but

forty when tense. Most popcorn chewers at Yankee Stadium stop

chewing momentarily just before the pitch. Gumchewers on

Macy's escalators stop chewing momentarily just before they get

off—to concentrate on the last step. Coins, paper clips, ball-point

pens, and little girls' pocketbooks are found by workmen when

¶ **A paragraph of**
they clean the sea lion's pool at the Bronx Zoo. A Park Avenue
details with no single topic sentence. What is the central unstated
doorman has parts of three bullets in his head—there since
topic?
World War I. Several young gypsy daughters, influenced by tele-

vision and literacy, are running away from home because they

don't want to grow up and become fortunetellers. Each month a

hundred pounds of hair is delivered to Louis Feder on 545 Fifth

Avenue, where blond hairpieces are made from German

women's hair; brunette hairpieces from Italian women's hair; but

no hairpieces from American women's hair which, says Mr.

¶ **A**
Feder, is weak from too frequent rinses and permanents. Some
separate paragraph here is not really necessary. Central topic mainly in
of New York's best informed men are elevator operators, who

subordinate clause.
rarely talk, but always listen—like doormen. Sardi's doormen listen to the comments made by Broadway's first-nighters walking by after the last act. They listen closely. They listen carefully. Within ten minutes they can tell you which shows will flop and
¶ An anecdotal paragraph with an introductory
which will be hits. On Broadway each evening a big, dark, 1948
sentence.
Rolls-Royce pulls into Forty-sixth Street—and out hop two little ladies armed with Bibles and signs reading, "The Damned Shall Perish." These ladies proceed to stand on the corner screaming at the multitudes of Broadway sinners, sometimes until three A.M., when their chauffeur in the Rolls picks them up and drives them
¶ In the last two paragraphs time is the impor-
back to Westchester. By this time Fifth Avenue is deserted by all
tant factor in the topic or introductory sentence.
but a few strolling insomniacs, some cruising cabdrivers, and a group of sophisticated females who stand in store windows all night and day wearing cold, perfect smiles. Like sentries they line Fifth Avenue—these window mannequins who gaze into the quiet street with tilted heads and pointed toes and long rubber
¶
fingers reaching for cigarettes that aren't there. At five A.M. Manhattan is a town of tired trumpet players and homeward-bound

bartenders. Pigeons control Park Avenue and strut unchallenged
                              ¶ **May be considered the topic sentence.**
in the middle of the street. This is Manhattan's mellowest hour.

Most *night* people are out of sight—but the *day* people have not

yet appeared. Truck drivers and cabs are alert, yet they do not

disturb the mood. They do not disturb the abandoned Rockefeller

Center, or the motionless night watchmen in the Fulton Fish Mar-

ket, or the gas-station attendant sleeping next to Sloppy Louie's

with the radio on.

GAY TALESE, "New York," *Esquire,* July 1960

45e Put the parts of a paragraph together in appropriate order.

Sentences can be arranged systematically in a number of ways.
Certain effects are produced from certain orders of sentences,
and what may be an appropriate arrangement for one kind of
paper will not be for another. Paragraphs with no system of order
are like motors with the parts randomly assembled: they function
poorly or not at all. Study below the various systems most often
used to arrange sentences in a paragraph.

Time

In paragraphs organized by time, things that happen first usually
come first in the paragraph. In many ways, this is the simplest
system because chronology is a ready-made pattern. Paragraphs
describing a process (how steel is made, how photographs are de-

veloped, and so forth) naturally are arranged sequentially. If you get steps out of order, the paragraph is confusing. Narratives usually begin at the first event and end with the last. In some instances, however, the writer may wish to create a special effect by describing a late event first and then coming back to the beginning.

The following paragraph is in strict chronological order.

> At the beginning of the cruise, the ship's engines seemed noisy, but the captain considered this a minor problem. He consulted with the chief engineer, who politely but firmly told him that he was imagining things. On the third day out, smoke was reported in the engine room, and the captain prepared the crew before giving orders to abandon ship. Shortly before the announcement was to be made, however, a large freighter came into view. It was an Italian ship, and few aboard spoke English, but they quickly discerned the problem, gave full assistance, and took the passengers on board their ship. Soon the fire was out and the *Ocean Wind* was in tow. After the two days that it took to reach Miami, the passengers agreed that they had never had better food, better quarters, or more attentive hosts.

Space

Descriptive paragraphs are most frequently organized according to spatial progression. If you are describing a scene or a person, you move from detail to detail of what you observed. As with time sequence, you must maintain the logical progression, in this instance the movement of the eye as it follows the object or scene. Getting sentences out of order may resemble counting 1, 2, 5, 4, 3 instead of 1, 2, 3, 4, 5. Notice how the paragraph below carries the eye from one wall of a room to another.

NOTE: Paragraphs with sentences arranged by time or space sometimes do not have conventional topic sentences.

> The right wall of the spacious office was covered completely with a mural of the most striking aspect. It was meant to represent a

city skyline, but the buildings resembled giant trees in winter, and the color red prevailed everywhere. The rear wall was composed of one piece of glass from floor to ceiling overlooking the real skyline. The contrast was immediate, but one could also see that in a strange sense the buildings did, indeed, look like a surrealistic forest. The left wall was taken up with bookshelves filled with volumes of various shapes and sizes. A closer look revealed that the top four shelves contained all first editions of famous works. The lower four shelves, however, were given to books of only two kinds—writings on architecture and on the cultures of certain Pacific islanders.

Climactic Order (increasing importance)

Sentences that progress according to importance are arranged in **climactic order.** This is an effective structure, based on sequence of importance (not chronological sequence). If you place a lesser sentence at the end of a paragraph, you may create confusion or unintentional humor. The strategy in arranging climactically is not to put down your thoughts simply as they occur to you, but to list them first, order them according to their relative importance, and then form the paragraph. Notice how the final sentence in the following paragraph dramatically acts as a climax.

> How successful one is in obtaining peace of mind and fulfillment depends upon which path is followed. Gratification of the physical appetites is vigorously pursued by some people as if this were the true route to happiness. Others eschew such a primitive attempt and give themselves over to the accumulation of material wealth. Their rewards may be somewhat more long lasting, but their disappointment is inevitable, for money is notoriously lacking in the food that feeds the inner person. Having recognized this basic truth, other seekers aim at what they consider a higher goal—the acquisition of power and influence, in which they find challenge and excitement. Power admittedly brings more satisfaction to the ego than does money. Those most likely to find their way will do so not through physical gratification, money, or power, but through the development of self-understanding and self-esteem.

The topics which are ordered according to increasing importance (climactically) are the following: physical appetites, material wealth, acquisition of power and influence, self-understanding and self-esteem.

General to Particular, Particular to General

Paragraphs in which the sentences progress from a general statement to particular details are related to deductive reasoning, and those which progress from several details to a generalization about them are related to inductive reasoning (see **44**). Writers often compose a topic sentence and then support and explain it with details, reasons, and illustrations. This sequence moves from the general to the particular (see paragraph **A** below). The reverse order usually has the topic sentence at the end of the paragraph with particulars coming first (as in paragraph **B** below). A more frequent pattern moves from the general to the particular and back to the general again, as in illustration **C**.

(A)

Never was there a more outrageous or more unscrupulous or more ill-informed advertising campaign than that by which the promoters for the American colonies brought settlers here. Brochures published in England in the seventeenth century, some even earlier, were full of hopeful overstatements, half-truths, and downright lies, along with some facts which nowadays surely would be the basis for a restraining order from the Federal Trade Commission. Gold and silver, fountains of youth, plenty of fish, venison without limit, all these were promised.

DANIEL BOORSTIN,
Democracy and Its Discontents

(B)

Photocopying makes it possible for a researcher to reproduce a long passage instantly instead of laboriously copying it in longhand or dragging along the entire book so that the section can be copied later. Ball-point and felt-point pens, now used widely instead of old-fashioned ink pens, are economical, convenient, and generally neater. The wide variety of colors in these pens enables writers to distinguish notes on one subject from another. Word-processing machines then allow the change of single words or the revision of a line or a passage long after the original typing. Transparent tapes are now available that can be written or typed on. A great number of conveniences have been developed for researchers and writers in the last few decades.

(C)

Mankind's most enduring achievement is art. At its best, it reveals the nobility that coexists in human nature along with flaws and evils, and the beauty and truth it can perceive. Whether in music or architecture, literature, painting or sculpture, art opens our eyes and ears and feelings to something beyond ourselves, something we cannot experience without the artist's vision and the genius of his craft. The placing of Greek temples like the Temple of Poseidon on the promontory at Sunion outlined against the piercing blue of the Aegean Sea, Poseidon's home; the majesty of Michelangelo's sculptured figures in stone; Shakespeare's command of language and knowledge of the human soul; the intricate order of Bach, the enchantment of Mozart; the purity of Chinese monochrome pottery with the lovely names—celadon, oxblood, peach blossom, clair de lune; the exuberance of Tiepolo's ceiling where, without the picture frames to limit movement, a whole world in exquisitely beautiful colors lives and moves in the sky; the prose and poetry of all the writers from Homer to Cervantes to Jane Austen and John Keats to Dostoevsky and Chekov—who made all these things? We—our species—did.

BARBARA TUCHMAN,
Thomas Jefferson lecture, Washington, D.C.

45f Develop a paragraph by a method that will appropriately enable it to fulfill its function.

Each paragraph has its own distinctive identity, and yet it must carry out its duty in the paper as a whole. Many methods of development are useful in working with different kinds of content. Long-established practices may at times be helpful in planning and arranging your thoughts. Several particular modes of developing paragraphs are discussed below.

Definition

Whether you are using a new word or a new meaning for an old one, a definition explains a concept. It avoids the problems that arise when two persons use the same term for different things. Be as specific as possible; exemplify. Avoid definitions which are uniquely your own (unless you are willing to be challenged). Definitions, of course, may be much more elaborate than those given in dictionaries. Avoid the expression "According to Webster. . . ."

> Romantic love may be described as an emotion; it is translated into behavior. A person in love wants to do something to or with his loved one. The behavior a couple settles upon comprises their love. The better the translation of emotion into behavior, the less residual emotion will remain. Paradoxically, then, people who love each other do not feel love for each other.
>
> ADAPTED FROM GEORGE W. KELLING,
> *Blind Mazes: A Study of Love*

Comparison, Contrast

Two basic methods can be used in developing a paragraph by comparison and contrast: writing everything about one point and then everything about the other (XXXX YYYY) or writing about alternating points throughout the paragraph (XY XY XY XY). Either method can be effective, but in long and complex comparisons and contrasts the alternating method is generally better because it keeps both aspects in mind at the same time throughout.

The degree of comparison or of contrast may vary a great deal from one instance to another. You might write, for example, that there are a great many likenesses between two things but only one or two strong contrasts. Your organization, then, might be represented this way (with likenesses represented by X and contrasts by Y): XXXXX YY. Or the reverse could be true, with a great many contrasts but one or a few striking likenesses. Whatever your methods of recounting comparisons and contrasts, be certain that it is in appropriate representation.

> Hot water is the most satisfactory form of heat for the small greenhouse. The heat is more evenly distributed than in the case of steam heat and there is less danger of a sudden drop in temperature. And it is an accepted fact that practically all plants thrive better under a system of hot water heat than under steam heat. It is a more natural kind of heat and is more nearly like the heat of the sun. Hot water heat has the added advantage of being more economical than steam, as it is possible to maintain a very low fire in mild weather.
>
> JAMES BUSH-BROWN AND LOUISE BUSH-BROWN,
> *America's Garden Book*

Causes and Effects

Generally a paragraph of this kind may state a condition or effect and then proceed by listing and explaining the causes. On the other hand, the first sentences may list a cause or causes and then conclude with the consequence, the effect. In either method of development, the writer usually begins with a phenomenon which is generally known and which moves on to the unknowns.

The following paragraph begins with an effect and proceeds to examine the causes.

> This close-knit fabric [of the city] was blown apart by the automobile, and by the postwar middle-class exodus to suburbia which the mass-ownership of automobiles made possible. The automobile itself was not to blame for this development, nor was the desire for suburban living, which is obviously a genuine aspiration of many Americans. The fault lay in our failure, right up to the present time, to fashion new policies to minimize the disruptive effects of the automobile revolution. We have failed not only to tame the automobile

itself, but to overhaul a property-tax system that tends to foster automotive-age sprawl, and to institute coordinated planning in the politically fragmented suburbs that have caught the brunt of the postwar building boom.

EDMUND K. FALTERMAYER,
Redoing America

Examples

Some topic sentences state generalizations which may not seem clear or true without evidence and illustration. Proof can be provided by an extended example or several short examples. They must be accepted as true in themselves and as representative of the generalization. Examples can add concrete interest as well as proof.

It was during this period that some of our most notable examples of garden art were produced: the great villas of Italy, the palace gardens of Spain, the vast plaisances of the French châteaux, the careful parterres of the Dutch, and the beautiful manor house gardens of England.

JAMES BUSH BROWN AND LOUISE BUSH-BROWN,
America's Garden Book

Classification

Paragraphs which classify explain by arranging a number of things into groups and categories. Seeing the distinctions should lead to clear understanding of the component parts and, then, an understanding of the larger group or concept. Analysis explains one thing by naming its parts. Synthesis lists several categories and then puts them into a single concept or classification.

Modern pessimism and modern fragmentation have spread in three different ways to people of our own culture and to people across the world. *Geographically,* it spread from the European mainland to England, after a time jumping the Atlantic to the United States. *Culturally,* it spread in the various disciplines from philosophy to art, to music, to general culture (the novel, poetry, drama, films), and to theology. *Socially,* it spread from the intellectuals to the educated and then through the mass media to everyone.

FRANCIS A. SCHAEFFER
How Should We Then Live?

Opening and Closing Paragraphs

Opening and closing paragraphs of a paper are often difficult to write. The first paragraph is sometimes harder to compose than the next several pages. It must attract interest, state the purpose or thesis or argument, and then sometimes suggest the method of development which will be used in the entire paper. If the first paragraph is dull, mechanical, or obscure, your reader may decide immediately that the paper is not worth reading.

The concluding paragraph does not simply restate the opening paragraph. It does not add substantial new information not discussed previously in the paper. Instead, it gives a brief overview of what the paper has shown and makes a final assessment of the importance and the originality of the paper in regard to its subject matter.

Analogy

An analogy is a figurative comparison; it explains one thing in terms of another. It is likely to be most effective when you can show a resemblance that is not generally recognized between two things that have so many differences that they are not ordinarily likened. In the paragraph below, for example, the writer convincingly reveals an analogy between the game of football and war.

      A further reason for football's intensity is that the game is played like a war. The idea is to win by going through, around or over the opposing team and the battle lines, quite literally, are drawn on every play. Violence is somewhere at the heart of the game, and the combat quality is reflected in football's army language ("blitz," "trap," "zone," "bomb," "trenches," etc.). Coaches often sound like generals when they discuss their strategy. Woody Hayes of Ohio State, for instance, explains his quarterback option play as if it had been conceived in the Pentagon: "You know," he says, "the most effective kind of warfare is siege. You have to attack on broad fronts. And that's all the option is—attacking on a broad front. You know General Sherman ran an option through the South."

MURRAY ROSS,
"Football Red and Baseball Green"

Process

Several methods may be used in describing a process. Most processes are given in chronological order, step by step. The kind of writing should be adapted to the particular kind of process. The simplest perhaps is the type used in a recipe, usually written in second person or imperative mood. The necessity here is to get the steps in order and to state each step very clearly. This process tells *how to do* something. It is more instruction than exposition.

Another kind of process is the relation of *how something works* (a clock, the human nervous system). Here, the problems in writing are avoiding technical terms and intricate or incomprehensible steps in the process. This kind of process is explanation; the reader may at some time need to understand it or to use it.

Still another kind of process, usually written in the past tense, tells *how something happened* (how oil was formed in the earth, how a celebration or riot began). Usually a paragraph of this type is written in the third person. It is designed to reveal how something developed (once in all time or on separate occasions). Its purpose is to explain and instruct. The following paragraph explains one theory about the process that formed the

moon. The distinct steps are necessary for explanation here just
as they are for instruction in a paragraph that tells how to do
something.

> There were tides in the new earth long before there was an
> ocean. In response to the pull of the sun the molten liquids of the
> earth's whole surface rose in tides that rolled unhindered around the
> globe and only gradually slackened and diminished as the earthly
> shell cooled, congealed, and hardened. Those who believe that the
> moon is a child of earth say that during an early stage of the earth's
> development something happened that caused this rolling, viscid
> tide to gather speed and momentum and to rise to unimaginable
> heights. Apparently the force that created these greatest tides the
> earth has ever known was the force of resonance, for at this time the
> period of the solar tides had come to approach, then equal, the pe-
> riod of the free oscillation of the liquid earth. And so every sun tide
> was given increased momentum by the push of the earth's oscilla-
> tion, and each of the twice-daily tides was larger than the one before
> it. Physicists have calculated that, after 500 years of such monstrous,
> steadily increasing tides, those on the side toward the sun became
> too high for stability, and a great wave was torn away and hurled
> into space. But immediately, of course, the newly created satellite
> became subject to physical laws that sent it spinning in an orbit of its
> own about the earth. This is what we call the moon.
>
> RACHEL CARSON,
> *The Sea Around Us*

45g Use transitional devices to show the relationships
between the parts of your writing.

Transitional devices are connectors and direction givers. They
connect content words to other words, sentences to sentences,
paragraphs to paragraphs. Writings without transitions would be
like a strange land with no signs for travelers. Practiced writers
assume that they should keep their readers informed about
where a paragraph and a paper are going.

The beginnings of paragraphs can contribute materially to clarity, coherence, and the movement of the discussion. Some writers meticulously guide readers with a connector at the beginning of almost every paragraph. H. J. Muller, for example, begins a sequence of paragraphs about science as follows:

In this summary, science . . .
Yet science does . . .
Similarly the basic interests of science . . .
In other words, they are not . . .
This demonstration that even the scientist . . .
This idea will concern us . . .
In other words, facts and figures . . .

CONNECTIVE WORDS AND EXPRESSIONS

but	indeed	likewise
and	in fact	consequently
however	meanwhile	first
moreover	afterward	next
furthermore	then	in brief
on the other hand	so	to summarize
nevertheless	still	to conclude
for example	after all	similarly

DEMONSTRATIVES

this	that	these	those

References to demonstratives must be clear (see p. 63).

OTHER PRONOUNS

many	each	some	others	such	either

Repeated Key Words, Phrases, and Synonyms

Repetitions and synonyms guide the reader from sentence to sentence and paragraph to paragraph.

Parallel Structures

Repeating similar structural forms of a sentence can show how certain ideas within a paragraph are alike in content as well as structure. A sequence of sentences beginning with a noun subject or with the same kind of pronoun subject, a series of clauses beginning with *that* or *which,* a series of clauses beginning with a similar kind of subordinate conjunction (like *because*)—devices like these can achieve transition and show connection.

Excessive use of parallelism, however, is likely to be too oratorical, too dramatic. Used with restraint, parallel structures are excellent transitional devices.

The following paragraph on the subject of patriotism illustrates how various transitional devices can help create direction and coherence.

Synonym: citizenship for patriotism
There is no reason why patriotism has to be so heavily asso-

ciated, in the minds of the young as well as adults, with military ex-

ploits, jets, and missiles. Citizenship must include the duty to ad-

vance our ideals actively into practice for a better community,
connective word: And
country, and world if peace is to prevail over war. And this obliga-
synonym: obligation for duty   demonstrative: this
tion stems not just from a secular concern for humanity but from a

belief in the brotherhood of man—"I am my brother's keeper"—

that is common to all major religions. It is the classic confrontation:
repeated key word: patriotism
barbarism *vs.* the holy ones. If patriotism has no room for delibera-

tion, for acknowledging an individual's sense of justice and his relig-

ious principles, it will continue to close minds, stifle the dissent that
parallel structure: who challenge in order to/
has made us strong, and deter the participation of Americans who
who question in order to
challenge in order to correct and who question in order to answer.

repeated key word: patriotism

We need only to recall recent history in other countries where patri-

otism was converted into an epidemic of collective madness and de-

parallel structure: A patriotism . . . asks/   A new

struction. A patriotism manipulated by the government asks only

patriotism requires

for a service nod from its subjects. A new patriotism requires a

repeated key word: patriotism

thinking assent from its citizens. If patriotism is to have a "manifest

destiny," it is in building a world where all mankind is our bond in

peace.

RALPH NADER,
"We Need a New Kind of Patriotism"

General exercises

■ **Exercise 5**

Write three paragraphs on any of the following subjects. Use at least two methods of development and two kinds of order (see pp. 244–254). Name the method you use in each paragraph.

1. Wisdom
2. Boredom
3. Poverty
4. Politics and sincerity
5. Kinds of leisure
6. Security
7. Study
8. Carelessness

■ **Exercise 6**

Find three good paragraphs from three different kinds of writing: from a book of nonfiction, an essay, a review, or a newspaper article. Discuss how effective paragraphs differ in different kinds of writing.

■ **Exercise 7**

Find an ineffective paragraph in a book or article. Analyze it in a paragraph.

Papers

46 Writing Papers

A good paper is the result of four important steps: preliminary thinking and planning (including the gathering of materials), composing a draft, revising, and writing the paper in its final form. Classifications of papers are similar to those of paragraphs —argument, process, comparison and contrast, and so forth. Therefore, the explanation of paragraph types on pp. 248–254 applies also to the paper as a whole.

46a Select a significant and interesting subject.

A writer must have something worthwhile to say. Often the best papers come from the imaginative use of experience. Draw on your experience and memory, therefore, as well as on your knowledge and interests. Good subjects can come to mind at unexpected moments. You may think of one while you are eating a meal or while you are taking your clothes to the laundry. Never let a possible subject escape you. Reserve a page or two in your notebook for all the topics and titles which occur to you.

Even the less promising possibilities may evolve into good subjects. When a paper must be written, it is better to have an excess of ideas than a blank sheet of paper staring at you from your desk. You can avoid false starts and lost time by examining your list of possibilities and settling on one good topic at the outset. (For suggestions about subjects for papers, see pp. 285–288.)

46b Choose a specific topic.

Generally it is more difficult to write on a broad or abstract subject than on a specific one. You might not know where to begin if you choose "transportation," but if you select a more specific topic, such as Japan's famous fast trains, you will have an interesting and manageable subject. First pick the general area in which you want to work; then spend some time thinking about definite aspects of that broad subject.

Suppose a student has decided to write a paper on health. That subject has so many dimensions that it is unsuitable for a single paper; therefore it must be broken down into components, one of which might make a good topic. The evolution of this subject in the student's thinking could take the following form:

Health: Too broad . . .
Staying Healthy: Still not specific enough . . .
Health and Our Relationship to Nature: Might have something here, but "nature" is too general . . .
Human Health and Pets: That's it. A subject I'm interested in and up to date on. I could call the paper "The Animal Factor."

For an extended discussion of additional ways of selecting a specific topic, see **48a**.

Through association of ideas, this student arrived at what looks like a workable subject.

Even after the topic is thus limited, however, you cannot *know* that it is the right size until you have (1) considered its subdivisions and (2) sometimes actually written a draft. A subject which at first seems limited may open up into greater complexity and promise to yield a paper far beyond the assigned length. If so, you must turn to another subject—perhaps a still more limited aspect of the first.

Or you may reduce the length of the draft, usually by cutting out whole sections. But a paper shortened in this way is often confused, jerky, or badly proportioned because of omissions and condensations. A fresh start with a new topic may cost a high price in lost time.

46c Formulate a thesis.

The central idea of a paper can usually be expressed in a single sentence. Sometimes this statement can be phrased early in the planning process, sometimes not until you are near the actual writing. In any event, it should be expressed early in the written paper, often in the opening paragraph.

A good **thesis statement** is specific and concise. It brings the subject into focus for the reader, suggests the scope of the paper, and shows coherently the idea or ideas that the paper will develop.

UNFOCUSED
It is the purpose of this paper to discuss how pets can help us stay
    healthy.

VAGUE
Pets are important.

GOOD THESIS STATEMENT
Modern research in physical and psychological medicine is proving that
    pets may be far more important to human health than has been sus-
    pected.

46d Organize carefully.

Never set out to write a paper without some kind of plan, even if it is a simple one. It is your map; without it you may wander aimlessly before finding your way. Three of the most common types of outlines are described below.

Scratch Outline

This is the simplest kind of outline. It is a list of points you want to make, and they are listed in any form you wish. It is a quick way to order your thoughts and remind you of that order when you are writing the draft. For brief papers or those written during the class hour, a scratch outline will often suffice. You might use the following points for a scratch outline on "The Animal Factor":

pets as aid to health—three ways
their importance in helping children mature
easing loneliness in adults
effect on high blood pressure
helping the aged feel loved

You may wish to add further points (some of which you may not use in the paper) as thoughts occur to you at different times.

Topic Outline

This is a formal and detailed structure to help you organize your materials. In making a topic outline, observe the following rules:

Number the main topics with Roman numerals, the first subheadings with capital letters, the next with Arabic numerals. If further subheadings are necessary, use a, b, c, and (1), (2), (3).

```
I. ................................................................................
   A. ............................................................................
      1. .........................................................................
         a. ......................................................................
            (1) ..................................................................
            (2) ..................................................................
         b. ......................................................................
      2. .........................................................................
   B. ............................................................................
II. ...............................................................................
```

Use parallel grammatical structures.
Use topics, not sentences. Do not place periods after the topics. Punctuate as in the example that follows.
Check to see that your outline covers the subject completely.

Use specific topics and subheadings arranged in a logical, meaningful order.

Each indented level of the outline represents a division of the preceding level and has smaller scope.

Avoid single subheadings. Roman numeral I calls for II and so forth.

NOT
  I. Children's development and pets
     A. Love and maturation
                          ←———————— *B needed*
 II. Pets and loneliness

The following is an example of a topic outline with a title, a thesis statement, and a series of orderly and carefully developed topics.

The Animal Factor

Thesis Statement: Modern research in physical and psychological medicine is proving that pets may be far more important to human health than has been suspected.

  I. Modern medicine and the value of pets
 II. Children's development and pets
     A. Love and maturation
     B. Necessary ties with nature
III. Pets and loneliness
     A. Fuller and longer life
     B. Laughter
 IV. Effects of pets on problems of the aged and the emotionally disturbed
     A. Blood pressure
     B. Mental patients
     C. Nursing home patients

Sentence Outline

This kind of outline is an extensive form of preparation for writing a paper. More thinking goes into it than into a scratch or topic outline, but the additional effort offers a tight control over your writing and makes it harder to wander from the subject. As a rule, the more time you spend on your outline, the less time you will need to do the actual writing. The sentence outline follows the same conventions as the topic outline except that the entries are expressed in complete sentences. Place periods after sentences in a sentence outline.

The Animal Factor

Thesis Statement: Modern research in physical and psychological medicine is proving that pets may be far more important to human health than has been suspected.

   I. Pets serve as diversions, but research is showing that they are also invaluable in at least three areas of growth and health.
  II. Child psychologists now know that pets aid children in the maturing process.
     A. Love for animals plays an important part in growing up.
     B. A pet is a vital link to the nonhuman world.
 III. Pets alleviate the loneliness that often accompanies adulthood.
     A. Life insurance companies have found that single people with pets live longer than single people without pets.
     B. As provokers of laughter, pets make life more bearable.
 IV. Among those reaching advanced age, among those mentally disturbed, and among those confined to nursing homes, pets have proven to be excellent medicine.
     A. Researchers report that holding and caressing pets lowers blood pressure.
     B. In mental institutions pets have served to make patients happier and less violent.
     C. Chronically depressed old people in nursing homes often find a new interest when they are allowed to be with animals.

46e Preliminary to writing the final version, compose a draft.

A rough draft is a necessary step toward the finished paper. Writers who go directly from outline to what they consider the

Paper is longer than
assignment calls for —
cut some.

This paragraph is little
off subject and outline.
Delete all but the
ending of it. $\longrightarrow$
It is also too informal
in places. Get rid of
contractions and slang.
Leave "I" out.

The Animal Factor

I don't know why some people don't like pets. They're as interesting and individualistic as people. I know a man who has a dog that looks just like he does. The case for pets is not always accepted, however. I know a married couple who not only will not allow any pets in their household but who will not go around them. They say that pets smell and carry diseases and they find it hard to understand why anyone would want an extra burden. On the other hand, some people go too far and let animals take the place of humans. They do all sorts of silly things from feeding them expensive food from plates to letting them sleep in beds. Such people talk baby talk to their pets and treat them as children. In the winter they put these cute little wool sweaters on the dogs and if there is the slightest sniffle or loss of appetite they rush him to their high-priced vet, who probably charges as much as a brain surgeon. When the pet dies, such people have a regular funeral complete with coffin, flowers, service, and so on. I just

Revise and make idea
of new first paragraph.

$\longrightarrow$

Too informal but
Keep idea.

$\longrightarrow$

get rid of "you"
and informality. $\longrightarrow$

Like "child" and
"children" better than
"kid" and "kids". $\longrightarrow$

2

think personally this is going too far. Somewhere
in between these two extremes of the pet hater and
the pet idolizer is the person who enjoys his pet
but doesn't carry it too far. This is the person
with his head screwed on straight. I know where a
person like this is coming from. He has already
found out for himself what alot of modern research
into medicine and psychology has uncovered in its
experiments and surveys. What that is is what the
rest of this paper is about.

First of all, everybody knows or should know
that pets are good for kids. Every kid ought to
have a pet. Some parents are bannanas on the subject and won't let their children have a pet. But
pets are marvelous for kids. You have to be careful of the kind you get, however, because some kinds
are better with small children than others. You
couldn't go wrong with a golden retriever. Such an
animal will be patient and kind and they are
thoroughly reliable. What this does for kids is to
give them another object to love. The more things
around a little kid that he can love, the better.
And it teaches a child to be kind and considerate.

make this example
of a lesson pets teach. ⟶

"Second" and "Third" ⟶
below too mechanical.

get rid of "you"
and "I". ⟶

3

A dog is representative of nature and so if a kid has a dog he is close to nature. This is especially important if a child lives in the big city where there are so few animals. A pet can also teach loyalty.

Second, as a person grows older, he may find that he is lonely due to living alone. Going to work, coming home to an empty house, and having no one there can be terrible. Such an individual definitely needs a pet to keep him company. It has been shown through various surveys conducted by Life Insurance Companies that single people who have pets actually live longer than people who do not have pets. This is because a pet lets you get outside yourself and forget your problems. It gives you something to love and care for. I believe in addition that laughter is one of the best medicines, and pets, dogs in particular, are great for making you laugh. A funny dog is one of the funniest things around. He never laughs at his own jokes. I mean, of course, that animals are often unconsciously funny. At any rate, lonliness is a terrible thing, and a pet can really help.

Some misspelling
and slang here. ⟶

Get rid of offensive
words. ⟶

4

    <u>Third and finally</u>, and this is especially pertinent to those who are senior citizens, pets are a means for reducing your high blood pressure. Alot of people may laugh at this idea, but lately medical doctors have found that petting and caring for a pet calms a person and makes him happier. Experimenters have also found that putting pets in a funny farm, especially where there are violent patients, works wonders. I saw a segment on TV about one of these places where there were the most violent kinds of loonies who had done all sorts of grusome things. They were given pets to look after and most of them became much more manageable and stable. Some of them were transformed. But to get back to blood pressure, it is a proven fact that if you have a dog you are going to do better in that category. Pets brought into the nursing homes make the old people feel loved and wanted when they felt pretty much deserted before. Certain organizations are bringing animals to these nursing homes for the old people to hold and caress. So remember, we need these creatures they do more good for us than we do for them.

final copy will usually produce a much less effective paper. Without worrying about how you are expressing your ideas, simply get them down on paper first. After that you can make improvements.

Read the rough draft of a paper on "The Animal Factor," on pp. 266–273. Study it and the notes that the student made in order to guide the writing of the final version.

46f Revise the draft.

Once you have put your ideas on paper, you are ready to revise and rewrite. Revising sometimes requires extensive deletions or additions, sometimes minor changes. Occasionally you will need to throw away an entire draft and begin over. Revising your draft (or drafts) is in some ways the most important stage in the writing process, for here your ideas and language are shaped into their final form.

After revising and just before submitting your paper, read over it two or three times, at least once aloud for sound. Watch especially for misspellings, typographical errors, faulty punctuation, and omissions made in revising or copying. You will find the following checklist helpful during the process of writing and revising as well as during the period just before turning your paper in.

Checklist

Title

The title should accurately suggest the contents of the paper.

It should attract interest without being excessively novel or clever.

It should not be too long.

NOTE: Do not underline the title of your own paper, and do not put quotation marks around it.

Introduction

The introduction should be independent of the title. No pronoun or noun in the opening sentence should depend for meaning on the title.

It should catch the reader's attention.

It should properly establish the tone of the paper as serious, humorous, ironic, or otherwise.

It should include a thesis statement which declares the subject and the purpose directly but at the same time avoids worn patterns like "It is the purpose of this paper to. . . ."

Body

The materials should develop the thesis statement.

The materials should be arranged in logical sequence.

Strong topic sentences (see **45a**) should clearly indicate the direction in which the paper is moving and the relevance of the paragraphs to the thesis statement.

Technical terms should be explained.

Paragraphs should not be choppy.

Adequate space should be devoted to main ideas. Minor ideas should be subordinated.

Concrete details should be used appropriately. Insignificant details should be omitted.

Transitions

The connections between sentences and those between paragraphs should be shown by good linking words and by repetition of parallel phrases and structures. (See **45g.**)

The Animal Factor

THESIS STATEMENT: Modern research in physical and psychological medicine is proving that pets may be far more important to human health than has been suspected.

Modern research in physical medicine and in psychological medicine is proving that pets may be far more important to human health and happiness than has been suspected before, even by those who have always loved animals, which most of us do. In at least 3 major phases of life, pets appear to serve their owners in ways that go far beyond mere diversion.

It has long been realized that pets are good for children. There is a lot of sentimental material on children and their pets. Child psychologists say that an animal does actually help in the normal maturing processes of children. A gentle breed of dog such as a golden retreiver, will be patient and kind usually with its young owner. Such a pet becomes an object of love and will help the child to mature normally and happily.

2

Young owners of pets learn to be kind and considerate toward other creatures. Parents can use pets to teach the child the meaning of responsibility. For the younster who lives in a large city, a pet may be the only nonhuman life frequently encountered. It is vital that children learn to relate to nature's creatures as sell as to other human beings; a pet can be invaluable in this way. Since different pets display different qualities, a child may pick up valuable lessons. For instance, a faithful dog teaches the value of loyalty.

As persons grow into adulthood and leave home, they frequently are confronted with one of the most painful and difficult of emotional states--loneliness. For a person living alone, nothing is more depressing than to come home each day after work to an empty house where there is no greeting, no signs of kindness or love. In recent years Life Insurance Companies have conducted surveys, which show that single people with pets actually live longer than those without pets. A dog, a cat, or even a bird, takes the focus from oneself for awhile, allows a person to forget personal cares

and to be interested in some other living thing.
Laughter has always been highly valued, but now we
know that it has a definite therapeutic effect.
Animals are famous for provoking laughter, causing
us to feel good. Many of them are naturally and
unconsciously funny, and they tend to bring out
our good natured side.

For those who have reached an advanced age or
who have severe emotional problems, pets may be
among the best medicines available. Medical research has discovered that pets not only alleviate
loneliness but actually have a positive effect on
blood pressure readings. Studies reveal that while
persons are caring for or simply caressing a pet,
blood pressure readings go down. Animals appear to
have a calming effect that can help one live longer.
Pets also have a positive influence on patients
with emotional problems, especially those who tend
to be violent. Recently a number of pets were
placed in an institution for the criminally insane
to determine how they would react. They became
happier and more manageable, and they cared well
for the animals. A few of them were almost

transformed, because they found something to love and take care of that asked nothing in return from them. Elderly men and women, who have been placed in nursing homes and who seldom if ever see a caring relative have profited greatly from visitors who bring calm and friendly animals. Humane societies and other organizations have had remarkable results when they brought pets to such nursing homes for the old and forgotten to hold. They seem renewed when a dog or cat notices them and gives them affection that they do not receive from the human world of people. They no longer feel deserted and unloved. For these and numerous other reasons, human beings need pets; they do for more for people than people do for them.

Conclusion

The conclusion should usually contain a final statement of the underlying idea, an overview of what the paper has demonstrated.

The conclusion may require a separate paragraph; but if the paper has reached significant conclusions all along, such a paragraph is not necessary for its own sake.

The conclusion should not merely restate the introduction.

Proofreading

Allow some time, if possible at least one day, between the last draft of the paper and final finished copy. Then you can examine the paper objectively for wordiness, repetition, incorrect diction, misspellings, faulty punctuation, choppy sentences, vague sentences, lack of transitions, and careless errors.

Notice how the author of "The Animal Factor" revised the draft to make a tighter and better written paper. Study the paper, on pp. 276–279, for its improvements over the draft but also for mistakes and weaknesses that remain.

46g Learn from your mistakes.

The process of composition is not complete until you have carefully examined your paper after it is returned to you, looked up your errors in this book and in a dictionary so that you understand how to correct them, and revised along the lines suggested by your instructor. Learn from your mistakes so that the same problems do not turn up in future papers.

Following is the paper on "The Animal Factor" after it was returned to the student. The instructor's marks in red are generally numbers that refer to sections in this book that the student needs to refer to. The student's revisions are in black.

The Animal Factor

THESIS STATEMENT: Modern research in physical and psychological medicine is proving that pets may be far more important to human health than has been suspected.

Modern research in physical *and psychological* medicine ~~and in psychological medicine~~ is proving that pets may be **38** far more important to human health and happiness than has been suspected before, even by those who **38** have always loved animals, ~~which most of us do.~~ In at least *three* major phases of life, pets appear to **36** serve their owners in ways that go far beyond mere diversion.

It has long been realized that pets are good for children. ~~There is a lot of sentimental~~ **44e** ~~material on children and their pets.~~ Child psychologists say that an animal does actually help in the normal maturing processes of children. A **31** gentle breed of dog such as a golden *retriever* will be patient and kind (usually) with its young owner. Such a pet becomes an object of love and will help the child to mature normally and happily.

2

Young owners of pets learn to be kind and considerate toward other creatures. Parents can use pets to teach the child the meaning of responsibility. For the *youngster* ~~younster~~ who lives in a large city, 3¶ a pet may be the only nonhuman life frequently encountered. It is vital that children learn to relate to nature's creatures as *w*ell as to other ✗ human beings; a pet can be invaluable in this way. Since different pets display different qualities, a child may pick up valuable lessons. For instance, a faithful dog teaches the value of loyalty.

As persons grow into adulthood and leave home, they frequently are confronted with one of the most painful and difficult of emotional states--loneliness. For a person living alone, nothing is more depressing than to come home each day after work to an empty house where there is no greeting, no signs 34 of kindness or love. In recent years *L*ife *I*nsurance 2li *C*ompanies have conducted surveys, which show that single people with pets actually live longer than those without pets. A dog, a cat, or even a bird, takes the focus from oneself for 49 *a while* ~~awhile,~~ allows a person to forget personal cares

3

and to be interested in some other living thing. Laughter has always been highly valued, but now we know that it has a definite therapeutic effect. 38 Animals are famous for provoking laughter/. ~~causing us to feel good.~~ Many of them are naturally and unconsciously funny, and they tend to bring out our good-natured side. 32b

For those who have reached an advanced age or who have severe emotional problems, pets may be among the best medicines available. Medical research has discovered that pets not only alleviate loneliness but actually have a positive effect on 38 blood pressure. ~~readings.~~ Studies reveal that while persons are caring for or simply caressing a pet, blood pressure readings go down. Animals appear to have a calming effect that can help one live longer. Pets also have a positive influence on patients with emotional problems, especially those who tend to be violent. Recently a number of pets were placed in an institution for the criminally insane 8g to determine how ~~they~~ *these patients* would react. They became happier and more manageable, and they cared well for the animals. A few of them were almost

4

2/ transformed, because they found something to love
and take care of that asked nothing in return from
them. Elderly men and women, who have been placed 2/i
in nursing homes and who seldom if ever see a
caring relative have profited greatly from visitors
who bring calm and friendly animals. Humane societies and other organizations have had remarkable
results when they brought pets to such nursing
homes for the old and forgotten to hold. They seem
renewed when a dog or cat notices them and gives
them affection that they do not receive from the
3q human world. ~~of people.~~ They no longer feel
deserted and unloved. For these and numerous other
reasons, human beings need pets; they do for more
3/ <u>for</u> people than people do for them.

Subjects for papers

Keep a notebook of items which you think may be useful to you
as possible subjects and materials for papers. Some suggestions
follow.

Inadequate Studying	Taking Risks
Rootlessness	Living for the Moment
Living for the Future	Living in the Past
Deceitful Appearances	Helping Others
Daydreaming	Handling Disappointment
True Beauty	Laughter as Medicine
Peer Pressure	The Illusion of Equality
Egotism—Its Results	The Average Person

Fewer Years for College	City Folklore
Old Photographs	The Center City
Fair Journalism	Bad Teaching
Return to the Country	Abortion
Political Cartoons	Television Commercials
The New Music	An Ice Storm
Divorce	Working in a Political Campaign
The New Freedoms	Good Fences and Good Friends
Blackness	Educating the Parent
Patterns of Humor	Camping Out

Walking	Parks
A Deserted House	Censorship
Crime	The Subway at Night
Exploring	Credit
The Scientific Attitude	Welfare
The Emergency Ward	Acting in a Play
Trip Down River	A Description of a Painting

Each of the following groups presents three points of view. In selecting a topic from one of the groups you may wish to choose A,
B, or C.

1. A. Each generation passes on to its children a better world.
   B. Each generation passes on to its children a world in worse condition than it was before.
   C. The condition of the world, everything considered, is always just about the same. Changes are superficial.

2. A. The best way to win an argument is never to let the opponent talk much.
   B. Silence wins the most arguments.
   C. In any argument, say just a little, but say it well.

3. A. A democracy is obligated to give every person an education.
   B. Educational institutions and agencies should carefully supervise admissions according to talent and abilities.
   C. Colleges should not bother to educate students who are below average in mentality or learning.

4. A. Optimism and belief in progress have long characterized most American thought.
   B. Optimism and belief in progress have greatly declined in the last two decades.
   C. Modern problems make it necessary for Americans who strongly believe in optimism and progress to temper their views.

5. A. The editorial page is the wisest section of a newspaper.
   B. The comics are the wisest section of a newspaper.
   C. The front page is the wisest section of a newspaper.

6. A. Neither a borrower nor a lender be.
   B. A good neighbor borrows or lends freely.
   C. Borrow freely or lend freely; no one can do both well.

Quotations to suggest subjects for papers

The following quotations may help you develop subjects for themes. Support, refute, exemplify, or use these quotations in any appropriate way. You may think of a subject only remotely related to what the author says.

For the 15 per cent of adolescents who learn well in schools and are interested in subjects that are essentially academic . . . catch-all high schools are wasteful.

PAUL GOODMAN,
"Freedom and Learning:
The Need for Choice"

Never have the burdens of wealth been greater than they are today, and never have its rewards been slimmer.

JEAN PAUL GETTY,
"The World Is Mean to Millionaires"

Women's emancipation has in various ways made marriage more difficult.

BERTRAND RUSSELL,
Marriage and Morals

Problems are never solved by returning to a stage which one has already outgrown.

ERICH FROMM,
"Our Way of Life Makes Us Miserable"

We are not so weak and timorous as to need to be free of fear; we need only use our capacity to not be afraid of it and so relegate fear to its proper perspective.

WILLIAM FAULKNER,
"Faith or Fear"

Religion will not regain its old power until it can face change in the same spirit as does science.

ALFRED NORTH WHITEHEAD,
"Religion and Science"

No great and enduring volume can ever be written on the flea, though many there be who have tried it.

HERMAN MELVILLE,
Moby-Dick

Whoso would be a man, must be a nonconformist.

RALPH WALDO EMERSON,
"Self-Reliance"

Stay, stay at home, my heart and rest; / Homekeeping hearts are happiest.

HENRY WADSWORTH LONGFELLOW

A prophet is not without honor, save in his own country, and in his own house.

MATTHEW 13:57

Home life as we understand it is no more natural to us than a cage is natural to a cockatoo.

GEORGE BERNARD SHAW,
Getting Married

To some extent a citizen of any country will feel that the tourist's view of his homeland is a false one.

MARY MCCARTHY,
"America the Beautiful"

Labor disgraces no man; unfortunately you occasionally find men disgrace labor.

ULYSSES S. GRANT,
Speech at Birmingham, England

The mass of men lead lives of quiet desperation. What is called resignation is confirmed desperation.

HENRY DAVID THOREAU,
Walden

Our life is frittered away by detail.

THOREAU,
Walden

The preservation of the English language in its purity throughout the United States is an object deserving the attention of every American who is a friend to the literature and science of his country.

JOHN PICKERING,
A Vocabulary

Literature

47   Writing About Literature

This section is not intended to provide you with the basis for an entire course in literature or for a major in English. Instead, it is an introduction to the writing of essays on literary subjects.

Casual readers of poetry, fiction, and drama merely see the surface of the work. Though nothing is wrong with this kind of quick and pleasurable reading, a deeper and more careful probing brings a different kind of satisfaction. In writing about literature, you should express your own reactions in a way that does justice to the richness and the complexity of the work. A good paper is not purely subjective although it does state the writer's opinions. It convinces others by solid evidence and proof cited or quoted from the work.

A poem, a work of fiction, or a play does not mean just anything a reader wishes it to. Although works of literature permit more than one correct interpretation, some readings are clearly more true to the purpose of the poem or story, and some criticisms can be shown to be erroneous.

47a   Choose a literary work which interests you. Write about the feature of the work which interests you most.

You can never hope to write about all you see in a work of literature. Choose the best topic you can find. What is dull to you is almost certain to be dull also to your reader. If your teacher permits you to select your own topic, discard anything which does not have for you some degree of intellectual and perhaps even emotional excitement. Do not give up too soon in your search for a topic, however; for what seems uninteresting at first may later develop into a promising subject.

Usually it is best to select one area (such as structure or theme or imagery) rather than to try to cover several. You may decide to write about the function of just one aspect of the complete work. At any rate, focusing sharply in this manner often leads to a good paper topic. A short paper on one crucial paragraph in fiction, the setting (or place of one scene), or one speech may provide perspective on an entire work.

Between the first reading of the work and the writing of your paper, study in detail every item which relates to your topic. Take notes. Do not read a work and then think that you can remember it well enough to write your paper from your memory and second looks at the printed page. As you read further into the work, it is natural to forget ideas that occurred to you at first; so it is important to write them down as you go along. Many first impressions will be proved wrong by what happens later in the work. Discard these and save the good ones.

Ideas for a paper should percolate before you write. It is difficult to produce an instant topic that is good. Keep the literary work on your mind even while you are doing other things besides sitting at your desk. Think about it in idle moments. The best idea you have for a paper may come while you are engaged in a trivial task or when you are not much aware that you are thinking about your paper at all. The actual composing of the paper will be much simpler and the results much better if you plan well before you start your first draft. The more thinking ahead of time, the more thoughtful the essay may be.

47b Determine the kind of essay you wish to write

Writings about literature fall into several categories. Explanations of a few of the more significant ones follow.

An interpretation

Most papers result from a close study of the work. An interpretative paper identifies methods and ideas. Through analysis, the writer presents specific evidence to support the interpretation.

Distinguish carefully between the thinking of a character and that of the author. Unless an author speaks in his or her own person, you can deduce what the author thinks only from the work as a whole. Many works of literature depict a character whose whole way of life and thinking is the opposite of the author's views. To confuse the character with the author in this kind of work is to make a crucial mistake. Sometimes it is clear immediately what authors think about their characters, but not always.

A review

A good review of a book or an article is both description and evaluation. It tells precisely what the author attempts to do and what methods are followed in carrying out the aim. Include a brief summary or outline of the contents, especially when an overview is needed for clarity, but follow up such information with your own estimate of the author's accomplishment.

A character analysis

A character sketch is a tempting kind of paper to write. Actually it is very difficult to compose a truly good character analysis. This kind of paper lends itself to superficiality. A critic accomplishes little by merely summarizing a character's traits and recounting actions without considering motivations, development, and interrelationships with other characters. Describe the method of characterization—*how* the author develops the character. Distinguish between *character* and *characterization.* Do not characterize; the author of the work is the one who characterizes.

Setting

Often the time and place in which a work is set tell something important about the way people interact with their environments. If you write about setting, you should do far more than merely describe it. Show how it brings out important meanings, moods, and so forth.

Technical analysis

The analysis of technical elements in literature—imagery, symbolism, point of view, structure, prosody, and so on—requires special study of the technical term or concept as well as of the literary work itself. You might begin by looking up the term in a good basic reference book like C. Hugh Holman's *A Handbook to Literature.*

Combined approaches

Many papers combine different kinds of approaches. A thoughtful paper on imagery, for example, does more than merely point out the images, or even the kinds of images, in the work under study. Rather, it uses the imagery to interpret, analyze, or clarify something else as well—theme, structure, characterization, mood, relationship, recurrent patterns, and so on.

47c Give the paper a precise title.

Do not search for a fancy title at the expense of meaning. Authors of literary works often use figurative titles like *Death in the Afternoon* and *The Grapes of Wrath,* but you would be wise to designate your subject more literally.

Vague and general titles of literary papers may be puzzling. As a title, "A Criticism of *The Color Purple*" provides no information about the subject except the name of the novel. "The Ending of *The Color Purple*" stands a better chance of revealing what the paper is about.

Stick to the topic named in the title. The topic sentence of every paragraph should point back to the introduction and to the title. Every paragraph should develop the announced subject.

47d Organize and develop the paper according to significant ideas.

Do not automatically organize your paper by following the sequence of the story or the poem. Sometimes the result of this kind of order may be poor topic sentences, summary rather than thought, mechanical organization, and repetitive transitional phrases.

Consider whether it would be better to break up your overall argument or thesis into several aspects and to move from the discussion of one of these topics on to the other.

Do not begin papers or paragraphs with automatic and dull sentences. Start writing with interest and substance, not with mechanical expressions like the following:

"In the first stanza . . . ."
"In the second stanza . . . ."
"To begin with, . . ."
"In 'The Rape of the Lock,' a poem written by Alexander Pope in the eighteenth century, . . ."

47e Do not summarize and paraphrase excessively.

A certain amount of summarizing is usually necessary. To a slight extent, summary may even involve interpretation. At least it selects, and selection points out the subjects of discussion.

Tell only as much of the story as is necessary, however, to clarify your interpretations and prove your arguments. Mere detailed summary is inadequate as the basis for a paper. Your thoughts are the crucial measure of your essay. When you paraphrase, make clear what you are doing so that someone else's thinking will not be taken as yours.

NOTE: Ordinarily you should use the historical present tense when you tell what *happens* in a work—not what *happened.* See **4.**

47f Think for yourself.

The excellence of your paper will depend finally on the significance of *your* thinking. Your readers will determine for themselves the importance of your paper according to your ideas and your evidence.

47g Write about the literature, not about yourself or the reading process.

Your reader will not be interested in the difference between what you saw in a work on a first reading and your insight after a second reading. Generally, do not write about how others *might* read or misread the work. Omit such irrelevant information. Only your final and considered views should be presented in your paper. Spend little or no time telling your reader that it is your belief; it is understood that opinions expressed are your own. It is a good idea to avoid frequent use of the first-person pronouns *I* and *we.*

Excessive concern with your own methods and the development of your own thoughts detracts from what you say about literature and causes irrelevance and wordiness.

47h   Provide sufficient evidence to support your ideas.

Strike a proper balance between generalizations and detailed support of your points. Make a point; develop its particularities and ramifications; quote the work; and show how your idea is supported by the quotation. Avoid long quotations.

Papers, or even paragraphs, usually should not begin with a quotation. Readers prefer to see what you have to say first. Then you can work in quotations to support your argument. As a rule, do not conclude paragraphs with quotations either.

47i   Do not moralize.

Good criticism is not preachy. Do not use your paper as a platform from which to moralize on the rights and wrongs of the world. A literary paper that is otherwise excellent can be spoiled by an attempt to teach a moral lesson.

It is especially ineffective to begin with your own philosophical view of the world and then to discuss the work as an illustration of views you already had before you read it.

47j   Acknowledge your sources.

Define the difference between what other critics have written and what you think. State your contribution. Avoid beginning papers or paragraphs with the names of critics and their views before you present your own.

Develop your own thesis. Stress your views, not those of others. Use sources to show that other critics have interpreted correctly, to correct errors in some criticism that is otherwise excellent, to show that a critic is right but that something needs to be added, or to show that no one has previously written on your subject at all.

If no critic has written about the work or the point you are making, that is no problem (unless your instructor requires that you have a number of sources). On the other hand, it is a serious error to state that nothing has been written about your subject when something has. Be thorough in your investigation.

For bibliographies of writings about literature, see **48b.** For information about plagiarism and documentation, see **48f** and **48g.**

Some hints about reading a work and planning to write a paper

Let your subject grow out of your reading of the work and your questions about it. Do not begin with preconceived ideas about what you will write on. You may discover that the subject you had hoped to write about is not appropriate. If you plan to discuss setting, for example, a close reading of the work may show that setting is not important.

Preparing to write a paper—an example

Read the following poem.

My Papa's Waltz

The whiskey on your breath
Could make a small boy dizzy;
But I hung on like death:
Such waltzing was not easy.

We romped until the pans
Slid from the kitchen shelf;
My mother's countenance
Could not unfrown itself.

The hand that held my wrist
Was battered on one knuckle;
At every step you missed
My right ear scraped a buckle.

You beat time on my head
With a palm caked hard by dirt,
Then waltzed me off to bed
Still clinging to your shirt.

THEODORE ROETHKE

Study the following questions. Write down the answers to
the ones that seem most significant to you.

1. Who is the speaker of the poem? Is it the poet? A boy?
2. Why did the poet choose this speaker?
3. Considering the great number of words which may be used
   for a father, what is the effect of calling him "Papa"?
4. Why does the poet refer to the movements around the room
   as a waltz?
5. That is, what kind of dance is a waltz, and how is it appropriate to the poem? Is it a happy dance? Graceful?
6. To whom is the poem addressed? Why?
7. What does "like death" mean in the poem?
8. Is the boy literally afraid, or is he exaggerating?
9. How long after the waltzing is the boy remembering the
   dance with his papa?
10. What does the falling of the pans show about the manner of
    dancing?
11. What is the reaction of the mother?
12. Later the boy or the man he becomes remembers that his fa-
    ther held him by the wrist. How does he probably hold him?
    Why? Is there a difference between his intentions in the
    holding and his manner of holding?
13. The speaker remembers that one of the father's knuckles was
    battered. What does this suggest? A fight? A fall?

14. Why does the father miss steps in the dance, and why does the boy remember his missing them?
15. What does *beat time* mean?
16. What is the significance of the father's dirty hands?
17. What is the point to the boy's right ear scraping a belt buckle?
18. What emotions are attached to the father's waltzing the boy off to bed?
19. What is the attitude of the speaker toward the drunken father?
20. What is the character or nature of the father, the boy, the situation, the emotions of the two, the memories of the boy when he is older? To sum up, what is the poem about?

■ Exercise 1

Using your answers to the questions above, write a paper about "My Papa's Waltz."

Writing a paper an example

Read the following short story.

The Open Window

"Saki" (H. H. Munro)

"My aunt will be down presently, Mr. Nuttel," said a very self-possessed young lady of fifteen; "in the meantime you must try and put up with me."

Framton Nuttel endeavoured to say the correct something which should duly flatter the niece of the moment without unduly discounting the aunt that was to come. Privately he doubted more than ever whether these formal visits on a succession of total strangers would do much towards helping the nerve cure which he was supposed to be undergoing.

"I know how it will be," his sister had said when he was preparing to migrate to this rural retreat; "you will bury yourself down there and not speak to a living soul, and your nerves will be worse than ever from moping. I shall just give you letters of introduction to all the people I know there. Some of them, as far as I can remember, were quite nice."

Framton wondered whether Mrs. Sappleton, the lady to whom he was presenting one of the letters of introduction, came into the nice division.

"Do you know many of the people round here?" asked the niece, when she judged that they had had sufficient silent communion.

"Hardly a soul," said Framton. "My sister was staying here, at the rectory, you know, some four years ago, and she gave me letters of introduction to some of the people here."

He made the last statement in a tone of distinct regret.

"Then you know practically nothing about my aunt?" pursued the self-possessed young lady.

"Only her name and address," admitted the caller. He was wondering whether Mrs. Sappleton was in the married or widowed state. An undefinable something about the room seemed to suggest masculine habitation.

"Her great tragedy happened just three years ago," said the child; "that would be since your sister's time."

"Her tragedy?" asked Framton; somehow in this restful country spot tragedies seemed out of place.

"You may wonder why we keep that window wide open on an October afternoon," said the niece, indicating a large French window that opened on to a lawn.

"It is quite warm for the time of the year," said Framton; "but has that window got anything to do with the tragedy?"

"Out through that window, three years ago to a day, her husband and her two young brothers went off for their day's shooting. They never came back. In crossing the moor to their favourite snipe-shooting ground they were all three engulfed in a treacherous piece of bog. It had been that dreadful wet summer, you know, and places that were safe in other years gave way suddenly without warning. Their bodies were never recovered. That was the dreadful part of it." Here the child's voice lost its self-possessed note and became falteringly human. "Poor aunt always thinks that they will come back some day, they and the little brown spaniel that was lost with them, and walk in at that window just as they used to do. That is why the window is kept open every evening till it is quite dusk. Poor dear aunt, she has often told me how they went out, her husband with his white waterproof coat over his arm, and Ronnie, her youngest brother, singing, 'Bertie, why do you bound?' as he always did to tease her, because she said it got on her nerves. Do you know, sometimes on still, quiet evenings like this, I almost get a creepy feeling that they will all walk in through that window—"

She broke off with a little shudder. It was a relief to Framton when the aunt bustled into the room with a whirl of apologies for being late in making her appearance.

"I hope Vera has been amusing you?" she said.

"She has been very interesting," said Framton.

"I hope you don't mind the open window," said Mrs. Sappleton briskly; "my husband and brothers will be home directly from shooting, and they always come in this way. They've been out for snipe in the marshes today, so they'll make a fine mess over my poor carpets. So like you men-folk, isn't it?"

She rattled on cheerfully about the shooting and the scarcity of birds, and the prospects for duck in the winter. To Framton, it was all purely horrible. He made a desperate but only partially successful effort to turn the talk on to a less ghastly topic; he was conscious that his hostess was giving him only a fragment of her attention, and her eyes were constantly straying past him to the open window and the lawn beyond. It was certainly an unfortunate coincidence that he should have paid his visit on this tragic anniversary.

"The doctors agree in ordering me complete rest, an absence of mental excitement, and avoidance of anything in the nature of violent physical exercise," announced Framton, who laboured under the tolerably wide-spread delusion that total strangers and chance acquaintances are hungry for the least detail of one's ailments and infirmities, their cause and cure. "On the matter of diet they are not so much in agreement," he continued.

"No?" said Mrs. Sappleton, in a voice which only replaced a yawn at the last moment. Then she suddenly brightened into alert attention—but not to what Framton was saying.

"Here they are at last!" she cried. "Just in time for tea, and don't they look as if they were muddy up to the eyes!"

Framton shivered slightly and turned towards the niece with a look intended to convey sympathetic comprehension. The child was staring out through the open window with dazed horror in her eyes. In a chill shock of nameless fear Framton swung round in his seat and looked in the same direction.

In the deepening twilight three figures were walking across the lawn towards the window; they all carried guns under their arms, and one of them was additionally burdened with a white coat hung over his shoulders. A tired brown spaniel kept close at their heels. Noiselessly they neared the house, and then a hoarse young voice chanted out of the dusk: "I said, Bertie, why do you bound?"

Framton grabbed wildly at his stick and hat; the hall-door, the gravel-drive, and the front gate were dimly noted stages in his headlong retreat. A cyclist coming along the road had to run into the hedge to avoid imminent collision.

"Here we are, my dear," said the bearer of the white mackintosh coming in through the window; "fairly muddy, but most of it's dry. Who was that who bolted out as we came up?"

"A most extraordinary man, a Mr. Nuttel," said Mrs. Sappleton; "could only talk about his illnesses, and dashed off without a word of good-bye or apology when you arrived. One would think he had seen a ghost."

"I expect it was the spaniel," said the niece calmly; "he told me he had a horror of dogs. He was once hunted into a cemetery somewhere on the banks of the Ganges by a pack of pariah dogs, and had to spend the night in a newly dug grave with the creatures snarling and grinning and foaming just above him. Enough to make any one lose their nerve."

Romance at short notice was her specialty.

Write down a list of questions like those above on "My Papa's Waltz." Make a list of subjects for papers about Munro's story. List them in the order of your preference, the best first and so on. Write a paper on "The Open Window" before you read the sample paper on page 304.

Fact and Fancy: Terror and a Joke

Surprise endings are common in short stories,
but it requires skill to begin a tale in a way so
that it seems to be one thing and then to reverse
it so that it becomes not at all what it seemed to
be at first. In the short story "The Open Window,"
H. H. Munro starts out solemnly and turns his work
into a surprisingly humorous piece of fiction. The
story is effective largely because of the central
image of a window, the setting, and the characterization of a "very self-possessed young lady of fifteen" who is both an accomplished story-teller and
a practical joker.

The three main parts of the story involve a
stranger's visit to an aristocratic home in England,
the young lady's account of a tragic disappearance
and death, and the unexpected arrival of those she
implies had died. The visitor is Framton Nuttel,
an extremely nervous man who has come to the
country in an effort to become more tranquil. In
the opening scene, it is difficult to say which
character--Mr. Nuttel or the young lady--is the
better model of good manners and propriety, but she

is actually setting him up for a nerve-racking experience.

An open window in the room suggests an entry
into a scary world, where she is about to have him
look. As soon as she learns of his complete and
convenient ignorance about the family, she tells
him that her aunt had a "great tragedy" three years
before and that this explains why the window is
kept open even in the chill of October afternoons.
The sorrow began, the "self-possessed" and apparently solemn young woman says, when "out through
that window, three years ago to a day, her husband
and her two young brothers went off for their day's
shooting. They never came back." In a carefully
calculated sad manner, she continues to relate that
the three men sank into a bog and that even "Their
bodies were never recovered"--a likely enough
tragedy but also good preparation for some super-
natural occurrence. The nervous visitor never de-
tects a clue that the "self-possessed" (a term
Munro uses several times) girl may be putting him
on. But she is. Masterfully in her perverse
spirit of fun, she describes her "creepy feeling

that they will all walk in through that window."

The open window is her instrument for a good joke, but Mr. Nuttel regards it now suspiciously and somewhat eerily. The aunt has no feelings about it one way or the other. She simply declares her hopes for the early return of her relatives. Cheerfully (but horribly to the deceived Framton Nuttel), the aunt chats with her visitor while she intently watches the window for her returning men. Naturally he thinks that she is crazy, at least on this subject. At this point, the reader tends to hold the same view.

The climactic moment in the story occurs when the three figures actually stride across the lawn. The aunt remains her normal self, but the mood of everyone else undergoes a transformation. At last the reader comprehends that the niece has invented a story of tragedy in order to make the returning men appear as ghosts. She maintains her formal composure, stares out the window, an accomplished actress with "dazed horror in her eyes" and, one should assume, secret glee in her heart at the success of her prank—though Munro never describes it

4

as such. Poor Framton "grabbed wildly at his stick
and hat" and fled. The aunt, amazed at his be-
havior, ironically comments that "one would think
he had seen a ghost." The imaginative niece--per-
haps a little horrible in her calm telling of
horror tales--rambles on about the nervous Mr.
Nuttel's "horror of dogs," his being chased by a
pack of them into a cemetery on the Ganges, and his
finding safety in "a newly dug grave." Apparently
she creates such stories even for her own family.

The open window has become the symbol of her
limitless inventiveness: "Romance at short notice
was her specialty." Her romances, however, are
full of horror; the "short notice" reveals her
quick imagination, and the "specialty" may range
from play to cruel eccentricity. Munro's story is
a remarkably complex tale. It contains simultan-
eously most of the ingredients of ghost stories, of
formal and social comedies, and of jokes in which
the humor becomes apparent so gradually that the
author never precisely reveals where the tone
should change from formality to horror to humor.

Some final hints on writing about literature

Read the work once carefully.

Decide on a subject generally.

Narrow the subject as much as you can before a second reading.

Ask yourself questions as you read the work the second time, the third, and so on.

Write down the answers to your questions.

Arrange the answers by topics.

Decide on a final approach, topic, title, and thesis.

Discard the erroneous answers to your questions.

Discard the irrelevant points. Choose the one you wish to discuss.

Select the best topics.

Put them in logical order.

Rearrange them as you carry out the creative process of thinking through the subject and writing the paper.

Revise as many times as necessary.

Do not display or emphasize technical terms, which may sometimes be as distracting as they are helpful. Your reader will not be impressed by attempts to show off. That is no substitute for straight thinking and clear writing.

Be sure to name the work which you write about and the author. Do not misspell the author's name—as often happens. Ernest Hemingway, for example, spelled his last name with only one *m*.

In the body of your paper do not rely on your title for information. Do not assume that your reader knows anything about the work or the author except what you tell him or her.

Research

48   Writing the Research Paper

The research paper is based on a systematic process of investigation. It uses materials from various sources, such as government repositories, laboratories, field trips, and surveys. Most frequently, however, research papers grow out of materials readily available in a library.

As you begin your work, keep in mind the following admonition from the *MLA Handbook for Writers of Research Papers* (1984): "The paper based on research is not a collection of others' thoughts but a carefully constructed presentation of an idea—or a number of ideas—that relies on other sources for clarification and verification."

This section provides instructions about the way to assemble materials from sources and to document them.

48a Choose a subject which interests you. Limit it to manageable size.

Your subject should allow you to use the library extensively, think for yourself, and come to a significant conclusion which will be of interest to your reader. Above all, it should engage your attention so that you enjoy reading and thinking about it and writing it up for others. Your final paper should not consist mainly of paragraphs cut and pasted from the materials you have used. The finished product should be mostly written in your own words. Avoid excessive quoting and paragraphing.

Begin by choosing a general subject area.

If you have long had a particular interest, it may be your starting point: photography, perhaps; or literature; or painting; or architecture. If nothing comes to mind, start with a list of broad areas, such as the following, decide on one you like, and then focus on a limited aspect of it.

art	government	industry
literature	sociology	science
philosophy	anthropology	archaeology
history	economics	medicine
religion	geography	ecology

At this stage you are trying to relate your investigation to an active interest.

Limit your subject adequately.

Suppose you have chosen photography as your general area. After a little thought and reading and a look at the card catalog of the library, you will see that this is too broad a topic for one paper. So you may begin by narrowing it to color photography, or aerial photography, or the history of photography. Any of these topics could be further restricted: for example, "The Effect of Color Photography on Advertising" or "Aerial Photography in World War II." Still further limitation may be desirable, depending on the length of your paper and the resources of your library.

If you are starting with a broad area, such as anthropology, history, science, or literature, you may move gradually toward your final subject in a process like the following:

Anthropology—tribal societies—a tribal people still surviving—American Indians—the Navajo—the lore of the Navajo—Navajo songs.

Science—a study of science in some historical period—biology—evolution—evolution before Darwin—reactions to evolution in popular periodicals before Darwin.

Art—popular art—cartoons—American cartoonists—James Thurber's drawings.

In practice, narrowing down from a general to a specific subject is seldom smooth and orderly. Glean ideas for limiting a

broad idea by skimming an article in an encyclopedia or the subject headings in the card catalog. You may even be well into your
preliminary research (see **48b**) before you arrive at the final topic.

As you read and work, consider whether you are trying to
cover too much ground or whether, at the other extreme, you are
too narrowly confined. If you are not satisfied with your subject
after you get into your preliminary reading, try with your instructor's help to work out an acceptable modification of it instead of
changing your topic completely.

Avoid inappropriate subjects.

Beware of subjects highly technical, learned, or specialized. Only
a specialist can handle modern techniques in genetic research or
experimental psychology. Avoid topics that do not lead to a wide
range of source materials. If you find that you are using one or
two sources exclusively, the fault may be with your method—or
with your topic. For example, a process topic (how to do something) does not lend itself to library investigation. Instead of writing on "How to Ski," a student might harness an interest in skiing
to a study of the effect of skiing on some industry or region in the
United States.

48b Become acquainted with the reference tools of the
library and use them to compile a working bibliography.

Certain guides to knowledge are indispensable to library investigation. From them you can compile a **working bibliography,** a
list of publications which contain material on your subject and
which you plan to read. The items on this list should have only
the author's name, the title, and the information you need in
order to find the source in the library.

The basic tool for finding books in the library is the **card catalog.** It leads you to the books in your library. Books are listed al-

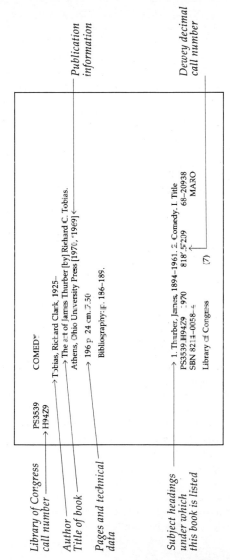

Subject Card
Subject (usually in red)

Publication information

Dewey decimal call number

Library of Congress call number

Author
Title of book

Pages and technical data

Subject headings under which this book is listed

PS3539
H94Z9

COMEDY

Tobias, Richard Clark, 1925–
  The art of James Thurber [by] Richard C. Tobias.
  Athens, Ohio University Press [1970, 1969]
  196 p. 24 cm. 7.50
    Bibliography: p. 186–189.

1. Thurber, James, 1894–1961. 2. Comedy. I. Title
PS3539.H9429 .970   818'.5209   68–20938
SBN 8214-0058-4   MARO
        (7)
Library of Congress

Another Subject Card

PS3539 H94Z9	THURBER, JAMES, 1894–1961

	Tobias, Richard Clark, 1925–
	    The art of James Thurber [by] Richard C. Tobias.
	Athens, Ohio University Press [1970, ⸢1969]
	
	    196 p. 24 cm. 7.50
	
	    Bibliography: p. 186–189.

      1. Thurber, James, 1894–1961. 2. Comedy. I. Title

PS3539.H94Z9   1970   818′.5′209   68–20938
SBN 8214–0058–4   MARO

Library of Congress   (7)

phabetically by author and title with helpful subject headings, subheadings, and cross-references which will steer you to new aspects of your topics. Reproduced on pp. 313–314, and p. 315 are four typical catalog cards—actually four copies of the same Library of Congress card filed for four different uses. Notice the typed title and subject headings.

In some libraries the card catalog has been supplemented or replaced by catalogs on microform. These new catalogs require comparatively little space and can be made available in locations outside the library. A COM (Computer Output Microform) catalog is commonly on microfiche or microfilm, and has author, title, and subject entries arranged in the same way as the card catalog. Computerized, or on-line, catalogs are being used by an increasing number of libraries to take advantage of the computer's capabilities to store and retrieve the information formerly contained in catalog cards. These systems allow the library user to sit at a terminal and search for material by author, title, subject, or any

Author Card

```
PS3539
H94Z9
        Tobias, Richard Clark, 1925–
              The art of James Thurber [by] Richard C. Tobias.
        Athens, Ohio University Press [1970, ᶜ1969]

              196 p. 24 cm. 7.50

              Bibliography: p. 186–189.




              1. Thurber, James, 1894–1961. 2. Comedy. I. Title

        PS3539.H94Z9      1970        818',5'209        68–20938
        SBN 8214–0058–4                                 MARO

        Library of Congress              (7)
```

Title Card

```
PS3539        The art of James Thurber
H94Z9
        Tobias, Richard Clark, 1925–
              The art of James Thurber [by] Richard C. Tobias.
        Athens, Ohio University Press [1970, ᶜ1969]

              196 p. 24 cm. 7.50

              Bibliography: p. 186–189.




              1. Thurber, James, 1894–1961. 2. Comedy. I. Title

        PS3539.H94Z9      1970        818',5'209        68–20938
        SBN 8214–0058–4                                 MARO

        Library of Congress              (7)
```

combination of these. Periodicals are indexed in special reference books, which list articles by author, title, and subject. The following periodical indexes are the most useful.

Periodical Indexes

Readers' Guide to Periodical Literature, 1900– .

An index to the most widely circulated American periodicals.

Nineteenth Century Readers' Guide to Periodical Literature, 1890–1899.

Author and subject index to some fifty English language general periodicals of the last decade of the nineteenth century.

Poole's Index to Periodical Literature, 1802–1906.

An index by subject to the leading British and American periodicals of the nineteenth century.

Humanities Index, 1974– .

Social Sciences Index, 1974– . Preceded by *Social Sciences and Humanities Index.*

Social Sciences and Humanities Index, 1965–1974. Formerly *International Index,* 1907–1965.

Author and subject index to a selection of scholarly journals.

British Humanities Index, 1962– .

Supersedes in part *Subject Index to Periodicals,* 1915–1922, 1926–1961.

Subject index to British periodicals.

Applied Science and Technology Index, 1958– .

Cumulative subject index to a selection of English and American periodicals in such fields as aeronautics, automation, chemistry, electricity, engineering, physics.

Art Index, 1929– .

"Cumulative Author and Subject Index to a Selected List of Fine Arts Periodicals."

Biography Index, 1946– .

"Cumulative Index to Biographical Material in Books and Magazines."

Biological and Agricultural Index, 1964– .
> Continues *Agricultural Index,* 1919–1964. "Cumulative Subject Index to Periodicals in the Fields of Biology, Agriculture, and Related Sciences."

Book Review Digest, 1905– .
> Index to book reviews. Includes excerpts from the reviews.

Book Review Index, 1965– .

Business Periodicals Index, 1958– .
> Cumulative subject index to periodicals in all fields of business and industry.

Current Index to Journals in Education, 1969– .
> Covers "the core periodical literature in the field of education" and "peripheral literature relating to the field of education."

Education Index, 1929– .
> "Cumulative Subject Index to a Selected List of Educational Periodicals, Proceedings, and Yearbooks."

General Science Index, 1978– .
> Science literature for the nonspecialist.

Industrial Arts Index, 1913–1957.
> In 1958 divided into the *Applied Science and Technology Index* and *Business Periodicals Index.* "Subject Index to a Selected List of Engineering, Trade and Business Periodicals."

Music Index, 1949– .
> Index by author and subject to a comprehensive list of music periodicals published throughout the world.

New York Times Index, 1851– .
> "Master-Key to the News since 1851."

Public Affairs Information Service. Bulletin, 1915– .
> Subject index to periodicals and government publications chiefly in the social sciences.

Suppose you are writing on the drawings of James Thurber. Looking under *Thurber, James* in the *Humanities Index,* Volume 2, April 1975 to March 1976, you find the following entry:

THURBER, James
James Thurber: artist in humor. L.
Hasley. South Atlan Q 73:504–15 Aut '74

Subject heading
Title of article
Author of article
Abbreviation of the name of the
     periodical in which the article
     appears. Learn the complete
     name by checking inside the
     front cover of the periodical
     index.
Volume number
Pages
Date

With this information, you should be able to find the article. Check the serials catalog to see whether the periodical is in your library. Of course, you will be unable to read through all the articles written about a broad subject. But you will be able to exclude some merely by studying their titles in the periodical indexes.

Besides using the card catalog and the periodical indexes, you will need to know about several **general reference aids.** Many of these will give you bibliographical listings as well as surveys of your subject.

General reference aids

Articles on American Literature, 1900–1950; 1950–1967; 1968–1975.
Cambridge Bibliography of English Literature, 1941–1957. 5 vols.; *New Cambridge Bibliography of English Literature,* 1969–1977. 5 vols.
Cambridge Histories: Ancient, 12 vols., rev. ed. in progress; Medieval, 8 vols.; Modern, 13 vols.; *New Cambridge Modern History,* 14 vols.
Collier's Encyclopedia.
Columbia Lippincott Gazetteer of the World, 1962.
Contemporary Authors, 1962– .
Current Biography, 1940– . "Who's News and Why."
Dictionary of American Biography, 1928–1937. 20 vols. Supplements 1–7, 1944–1981.

Dictionary of American History, rev. ed., 1976–1978. 8 vols.

Dictionary of National Biography, 1885–1901. 22 vols. main work and 1st supplement; supplements 2–7, 1912–1971.

Encyclopedia Americana. Supplemented by the *Americana Annual,* 1923– .

Encyclopaedia Judaica, 1972. 16 vols.

Encyclopedia of Philosophy, 1967. 8 vols.

Encyclopaedia of Religion and Ethics, 1908–1927. 13 vols.

Encyclopedia of World Art, 1959–1968. 15 vols. Supplement, 1983.

Encyclopedia of World History, 5th ed., 1972.

Essay and General Literature Index, 1900– . "An Index to . . . Volumes of Collections of Essays and Miscellaneous Works."

Facts on File; a Weekly World News Digest . . . , 1940– .

Information Please Almanac, 1947– .

International Encyclopedia of the Social Sciences, 1968. 17 vols. *Biographical Supplement,* 1979.

Literary History of the United States, 1974. 2 vols.

MLA International Bibliography of Books and Articles on the Modern Languages and Literatures, 1919– .

McGraw-Hill Encyclopedia of Science and Technology, 5th ed., 1982. 15 vols. Supplemented by *McGraw-Hill Yearbook of Science and Technology.*

McGraw-Hill Encyclopedia of World Drama, 1972. 4 vols.

The Mythology of All Races, 1916–1932. 13 vols.

New Catholic Encyclopedia, 1967–1979. 17 vols.

New Century Cyclopedia of Names, 1954. 3 vols.

New Encyclopaedia Britannica. Supplemented by *Britannica Book of the Year,* 1938– .

New Grove Dictionary of Music and Musicians, 1980. 20 vols.

Oxford Classical Dictionary, 2d ed., 1970.

Oxford Companion to Film, 1976.

Oxford History of English Literature, 1945– .

Princeton Encyclopedia of Poetry and Poetics, 1974.

Statesman's Yearbook: Statistical and Historical Annual of the States of the World, 1864– .

Statistical Abstract of the United States, 1878– .

Webster's Biographical Dictionary, 1980.

World Almanac and Book of Facts, 1868– .

Check your card catalog for special reference works in the area of your subject.

Your working bibliography should grow as you proceed. Be sure to include all the information that will help you find each item listed: along with the author and title, you will need the library call number for books and the date, volume, and page numbers for articles.

48c Distinguish between primary and secondary materials.

Primary materials are such things as a painting, a poem, a short story, a motor, a stock exchange, an animal, a fossil, a virus, or a public opinion poll. In a paper on gasolines, for example, the gasolines tested are primary materials; the writings of engineers about them are secondary. Primary materials for a study of tourists abroad would consist of published and unpublished diaries, journals, and letters by tourists; interviews of tourists; and anything that is part of the tourist's life. Select a topic which allows use of primary materials so that you can reach independent conclusions and not rely entirely on the thinking of others.

Secondary materials are those written *about* your topic. In a study of tourists abroad, for example, the writings of journalists and historians about them are called secondary sources. The significance and accuracy of such materials should be evaluated (see pp. 221–222). It is important to consider when a work was written; what information was available to its author at that time; the general scholarly reputation of the author; the extent of the author's knowledge and reliability as indicated in the preface, footnotes, or bibliography; the logic the author has demonstrated in proving points; and even the medium of publication. A general article in a popular magazine, for example, is likely to be less reliable than a scholarly article in a learned journal.

48d Locate source materials, read, evaluate, and take notes.

Before you begin to take notes, it is a good idea to do some broad **preliminary reading** in an encyclopedia or in other general introductory works. Try to get a general view, a kind of map of the territory within which you will be working.

After you have compiled a working bibliography (**48b**), located some of the sources you wish to use, and done some preliminary reading, you are ready to begin collecting specific material for your paper. If you are writing a formally documented paper, make a **bibliography card** for each item as you examine it. This will be a full and exact record of bibliographical information, preferably on a 3 × 5 inch filing card. From these cards you will later compile your list of works cited. A sample card is shown on p. 322. The essential information includes the name of the author, the title of the work, the place and date of publication, and the name of the publisher. If the work has an editor or a translator, is in more than one volume, or is part of a series, these facts should be included. For later checking, record the library call number.

For **note-taking,** your next step, use cards or slips of paper uniform in size. Cards are easier to use than slips because they withstand more handling. Develop the knack of skimming so that you can move quickly over irrelevant material and concentrate on pertinent information. Use the table of contents, the section headings, and the index to find chapters or pages of particular use to you. As you read and take notes, consider what subtopics you will use. The two processes work together: your reading will give you ideas for subtopics, and the subtopics will give direction to your note-taking. At this point you are already in the process of organizing and outlining the paper. Suppose you wish to make a study of the drawings of James Thurber. You might work up the following list of tentative topics:

Thurber's background
His beginnings as an artist
His stature as an artist
The nature and effects of his drawings
His most famous drawing
His world view as seen in the drawings

Bibliography Card

(reduced facsimile—actual size 3 × 5 inches)

Author's name ⟶ Bernstein, Burton. Thurber: A Biography ← Title

Place of
publication and ⟶ New York : Dodd, 1975. ← Date of
name of publisher   publication

Call number ⟶ PS 3539
H94Z57

*You may find it
convenient to keep
these cards separate
from those on which
you take notes. They
will eventually be
used in making up
the list of works cited
in your paper.*

These headings may not be final. Always be ready to delete, add, and change headings as you read and take notes. At this stage, it may be neither possible nor necessary to determine the final order of headings.

To illustrate the methods of note-taking, suppose you have found the following paragraph about James Thurber.

> Beyond question the foremost humorist of the twentieth century, James Thurber was a divided man. With minor exceptions he did not explore the century's large social and political problems. War, religion, crime, poverty, civil rights—these were not his subjects. Instead he struck at the immemorial stupidities, cruelties, and perversities of men that lie at the root of our ills. A disillusioned idealist, he satirized mean behavior to sound the clearest note of his discontent. Yet he considered himself an optimist or near kin to one. He insisted that the perceptive reader would detect in his work "a basic and indestructible thread of hope."
>
> LOUIS HASLEY,
> "James Thurber: Artist in Humor"

You may make a note on this passage by paraphrasing, by quoting, or by combining short quotations with paraphrasing.

To **paraphrase** is to express the sense of a passage entirely in your own words, selecting and summarizing only information and ideas that will be useful. The card on p. 324 identifies the source, gives a subject heading, indicates the page number, and then records relevant information in the student's own words. It *extracts* items of information instead of merely recasting the entire passage and line of thought in different words. Notice the careful selection of details and the fact that the paraphrase is considerably shorter than the original.

If at the time of taking notes you cannot yet determine just what information you wish to extract, you may copy an entire passage. For later reference you must then be careful to show by quotation marks that it is copied verbatim.

A photoduplicating machine can guarantee accuracy and save you time. At an early stage in research it is not always possi-

Paraphrased Notes

(reduced facsimile—actual size 3 × 5 inches)

Subject heading ───────

Identification of source.
Full bibliographical
information has been
taken down on the
bibliography card.

Page number ───────

→ James Thurber's Optimism

→ Hasley, "James Thurber: Artist in Humor"

→ 504 Though he dealt with the basic ills
of mankind, Thurber thought of himself
not as a pessimist but as an optimist.

ble to know exactly what information is needed. Photocopy some of the longest passages, and then you can study them and digest them during the writing of the first draft of the paper.

When writing your paper, you may either quote directly, as in the note at the top of p. 326, or paraphrase (see **28c**). Quoting and paraphrasing may be combined on a single note card, as in the card at the bottom of p. 326. It is most important to use quotation marks accurately when taking notes, to use your own words when not quoting, and to transfer quotations and quotation marks from card to paper with scrupulous care.

Any single card should contain notes from only one source, and all the notes on any single card should be about one single topic, such as James Thurber's subjects on the cards above. This will give you maximum flexibility in organizing materials as the plan of the paper takes shape. Arrange the cards by topic before you write the paper.

The accuracy of your paper depends to a great extent on the accuracy of your notes. Indicate on each card the source, the page numbers, and an appropriate subject heading.

Note-taking is not a mere mechanical process; it involves interpretation and evaluation. Two persons writing on the same subject and using the same sources would not be likely to take quite the same notes, and their papers would differ accordingly in content and organization.

Study the following passage, which deals with the similarity of Thurber's cartoons to dreams.

> Most of the drawings in *The Seal in the Bedroom* have a touch of that strange, dream-like quality which was always to be one of the hallmarks of Thurber's imagination. Neurosis, hallucination, the whole area of the irrational were subjects which held a particular fascination for him throughout his career. Many of his drawings haunt the imagination because they confront us directly with images which seem to have popped up from the unconscious or to have been recalled from dreams. His most famous cartoon, ''All right, have it your way—you heard a seal bark,'' shows a man and a woman in bed, and looming up behind the headboard, a pleasant-looking seal.

Quotation

James Thurber's subjects

Hasley
504 "With minor exceptions he did not explore
the century's large social and political problems.
War, religion, crime, poverty, civil rights —
these were not his subjects. Instead he
struck at the immemorial stupidities,
cruelties, and perversities of men that lie
at the root of our ills."

Quotation and Paraphrase

James Thurber's subjects

Hasley
504 "With minor exceptions he did not
explore the century's large social and political
problems." Instead of addressing himself
to such things as war or crime, he chose
to point out the basic weaknesses of human
nature.

> The woman is querulous and impatient at her husband's nonsense, and the man is silently exasperated because she won't believe him. The scene has that mixture of the familiar and the strange which is the essence of dreams, and like dream-images, it resists logical explanation.
>
> CHARLES S. HOLMES,
> *The Clocks of Columbus:*
> *The Literary Career of James Thurber*

From a passage as full of information as this one, it is possible to take several kinds of notes under different subject headings. Most of this material might eventually be used in a paper, but to a certain extent the material is adapted to the purposes of the paper by the way it is selected and classified under the student's subject headings. By the very process of reading and note-taking, the student is thinking about the subject and organizing thoughts. This is the supreme importance of taking notes, of quoting and paraphrasing. Now study the notes on pp. 328–329, all from the preceding paragraph by Holmes. Observe the variety in subject headings and treatment.

48e Construct an outline.

No step in the writing of a research paper is more helpful than the working out of a good outline. The purpose of an outline is not to hold you rigidly to a preconceived form but to enable you to think through your topic and organize it logically and interestingly *before you begin to write.* Writing too soon is the most common of all flaws in composing a research paper. The outline may therefore be the most important single step in the process. After you have worked out a tentative outline, study it carefully to be sure that you have included all the major points you wish to make and that you have arranged them so that your discussion will flow rationally from one to the other. If you have taken the time and effort to complete a full and effective outline, you will

Quotation

Thurber's drawings and dreams

Holmes, <u>Clocks</u>

134   "Most of the drawings in <u>The Seal in the
Bedroom</u> have a touch of that strange, dream-
like quality which was always to be one of
the hallmarks of Thurber's imagination."

Quotation

Thurber's interest in the irrational

Holmes, <u>Clocks</u>

134   "Neurosis, hallucination, the whole area
of the irrational were subjects which held
a particular fascination for him throughout
his career. Many of his drawings haunt
the imagination because they confront us
directly with images which seem to have
popped up from the unconscious...."

Paraphrase

> Thurber's Cartoon of the Seal
>
> Holmes, _Clocks_
> 135 Thurber's cartoon of the seal in the
>   bedroom is difficult to analyze because
>   it blends the real world with a world
>   of fantasy and is therefore much like
>   a dream.

Quotation and Paraphrase

> Thurber's Cartoon of the Seal
>
> Holmes, _Clocks_
> 135 "His most famous cartoon," of
>   the seal in the bedroom, "has that
>   mixture of the familiar and the strange"
>   that makes it too much like a dream
>   to be easily analyzed.

find that the writing of the paper itself will go much quicker and smoother and that the result will be a unified discussion. See the model outline on pp. 264–265.

48f Acknowledge your sources. Avoid plagiarism.

Acknowledge your indebtedness to others by giving full details of sources. Using others' words and ideas as if they were your own is a form of stealing called **plagiarism.**

Some of the principles of quoting and paraphrasing have already been discussed under the topic of taking notes (**48d**). They must be kept in mind during the writing and revision of your paper. Finally, quotations and paraphrases should be carefully checked for accuracy after the paper is written.

All direct quotations must be placed in quotation marks and acknowledged in your text.

Even when you take only a phrase or a single unusual word from a passage, you should enclose it in quotation marks. You may quote words, phrases, clauses, sentences, or even whole paragraphs. Generally you should quote a sentence or a paragraph only when a writer has phrased something especially well and when you need to supply all the information given. Do not quote excessively. A sequence of quotations strung together with a few words of your own is not satisfactory. Excessive quoting indicates that you have not properly digested your sources, thought about the ideas, and learned to express them in your own words and to relate them to your own ideas.

All paraphrases and citations must be acknowledged.

Credit a source when you cite ideas or information from it even when you do not quote directly. Altering the wording does not make the substance yours. An acknowledgement not only gives proper credit but also lends authority to your statement. Whenever you consult a source or a note card as you write, you are probably paraphrasing, and you probably need an acknowledgement.

In paraphrasing you are expressing the ideas of another writer in your own words. A good paraphrase preserves the sense of the original, but not the form. It does not retain the sentence patterns and merely substitute synonyms for the original words, nor does it retain the original words and merely alter the sentence patterns. It is a genuine restatement. Invariably it should be briefer than the source. In the example below, notice the difference between a satisfactory and an unsatisfactory paraphrase:

ORIGINAL

Hemingway's debt to journalism was a large one, and he always acknowledged it. Unlike many ex-newspapermen, however, he neither sentimentalized the profession nor misunderstood its essential threat to creative writing.

CHARLES A. FENTON,
The Apprenticeship of Ernest Hemingway

BADLY PARAPHRASED

Hemingway's indebtedness to journalism was very great, and he himself said so. Unlike so many writers who have been newspapermen, however, he did not sentimentalize journalism or misunderstand that it is a danger to creative talent.

BETTER

Hemingway admitted that he learned from newspaper work, but he also recognized that journalism can hurt writers as well as help them.

If the source has stated the idea more concisely than you can, you should quote, not paraphrase.

Do not make use of extended paraphrases. If a good many of your paragraphs are simply long paraphrases, your reader will assume that even your organization is taken from someone else, concluding that you have not assimilated your materials and thought independently about them—in short, that you have not done an acceptable piece of original work.

48g Follow an accepted system of documentation.

The forms of documentation vary with fields, periodicals, publishers, and indeed even instructors. The following style books and manuals are most frequently used in general studies.

MLA Handbook for Writers of Research Papers. 2d ed. By Joseph Gibaldi and Walter S. Achtert. New York: Modern Language Assn. of America, 1984.

Publication Manual of the American Psychological Association. 3d ed. Washington: American Psychological Assn., 1983.

Chicago Manual of Style. 13th ed. Chicago: U of Chicago P, 1982.

Words into Type. By Marjorie E. Skillin, Robert M. Gay et al. 3d ed. Englewood Cliffs: Prentice, 1974.

A Manual for Writers of Term Papers, Theses and Dissertations. By Kate L. Turabian. 4th ed. Chicago: U of Chicago P, 1973.

The system of documentation followed in this book is that of the *MLA Handbook,* 2d ed., which is the most widely used, especially in the humanities. Follow this method with exactness and precision, and you can then easily learn any other system.

48h Follow standard forms for listing sources at the end of your paper.

At the end of the paper, after the text itself and after the notes (or endnotes), comes the section called "Works Cited." Here you list alphabetically all the sources that you have referred to in the text. The list below includes models for many of the most common kinds of entries. The citations for the Smith book and the Watson article illustrate the most frequently used forms. (At the end of the model paper on Thurber's drawing you will also find other entries.)

ARTICLE IN WEEKLY OR MONTHLY MAGAZINE

Brien, Alan. "Take Me to Your Union Leader." *Punch* 3 May 1972: 610, 612.

NEWSPAPER ARTICLE

"Churchill's Account of His Early Wars Is Ridiculed in a Contemporary's Notes." *New York Times* 23 July 1972, sec. 1:12.

BOOK BY MORE THAN ONE AUTHOR

Cuskey, Walter R., Arnold William Klein, and William Krasner. *Drug-Trip Abroad: American Drug-Refugees in Amsterdam and London.* Philadelphia: U of Pennsylvania P, 1972.

INTRODUCTION TO A BOOK

Dobrée, Bonamy. Introduction. *The Mysteries of Udolpho.* By Ann Radcliffe. London: Oxford UP, 1966.

ESSAY IN A VOLUME OF ESSAYS

Emmet, Dorothy. "Coleridge and Philosophy." *S. T. Coleridge.* Ed. R. L. Brett. London: G. Bell, 1971, 195–220.

UNSIGNED BULLETIN OR PAMPHLET

Enforcement of the Selective Service Law. Special Monograph 14. Selective Service System. Washington: GPO, 1951.

BOOK BY MORE THAN THREE AUTHORS OR EDITORS

Hornstein, Harvey A. et al., eds. *Social Intervention: A Behavioral Science Approach.* New York: Free P, 1971.

BOOK THAT IS PART OF A SERIES

Hubler, Edward. *The Sense of Shakespeare's Sonnets.* Princeton Studies in English 33. Princeton: Princeton UP, 1952.

AN UNPUBLISHED DISSERTATION

Kenney, Catherine McGehee. "The World of James Thurber: An Anatomy of Confusion." Diss. Loyola of Chicago, 1974.

ARTICLE IN *DISSERTATION ABSTRACTS INTERNATIONAL*

Kenney, Catherine McGehee. "The World of James Thurber: An Anatomy of Confusion." *DAI* 35 (1974): 2276A. Loyola of Chicago.

SECOND OR LATER EDITION OF A BOOK

King-Hele, Desmond. *Shelley: His Thought and Work.* 2d ed. Teaneck: Fairleigh Dickinson UP, 1971.

UNSIGNED ARTICLE IN AN ENCYCLOPEDIA

"Midway Islands." *Encyclopedia Americana.* 1964 ed.

BOOK WITH A TRANSLATOR

Remarque, Erich Maria. *Shadows in Paradise.* Trans. Ralph Manheim. New York: Harcourt, 1972.

VOLUME IN A WORK OF MORE THAN ONE VOLUME WITH DIFFERENT PUBLICATION DATES

Schueller, Herbert M., and Robert L. Peters, eds. *The Letters of John Addington Symonds.* 3 vols. Detroit: Wayne State UP, 1967–69. Vol. 2.

VOLUME IN A WORK OF MORE THAN ONE VOLUME WITH SAME PUBLICATION DATE

Simcox, George A. *A History of Latin Literature from Ennius to Boethius.* 2 vols. New York: Harper, 1883. Vol. 1.

MODERN REPRINTING OF AN OLDER EDITION

Slosson, Edwin E. *Major Prophets of To-Day.* 1914. Freeport: Books for Libraries P, 1968.

STANDARD REFERENCE TO A BOOK

Smith, Henry Nash. *Mark Twain: The Development of a Writer.* Cambridge: Harvard UP, 1962.

SIGNED ARTICLE IN AN ENCYCLOPEDIA

Tobias, Richard C. "Thurber, James." *Encyclopedia Americana.* 1980 ed.

STANDARD REFERENCE TO AN ARTICLE

Watson, George. "Quest for a Frenchman." *Sewanee Review* 84 (1976): 465–75.

SIGNED BULLETIN OR PAMPHLET

Whieldon, Charles E., Jr., and William F. Eckard. *West Virginia Oilfields Discovered before 1940.* Bulletin 607. Bureau of Mines. U.S. Dept. of the Interior. Washington: GPO, 1963.

48i Document sources in parenthetical references in your text.

The list of works cited indicates clearly what sources you used, but precisely what you derived from each entry must also be revealed at particular places in the paper. Document each idea, paraphrase, or quotation by indicating the author (or the title if the work is anonymous) and the page reference at the appropriate place in your text.

The extent of dissension that year in Parliament has been pointed out before (Levenson 127). *[Writer cites author and gives author's name and page number in parentheses.]*

Accordingly, no "parliamentary session was without severe dissension" (Levenson 127). *[Writer quotes author and gives author's name and page number in parentheses.]*

Levenson points out that "no parliamentary session was without severe dissension" (127). *[Writer names author, places quotation marks at beginning of quotation and before parenthesis, and gives only page number in parentheses.]*

These references indicate that the quotation is to be found in the work by Levenson listed in Works Cited at the end of the text of the paper.

If two authors in your sources have the same last name, give first names in your references.

It has been suggested that the general's brother did not arrive until the following year (Frederick Johnson 235).
The authenticity of the document, however, has been questioned (Edwin Johnson 15).

If two or more works by the same author are listed in Works Cited, indicate which one you are referring to by giving a short title: (Levenson, *Battles* 131). The full title listed in Works Cited is *Battles in British Parliament, 1720–1721.*

If a work cited consists of more than one volume, give the volume number as well as the page: (Hoagland 2:173–74).

Some sources—the Bible and well-known plays, for example —are cited in the text of the paper but not listed as sources in Works Cited. Use the following forms:

. . . the soliloquy (*Hamlet* 2.2). [The numbers designate act and scene. Some instructors prefer Roman numerals: *Hamlet* II.ii.]

. . . the passage (1 Kings 4.3). [That is, chapter 4, verse 3.]

For further illustrations of parenthetical references to works cited, see the model research paper.

48j Follow accepted practices in using notes for comments, explanations, and references to supplementary sources.

You will probably need few numbered notes (called "footnotes" when at the bottom of the page, "notes" at the end of the paper) because sources are referred to in the text itself and listed after the body of the paper. Notes are used to explain further or to comment on something you have written. To include incidental information in the text itself would be to interrupt the flow of the argument or to assign undue importance to matters that add to the substance only tangentially. Make your decision as to where to place such information—in the text or in a note—on the basis of its impact and direct relevance.

Notes are also useful in referring to sources other than those mentioned in the text or in commenting on sources. If you wish to list several books or articles in connection with a point you are making, it may prove awkward to include all of this information in parentheses. Therefore, a note is preferable.

The sign of a note is an Arabic numeral raised slightly above the line at the appropriate place in the text. The *MLA Handbook* recommends that notes be grouped at the end of the paper. Notes should be numbered consecutively throughout.

Examples

[1]See also Drummond, Stein, Van Patten, Southworth, and Langhorne.

[Lists further sources. Full bibliographic information given in Works Cited at end of paper.]

[2]After spending seventeen years in Europe, he returned to America with a new attitude toward slavery, which he had defended earlier.

[Remark parenthetical to main argument but important enough to include in a note.]

[3]This biography, once considered standard, is no longer reliable because of recent discoveries.

[Evaluates a source.]

Model research paper.

A model research paper, with an outline and accompanying explanations, is given on the following pages.

GENERAL APPEARANCE AND MECHANICS

Allow ample and even margins.

Indent five spaces for paragraphs.

Leave two spaces after periods and other terminal punctuation.

Leave one space after other marks of punctuation.

Double-space between lines in the text, the notes, and entries in the section Works Cited.

Set off a quotation of five or more typed lines. Begin a new line, indent ten spaces from the margin, do not add quotation marks, and double-space unless your instructor specifies single spacing. If you quote only one paragraph, do not indent the first line.

Compose a title page for your research paper if your instructor requires it (MLA does not require it.) Balance the material on the page. Center the title and place it about one-third of the way down from the top of the page. Include your name and the name and section number of the course as indicated on the opposite page, or follow the specific preferences of your instructor.

Hope Through Fantasy in James Thurber's Drawings

By

Debra Warwick

English 101

Section 1

If your instructor requests that you submit an outline with your paper, it should occupy a separate, unnumbered page following the title page and should follow the form for the outline illustrated on pp. 264–265.

If your instructor requests that you include a thesis statement as part of your outline, place it between the title and the first line of the outline. A thesis statement for this outline might be: "Although the comic drawings of James Thurber seem simple, they actually embody a complex world view with strong suggestions of pessimism but with an even stronger sense of hope."

Hope Through Fantasy in James Thurber's Drawings

I.   Introduction--Thurber's career as a cartoonist

   A.   His one-man exhibition at the Valentine Gallery

   B.   Before the Valentine exhibit--beginnings

      1.   Collaboration with E. B. White

      2.   Praise by British artist Paul Nash

      3.   First collection of drawings: The Seal in the Bedroom

   C.   After the Valentine exhibit--later years

II.   The Nature of Thurber's drawings

   A.   Subject matter

   B.   Technique

   C.   Captions

III.   The effects of Thurber's drawings

   A.   Before careful analysis

   B.   After careful analysis

IV.   An examination of "The Seal in the Bedroom"

   A.   The woman

   B.   The man

   C.   The seal

V.   Thurber's world view

   A.   Reputation for bitterness

   B.   His complexity and affirmation

The writer has submitted a photocopy of the main cartoon which she writes about in order to provide a concrete example for the reader as well as to help establish a tone for the paper.

**"All Right, Have It Your Way—
You Heard a Seal Bark!"**

Center the title on the page. Allow four spaces between the title and the first line of the text.

The two parenthetical references to "Morose Scrawler" cite an unsigned article. No page number is given because the article is only one page long.

The source for the statement beginning "Nevertheless, this . . ." is given below. Notice how the quotation has been paraphrased in the paper.

> Gallery-goers, stepping sideways like crabs, passed from frame to frame in which were exposed the backs of old letterheads and odd sheets of scratch paper on which were scrawled the amiable bloodhounds, the horrid boneless women, the bald, browbeaten little men of Artist Thurber, associate editor and one of the two most successful members of the staff of *The New Yorker*.
>
> "MOROSE SCRAWLER," *Time*

Place note numbers slightly above the line of type and after marks of punctuation. Do not leave a space before the number; do not place a period after the number. Number notes consecutively throughout the paper.

After capturing the reader's interest by recounting the story of Thurber's one-man art exhibition, the writer uses the final lines of the first paragraph to state the central idea of the paper.

The next paragraph then takes up the subject of Thurber's background as an artist.

The page number for the first page may be omitted (in MLA style) or centered at the bottom.

Hope Through Fantasy in James Thurber's Drawings

In December of 1934 the highly respected Valentine Gallery in Manhattan held one of the most unusual exhibitions in all of its history. Less traditional than many of the art galleries in New York City, the Valentine "devoted itself to the more advanced of the socially acceptable left-wing artists" ("Morose Scrawler"). Nevertheless, this was a particularly odd one-man show: as viewers shuffled from one frame to another, they witnessed childlike reproductions of gentle dogs, aggressive women, and emasculated men all casually drawn as doodles on various sorts and sizes of sheets, even scratch paper ("Morose Scrawler"). Much puzzlement and disbelief ran through these lovers of art; but the exhibition was widely reviewed, and the artist, James Thurber, was in the end compared with such giants as Picasso and Matisse.[1] Since then, Thurber's position as a serious artist as well as a serious writer has been solidly established, although his cartoons, known best from the pages of The New Yorker, are deceptively simple. His fame

Place the page number in the upper right-hand corner, two lines above the first line of text. Use Arabic numerals; do not put a period after the number. (According to MLA style, you may add your first initial and last name before the page number on each page.)

The statement beginning with "Blending" illustrates the technique of combining in a sentence one's own words with quoted words.

The parenthetical reference to Holmes contains the word *Introduction* to distinguish between this work and Holmes's other work also cited in the paper.

has been accompanied by a reputation for bitterness, which is in some measure justified; but if
pessimism is reflected in Thurber's drawings, a
sense of hope is even stronger.

Thurber never took his role as an artist as
seriously as other people did. He was completely
self-taught. In fact, his brother William was sup-
posedly the Thurber with talent for drawing.
James's early doodles were not drastically different from the ones that brought him acclaim, but
his family dismissed them, and he was advised not
to waste his time. An urge so deep that he did not
himself understand it kept him at these spare, un-
detailed, outline figures. He produced them so
quickly and effortlessly that his respect for them
was slight compared to his feelings for his writing,
which came slowly and painfully. Yet others saw
depth in the drawings that seemed spontaneously
dredged up from the unconscious mind of a genius.
"Blending the worlds of reality and dream," as one
critic has put it, the drawings, not the writings,
"are the purest expression of his imagination"
(Holmes, Introduction 7).

3

The person most responsible for getting Thurber's drawings into magazines and books was E. B. White. While sharing an office with him at The New Yorker, White noticed that Thurber produced dozens of drawings, which were promptly crumpled up and tossed into the trash. One of these turned out to be a seal resting on a large rock and looking dreamily off into the distant sea where there were two approaching specks. The caption read, "Hm, explorers." White was so amused and so convinced of a profound comic talent in Thurber that he tried to get the editor of The New Yorker to publish the cartoon.[2] This failed, but when they collaborated in 1929 on a satirical book, White insisted to the publishers that Thurber do the illustrations. Both for the writing and the drawings, Is Sex Necessary? was a hit, and Thurber was on his way. Seeing how well the book was selling, the editor of The New Yorker then asked Thurber if he could publish the seal drawing. Thurber had thrown it away, however, and when he tried to reproduce it, it came out differently and was destined to be the most famous of all his cartoons, the seal in the bedroom.[3]

In the quotation, brackets have been used to indicate that the word *Nash* is not in the original text (see **26**). Brackets are also used to enclose the scholarly term *sic* when a word in a quotation has been misspelled. This assures your reader that the misspelling is not yours and that you are quoting accurately.

The reference to Eates illustrates the most frequently used form of parenthetical documentation: author's last name, no punctuation, page number.

4

The illustrations for Is Sex Necessary? and the cartoons that steadily appeared in The New Yorker magazine thereafter brought Thurber much attention as a funny and peculiar scrawler, but he was surprised to realize in 1931 that he was being taken seriously by artists and critics of high reputation. When the respected British artist Paul Nash came to America, he sought out Thurber. "In the paintings of his American contemporaries he [Nash] found little to attract him, and he shocked them by his insistence on the importance of James Thurber's comic drawings" (Eates 48). Nash was only one of many serious artists and art critics to see in the witty Thurber a profundity and a complexity only half recognized by the man himself. In 1932 Thurber's first and perhaps most impressive collection of drawings was published as The Seal in the Bedroom and Other Predicaments. With the success of that volume and the one-man exhibition at the Valentine Gallery the next year, it was difficult even for Thurber not to recognize that he had achieved stature as an original artist. His reputation continued to grow until the 1950's, when

The writer now moves from Thurber's career as an artist to the nature of his drawings.

When an ellipsis is used to indicate omitted words at the end of a sentence, the three spaced periods are preceded by a fourth with no space before it.

Be extremely careful with all quotations. For example, the word *Sex* with a capital "S" may look strange, but that is the way the author wrote it, the way it should be represented.

In quotations that are run in with the text (that is, not set off), use single quotation marks to designate a quotation within the quotation. Notice the word *psych.*

he was forced to give up drawing because of blindness.[4]

    Thurber's drawings present a world of men, women, and animals. The women tend to be large and angry. The men find themselves often intimidated by the female's size and manner. They appear constantly at odds with each other. The animals--frequently dogs but sometimes seals or penguins--are universally pleasant. In 1943, <u>Newsweek</u> called Thurber "America's most incredible artist," and described his typical woman figure as "a fiercely aggressive female with the figure of a potato sack, a face which is a cross between a weasel's and a swordfish's, and, the final indignity, perfectly straight and stringy hair. . . . She frowns grimly, smiles idiotically, and leers loomily. She stalks the male, rules him, bewilders him, and even, once, murders him" ("That Thurber Woman"). The man of the drawings, writes another critic, is "bothered most of all by Sex, with its marital concomitant, but also by all disciplines whose names begin with 'psych'; by mechanical devices; by the upper-middle-class ceremonials of suburbia; by the

Prose quotations of five lines or more should be set off ten spaces as indicated here. Leave the right margin unchanged. Double-space unless instructed otherwise. Do not indent the first paragraph; indent for paragraphs thereafter. Do not use quotation marks around quotations which are set off. When there are single quotation marks within double quotation marks in the original, use double quotation marks (as here) to replace the single ones.

6

bureaucratic organization of modern society, and by the deterioration of communications between man and man and between man and woman" (Yates 278). What the writer of one of Thurber's obituaries said about his dogs can also be said about most of the other animals: "His drawings of dogs, which he produced with abundance on the backs of envelopes, in telephone books and on tablecloths, had a quality that seemed to link them with no other beast on earth."[5]

If the general subject of Thurber's drawings is the war between men and women, with an animal of some sort frequently the innocent bystander, his technique is having no technique--that is, none that sophisticated training teaches. In answer to Alistair Cooke's question as to whether his cartoons had encouraged parents to submit their children's drawings, Thurber answered:

> It actually did--not only parents but very strange people. Some people thought my drawings were done under water; others that they were done by moonlight. But mothers thought that I was a little child

The period after a quotation which is set off comes *before* the parenthetical reference. In contrast, after a quotation which is not set off the period comes *after* the parentheses.

You may or may not begin a new paragraph after a quotation which is set off. Here the same paragraph continues, and *With* is not indented.

The two words quoted, "been through," do not need to be documented because the reader can clearly see that they are taken from the long quotation above for which the source has already been given.

7

> or that my drawings were done by my
> granddaughter. So they sent in their own
> children's drawings to the New Yorker,
> and I was told to write these ladies, and
> I would write them all the same letter:
> "Your son can certainly draw as well as I
> can. The only trouble is that he hasn't
> been through as much." ("James Thurber in
> Conversation" 39)[6]

With his usual tone of humility where his drawings
were concerned, he was indulging in satire of
others and himself, but he revealed nevertheless in
his comment about how much he had "been through"
and understanding of the relationship between his
deepest inner self and his drawings. "No one
understands," commented Dorothy Parker, "how he
makes his boneless, loppy beings, with their shy
kinship to the men and women of Picasso's later
drawings," and likewise, no one knows "from what
dark breeding-ground come the artist's ideas" (ix).
Like so many others, Dorothy Parker was intrigued,
if not spellbound, by the drawing of the seal in
the bedroom: "How is one to shadow the mental

Notice the handling of single and double quotation marks at the end of the paragraph. Ordinarily the question mark would not separate the single and double quotation marks, but it does so here because the entire sentence is a question.

The parentheses used in the quotation of the second paragraph indicate that the words *the one-line cartoon* were in parentheses in the source as well. If these words were not in the source but were added by the writer of this paper, they would be in brackets, not parentheses.

8

process of a man who is impelled to depict a seal
looking over the headboard of a bed occupied by a
broken-spirited husband and virago of a wife, and
then to write below the scene the one line: 'All
right, have it your way--you heard a seal bark'?"
(ix).

Thurber and his fellow artists who were drawing for The New Yorker created a "new kind of cartoon (the one-line cartoon), in which the words and
drawing were inextricable and neither was witty
without the other" (Becker 128). Many who have
admired Thurber's art and compared it to such
painters as Matisse have not realized the extent to
which the drawing depends upon the caption for its
effect. Dorothy Parker recalled that a friend of
hers had overheard one woman say to another on a
London bus: "Mad, I don't say. Queer, I grant you.
Many's the time I've seen her nude at the piano."
This was, she felt, precisely the kind of caption
Thurber would write under a drawing of two women
chatting, for Thurber, she argued, "deals solely in
culminations. Beneath his pictures he sets only
the final line. . . . It is yours to ponder how

After dealing with the nature of Thurber's drawings—their subject matter, their techniques, and their captions—the writer now moves to the next block of the discussion, the effects that the drawings produce on the viewers.

9

penguins get into drawing-rooms and seals into bed-
chambers. . . . He gives you a glimpse of the
startling present and lets you construct the
astounding past" (vii-viii).

The effect of a Thurber drawing is both immediate and long lasting. As his general popularity
suggests, his cartoons create laughter spontaneously in the viewer, who in most cases is not
interested in questioning why. If the question is
raised and if viewers contemplate the drawings over
a period of time, they discover that the cartoons
lose none of their humor with time but that other
emotions are evoked. After the initial amusement
comes the awareness of the characters' state of
mind or situation, which is usually that of confusion or unhappiness or both. "Thurber is almost
alone in using, as a comedian, material which in
other hands is tragic" (Black 16). On the heels of
this unpleasant recognition of predicament, however, follows that sense of wonder and mystery that
attracted Dorothy Parker. In his ability to evoke
this world of dreams, he has been called a "fantast"
and compared favorably with such artists as Goya,

Quoting an important critic of art here (E. M. Benson) is especially effective, for it indicates that Thurber is not merely a cartoonist drawing for the funny papers, that he is taken seriously as an artist for his ability to project the depths of his imagination.

The writer is now ready to illustrate much of what she has previously said with a close analysis of the drawing.

10

William Blake, and Pieter Bruegel the Elder.
Speaking of these as well as Thurber, one art
critic writes:

> Perhaps it is the fantast who, after all,
> gets closer to the truth than anyone
> else, for instead of giving us an
> idealized transmutation of reality or a
> photographically accurate record, he
> gives us only its most salient and
> telling features after they have been
> distilled in the alembic of his fantasy.
> (Benson 299)

The fantasy, of which innocence is frequently a
component, works to offset the pessimism of the
overt subject matter, and one is brought full
circle back to humor. Before and after contemplation and analysis, a Thurber drawing is comic--
in the best and deepest sense of the word.[7]

A detailed examination of one cartoon, the one
picturing a seal in the bedroom, will illustrate
more specifically the complexity of Thurber's art.
The only active figure in the scene is a woman in

Dorothy Parker has already been cited three times but it is clear that the writer is not relying too heavily on one source, for she has selected a subject for which there are abundant resources, and she is using a great variety of them. Do not pick a subject on which you cannot find adequate secondary research materials.

The drawing of the seal in the bedroom is primary material; the writings about Thurber and his art are secondary materials. The discussion of the specific cartoon is much enhanced by the fact that the writer included as an illustration a photocopy of the drawing.

11

bed with her husband. As is often the case in a
Thurber cartoon, she is large, almost formless.
Dorothy Parker wrote that Thurber's characters
"have the outer semblance of unbaked cookies" and
that "the women are of a dowdiness so overwhelming
that it becomes tremendous style" (viii). Thurber
himself claimed that he could not draw a beautiful
woman ("That Thurber Woman"). Her hair is represented by a few almost straight lines that add to
the overall impression of a person who has ceased
to be concerned about her appearance, one who could
not care less whether she is appealing to the opposite sex. The action of the drawing comes from her
mouth, opened angrily and snarling out the words of
the caption, "All right, have it your way--you
heard a seal bark!" Her hands, like those of most
Thurber figures, "do not look much like hands," as
one of his collaborators observed (Nugent). They
are more like the feet of a goat in this drawing.
Her impatience, her lack of tenderness and warmth
pervade the scene. She is what every man dreads,
a dominating, overbearing, loud-mouthed, insensi-
tive female.

It is evident that the writer has studied many of Thurber's drawings, not merely the one being analyzed, for she makes comparisons and contrasts. A good paper may center upon a single work or a single aspect of a subject, but the writer is wise to become familiar with other works of the same author or artist or other aspects of the general subject. Otherwise, the analysis will tend to be without that richness of reference that comes when the writer has become steeped in the subject.

12

The man is larger than many of Thurber's men, who tend to be smaller than the women. As usual, he is without hair, and that feature seems to increase the implied distance between the man and the woman. Thurber's figures are so much alike that the slightest difference in detail points up vast differences in the characters. They may be in the same bed, but they are worlds apart. One imagines that they have had such exchanges before, the man escaping her shrewish domination for a world of fancy. He does not understand this other world--nothing is so evident on his face as a sense of bewilderment--but at least he can experience it. The woman in the drawing does not represent women in general but a literal and unimaginative world, the real world.

The seal is the center of the drawing. It looms over the headboard of the bed, but it is not looking down at the man and woman. It stares out dreamily into space, with an expression of innocence. It is difficult to imagine how anyone could view it without smiling the kind of smile that comes from seeing a baby, the result of a feeling

Underlining for emphasis should be used sparingly, but since the writer has not used it previously and since both an original and crucial point is being made, it is effective here to underline the words.

This paragraph has no parenthetical reference because the writer found none of these ideas in a source. She is making an original contribution. If the ideas had been derived from secondary sources, however, documentation would have been necessary to avoid the serious act of plagiarism.

13

of comic tenderness. Something more is in that seal, however. It should not be there in the bedroom; it is out of place. A sense of mystery surrounds it. It is like a benign ghost that one person sees but another cannot. Perhaps it is something in the man that causes the seal to be there for him.

Probably the most striking discovery that one makes after viewing the cartoon for a while is that the seal looks very much like the man. In fact, the man's hands look more like flippers than hands. From that point one notices that neither the man nor the seal has any hair and that the shape of their heads is the same. The arc of their eyebrows is practically identical, making their eyes appear the same. They both look off in the distance as if expecting to hear something. Their mouths are both closed whereas the woman's is open. In fact, if the man's nose were made larger and given whiskers, he would be the seal.

The seal, then, is a projection of something in the man himself, that sense of wonder, that remarkable imagination that enables him to dwell for

With the paragraph beginning "Because," the writer moves into the concluding section of the paper where the charge of pessimism is rejected and the note of hope stressed.

The writer wished to use this anecdote about Churchill, which she first found in the Bernstein biography of Thurber, then in Holmes's book, and also in Morsberger's book. It can, therefore, be safely assumed that this is common knowledge, and thus there is no need for a reference.

14

a while in the realm of fantasy, a world of innocence and tenderness that is in stark opposition to
the actual world. This drawing, as a critic has
said of Thurber's works as a whole, "affirms the
power of imagination" (Tobias 172).

Because Thurber so often depicted the need to
escape the real world and perhaps because he was
known as an eccentric given to moments of sourness,
he acquired a reputation among some critics as a
pessimist. Time magazine referred to him as a
"morose scrawler," and commented that his drawings
are "enormously funny" but "are the products of an
unhappy mind" ("Morose Scrawler"). An acquaintance
once told Thurber that when Winston Churchill heard
Thurber's name called, he thought briefly and then
said, "Oh, that depraved and insane American
artist." Sometimes a pessimistic or abnormal out-
look is attributed to Thurber for other reasons.
For example, W. H. Auden severely criticized
Thurber because his drawings are so bare, because
they leave out details, "even sexual differences
almost disappear." To Auden, Thurber is a sample
of the "inward-looking artist" who draws as he does

The passage from W. H. Auden is given below to indicate how the writer condensed, paraphrased, and quoted a source. Also, comparing Auden's argument and the opinion of the writer of the paper shows how the writer took issue with Auden. Such disagreements should always be expressed tactfully. Sources can be used for purposes of disagreement as well as for agreement and support. The existence of a statement in print is no reason to accept it as true.

> Is it not, then, a little disconcerting to find how little of life has today any iconographic significance, that is, seems both universal and capable of inspiring reference and love? Not only landscape but the human figure itself has to be reduced to the barest outline—even sexual differences almost disappear. All detail, all portraiture belong to the world of the enemy, those unpleasant and powerful forces which Lear called "They" and Thurber calls the Liberators, the world whose art is the realistic bosh of society portraits and statues representing the workers of tomorrow. The realm of modern freedom is indeed limited. . . . Just as we have still to discover the proper relations of the private and public life, so the inward-looking artist has to unlearn his puritanical distrust of matter. . . . Logos and Eros have yet to be reconciled in a new Agape.
>
> W. H. AUDEN,
> "The Icon and the Portrait"

The three sentences before the reference to Hasley constitute a paraphrase with no actual quoting. The source is given below for comparison. Notice that the ideas have been followed but not the words.

> Beyond question the foremost humorist of the twentieth century, James Thurber was a divided man. With minor exceptions he did not explore the century's large social and political problems. War, religion, crime, poverty, civil rights—these were not his subjects. Instead he struck at the immemorial stupidities, cruelties, and perversities of men that lie at the root of our ills. A disillusioned idealist, he satirized mean behavior to sound the clearest note of his discontent. Yet he considered himself an optimist or near kin to one. He insisted that the perceptive reader would detect in his work "a basic and indestructible thread of hope."
>
> LOUIS HASLEY,
> "James Thurber: Artist in Humor"

15

because of a lack of "Agape" and because of a deep
distrust of the world. If an artist distrusts the
world, Auden suggests, he will reproduce as little
of its details as possible in his art (60, 61). If
this were true, then it would seem to follow that
all those artists who do reproduce fully the details of the external world are necessarily optimistic lovers of matter.

Thurber was not in love with the world of
ordinary activity, but Auden and many like him who
see bitterness behind Thurber's comedy have missed
something fundamental in his drawings. It is true
that the subjects of Thurber's work generally were
not political or social issues but the even larger
and more basic problems, the weaknesses of human
nature. He was something of an idealist who had
become disappointed. In spite of his discontent,
however, he thought of himself as an optimist
rather than as a pessimist, and he believed that a
sensitive audience would detect this positive note
in his works (Hasley 504). Admittedly he, like
many great writers and artists before him, despised
certain aspects of a modern mechanized existence,

Although it is tempting to end a paper with an eloquent quotation, it is generally more effective to end with your own words that express your own thoughtful conclusions.

16

but the very fact that he saw in mankind the
ability to transcend that realm into a world of
fantasy and innocence represents a strong and definite note of hope. There is both danger and
promise in human existence. He "insisted that the
menace to the individual lurks in the world of man-
made systems, whether mechanical or mental, and
that the promise waits in the uncircumscribed
realms of the instinct and the imagination (Elias
356). To the man in the drawing of the bedroom
scene, the woman is but a representation of a
threatening world of cold and harsh realities. But
in the drawing, and in mankind's existence, the
seal is just as real and is there to represent that
other world we can--whether we be man or woman--
experience if our ears are tuned aright.

The word *Notes* is centered on the page. Double-space throughout unless instructed otherwise.

Indent the first line of every note five spaces; do not indent succeeding lines. Note numbers are raised slightly above the line. Leave a space between the number and the first word of the note.

As note 1 illustrates, bibliographic references in notes are identical in form to parenthetical documentation in the body of the paper. This note gives additional background information.

In note 3 the writer wanted to use the Benchley quotation, but she did not have access to the telegram in which it appeared; she therefore correctly indicated that she found it quoted in a secondary source (Holmes, *Clocks*). Use original sources whenever possible. A number of references to items that are "quoted in" other works suggests inadequate research.

The information given in note 4 is to be found in all accounts of Thurber's life; therefore, it is not necessary to cite a source. Such information is called "common knowledge." Of course material like this may be used either in the text or in a note.

17

Notes

[1] In the previous year Smith College exhibited Thurber's drawings and those of George Grosz. Then after the one-man show at the Valentine Gallery, "it was clear that he had arrived as a comic artist" (Holmes _Clocks_ 163).

[2] Thurber recounted this incident in an interview with Alistair Cooke ("James Thurber in Conversation" 38).

[3] Burton Bernstein calls it "one of the most celebrated and often-reprinted cartoons of the twentieth century" (190). The eminent humorist Robert Benchley was so taken with it that he sent Thurber a telegram that read as follows: "Thank you for the funniest drawing caption ever to appear in any magazine" (quoted in Holmes, _Clocks_ 136).

[4] His older brother accidentally shot him in the eye with an arrow when they were children, causing the immediate loss of that eye. Thurber gradually lost the sight of the other eye because of complications from the accident and a cataract.

Although the information in note 7 is important, it does not belong in the text of the paper because it brings up a side issue. This note thus illustrates a primary function of notes. Deciding whether to include certain information in the body of the paper or in a note will help you define your focus. Notes assist you in preserving a tight argument in the text without having to give up slightly extraneous material that adds color and interest.

18

5 An art critic remarked that Thurber's dog figure is "a fantasy dog, which arouses sympathy and laughter in many people and faintly depresses others" (Priest 261).

6 In "The Lady on the Bookcase," Thurber wrote that a rumor was abroad that he wrote the captions while his nephew made the drawing (67).

7 It is natural to question whether Thurber's failing eyesight, and not some deeper reason, was responsible for his sparse, unrealistic drawings. Robert E. Morsberger points out, however, the following: "Thurber's visual problems had no relation to the technique of his art. His drawings were most devoid of detail when his sight was strongest; and his later illustrations, even after the operation, have considerably more detail than the earlier ones" (170).

FORM FOR LIST OF WORKS CITED

Begin on a new page for the list of works cited. Center the title. Double-space throughout unless instructed otherwise.

Do not indent the first line of an entry; indent succeeding lines five spaces.

List only those sources actually used in your paper and referred to in parenthetical documentation.

Authors are listed with surnames first. If a book has more than one author, the names of authors after the first one are put in normal order.

List entries alphabetically. When more than one book by the same author is listed, do not repeat the name but type three unspaced hyphens in place of the author's name in entries after the first. An entry without an author (for example an unsigned magazine article) is listed alphabetically by the first word (see, for example, the entry for "That Thurber Woman").

Give the inclusive pages for articles.

Notice that the important divisions of entries are separated by periods.

The first entry illustrates the proper way to list a previously published essay included in a collection.

Other types of entries in this list are explained in the sample list on pp. 333–335.

19

Works Cited

Auden, W. H. "The Icon and the Portrait." Nation,
     13 Jan. 1940: 48. Rpt. in Thurber: A Col-
     lection of Critical Essays. Ed. Charles S.
     Holmes. Twentieth Century Views. Englewood
     Cliffs: Prentice, 1974. 59-61.

Becker, Stephen. Comic Art in America. Introd.
     Rube Goldberg. New York: Simon, 1959.

Benson, E. M. "Phases of Fantasy." American Maga-
     zine of Art 28 (1935): 290-99.

Bernstein, Burton. Thurber: A Biography. New
     York: Dodd, 1975.

Black, Stephen A. James Thurber: His Masquerades.
     Studies in American Literature 23. The Hague:
     Mouton, 1970.

Eates, Margot. Paul Nash: The Master of the
     Image, 1889-1946. London: Murray, 1973.

Elias, Robert H. "James Thurber: The Primitive,
     the Innocent, and the Individual." American
     Scholar 27 (1958): 355-63.

Hasley, Louis. "James Thurber: Artist in Humor."
     South Atlantic Quarterly 73 (1975): 504-15.

The entry for "James Thurber Is Dead" lists no section number (or letter) because this issue of the *New York Times* is not divided into sections and is numbered consecutively. For contrast, see the Nugent entry.

20

Holmes, Charles S. The Clocks of Columbus: The
     Literary Career of James Thurber. New York:
     Atheneum, 1972.

---. Introduction. Thurber: A Collection of
     Critical Essays. Ed. Charles S. Holmes.
     Twentieth Century Views. Englewood Cliffs:
     Prentice, 1974.

"James Thurber in Conversation with Alistair
     Cooke." Atlantic Aug. 1956: 36-40.

"James Thurber Is Dead at 66; Writer Was Also Comic
     Artist." New York Times 3 Nov. 1961, late
     ed.: 1, 35.

"Morose Scrawler." Time 31 Dec. 1934: 38.

Morsberger, Robert E. James Thurber. Twayne's
     United States Authors Series 62. New York:
     Twayne, 1964.

Nugent, Elliott. "Notes on James Thurber the Man,
     or Men." New York Times 25 Feb. 1940, late
     ed., sec. 9:3.

Parker, Dorothy. Introduction. The Seal in the
     Bedroom and Other Predicaments. By James
     Thurber. New York: Harper, 1932.

The entry for "Thurber, James" lists an item in a book that is a collection of works by the same author.

21

Priest, Alan. "Mr. Thurber's Chinese Dog." Metro-
politan Museum of Art Bulletin 4 (1946): 260-
61.

"That Thurber Woman." Newsweek 22 Nov. 1943:
84-86.

Thurber, James. "The Lady on the Bookcase." The
Beast in Me and Other Animals. New York:
Harcourt, 1948, 66-75.

Tobias, Richard C. The Art of James Thurber.
Athens: Ohio UP, 1969.

Yates, Norris W. The American Humorist: Conscience of the Twentieth Century. Ames:
Iowa UP, 1964.

Glossary of Usage

<table>
<tr><td>

49

</td><td>

Glossary of Usage   *gl / us*

</td></tr>
</table>

Many items not listed here are covered in other sections of this book and may be located through the index. For words found neither in this glossary nor in the index, consult a good dictionary. The usage labels (*informal, dialectal,* and so on) affixed to words in this glossary reflect the opinions of two or more of the dictionaries listed on p. 189.

A, an   Use *a* as an article before consonant sounds; use *an* before vowel sounds.

a nickname	*an* office
a house	*an* hour
(the *h* is sounded)	(the *h* is not sounded)
a historical novel	*an* honor
(though the British say *an*)	*an* uncle
a union	
(long *u* has the consonant sound of *y*)	

Accept, except   As a verb, *accept* means "to receive"; *except* means "to exclude." *Except* as a preposition also means "but."
Every legislator *except* Mr. Whelling refused to *accept* the bribe.
We will *except* (exclude) this novel from the list of those to be read.

Accidently   A misspelling usually caused by mispronunciation. Use *accidentally.*

Advice, advise   Use *advice* as a noun, *advise* as a verb.

Affect, effect   *Affect* is a verb meaning "to act upon" or "to influence." *Effect* may be a verb or a noun. *Effect* as a verb means "to cause" or "to bring about"; *effect* as a noun means "a result," "a consequence."
The patent medicine did not *affect* (influence) the disease.
The operation did not *effect* (bring about) an improvement in the patient's health.
The drug had a drastic *effect* (consequence) on the speed of the patient's reactions.

Aggravate   Informal in the sense of "annoy," or "irritate," or "pester." Formally, it means to "make worse or more severe."

Agree to, agree with   *Agree to* a thing (plan, proposal); *agree* with a person.

He *agreed to* the insertion of the plank in the platform of the party.
He *agreed with* the senator that the plank would not gain many votes.

Ain't Nonstandard or illiterate.

All ready, already *All ready* means "prepared, in a state of readiness";
already means "before some specified time" or "previously" and describes an action that is completed.
The riders were *all ready* to mount. (fully prepared)
Mr. Bowman had *already* bagged his limit of quail. (action completed at
time of statement)

All together, altogether *All together* describes a group as acting or ex-
isting collectively; *altogether* means "wholly, entirely."
The sprinters managed to start *all together.*
I do not *altogether* approve the decision.

Allusion, illusion An *allusion* is a casual reference. An *illusion* is a false
or misleading sight or impression.

Alot Nonstandard for *a lot.* See **Lot of , lots of.**

Alright Nonstandard for *all right.*

Among, between *Among* is used with three or more persons or things;
between is used with only two.
It will be hard to choose *between* the two candidates.
It will be hard to choose *among* so many candidates.

Amount, number *Amount* refers to mass or quantity; *number* refers to
things which may be counted.
That is a large *number* of turtles for a pond which has such a small *amount*
of water.

An See **A.**

And etc. See **Etc.**

Anyways Prefer *anyway.*

Anywheres Prefer *anywhere.*

As Weak or confusing in the sense of *because.*
The client collected the full amount of insurance *as* her car ran off the
cliff and was totally demolished.

At this (*or* that) **point in time** Avoid. Wordy and trite.

Awful A trite and feeble substitute for such words as *bad, shocking, lu-
dicrous, ugly.*

Awhile, a while   *Awhile* is an adverb; *a while* is an article and a noun.
Stay *awhile*.
Wait here for *a while*. (object of preposition)

Bad, badly   See p. 78.

Because   See **Reason is because.**

Being as, being that   Use *because* or *since*.

Beside, Besides   *Beside* means "by the side of," "next to"; *besides* means
"in addition to."
Mr. Potts was sitting *beside* the stove.
No one was in the room *besides* Mr. Potts.

Between   See **Among.**

Between you and I   Wrong case. Use *between you and me*.

Bug   Informal or slang in almost every sense except when used to name
an insect.

Bunch   Informal for a group of people.

Bust, busted   Slang as forms of *burst*. *Bursted* is also unacceptable.

Can, may   In formal English, *can* is still used to denote ability; *may*, to
denote permission. Informally the two are interchangeable.

FORMAL
May (not *can*) I go?

Capital, capitol   *Capitol* designates "a building which is a seat of government"; *capital* is used for all other meanings.

Center around   Illogical: use *center in* (or *on*) or *cluster around*.

Climactic, climatic   *Climactic* pertains to a climax; *climatic* pertains to
climate.

Compare, contrast   Do not use interchangeably. *Compare* means to look
for or reveal likenesses; *contrast* treats differences.

Continual, continuous   *Continual* refers to a prolonged and rapid succession; *continuous* refers to an uninterrupted succession.

Contractions   Avoid contractions (*don't, he's, they're*) in formal writing.

Contrast   See **Compare.**

Cool   Slang when used to mean excellent or first-rate.

Criteria, phenomena   Plurals. Use *criterion, phenomenon* for the singular. *Data*, however, can be considered singular or plural.

Cute, great, lovely, wonderful   Often poor substitutes for words of approval.

Don't   Contraction of *do not;* not to be used for *doesn't,* the contraction of *does not.*

Double negative   Avoid such uneducated phrases as *can't help but, didn't have scarcely,* and so on.

Due to   Objectionable to some when used as a prepositional phrase modifying a verb.

OBJECTIONABLE

Due to the laughter, the speaker could not continue.

BETTER
Because of the laughter, the speaker could not continue.

Each and every   Redundant. Use one or the other, not both.

Early on   Redundant. Use *early.* Omit *on.*

Effect   See **Affect.**

Enthused   Use *enthusiastic* in formal writing.

Etc.   Do not use *and etc. Etc.* means "and so forth."

Ever, every   Use *every* in *every day, every other, everybody, every now and then;* use *ever* in *ever and anon, ever so humble.*

Every day, everyday   *Every day* is used as an adverb; *everyday,* as an adjective.
He comes to look at the same picture in the gallery *every day.*
His trip to the gallery is an *everyday* occurrence.

Exam   Considered informal by some authorities. *Examination* is always correct.

Except   See **Accept.**

Expect   Informal for *believe, suspect, think, suppose,* and so forth.

Fabulous   Informal for *extremely pleasing.*

Fantastic   Informal for *extraordinarily good.*

Farther, further   Generally interchangeable, though many persons prefer *farther* in expressions of physical distance and *further* in expressions of time, quantity, and degree.
My car used less gasoline and went *farther* than his.
The second speaker went *further* into the issues than the first.

Fewer, less Use *fewer* to denote number; *less,* to denote amount or degree.
With *fewer* advertisers, there will also be *less* income from advertising.

Finalize Bureaucratic. Avoid.

Fine Often a poor substitute for a more exact word of approval or commendation.

Fix Informal for the noun *predicament.*

Flunk Informal: prefer *fail* or *failure* in formal usage.

Funny Informal for *strange, remarkable,* or *peculiar.*

Further See **Farther.**

Good Incorrect as an adverb. See p. 76.

Great Informal for *first-rate.*

Hardly See **Not hardly.**

Himself See **Myself.**

Illusion See **Allusion.**

Imply, infer *Imply* means "to hint" or "suggest"; *infer* means "to draw a conclusion."
The speaker *implied* that Mr. Dixon was guilty.
The audience *inferred* that Mr. Dixon was guilty.

In, into *Into* denotes motion from the outside to the inside; *in* denotes position (enclosure).
The lion was *in* the cage when the trainer walked *into* the tent.

Infer See **Imply.**

In regards to Unidiomatic: use *in regard to* or *with regard to.*

Into See **In.**

Irregardless Nonstandard for *regardless.*

Is when, is where Ungrammatical use of adverbial clause after a linking verb. Often misused in definitions and explanations.

    NONSTANDARD
Combustion *is when* (or *is where*) oxygen unites with other elements.

    STANDARD
Combustion occurs when oxygen unites with other elements.
Combustion is a union of oxygen with other elements.

Its, it's   *Its* is the possessive case of the pronoun *it; it's* is a contraction of *it is* or *it has.*
It's exciting to parents when their baby cuts *its* first tooth.

Kind of, sort of   Informal as adverbs: use *rather, somewhat,* and so forth.

INFORMAL
Mr. Josephson was *sort of* disgusted.

FORMAL
Mr. Josephson was *rather* disgusted.

FORMAL (not an adverb)
What *sort of* book is that?

Kind of a, sort of a   Delete the *a;* use *kind of* and *sort of.*
What *kind of* (not *kind of a*) pipe do you smoke?

Lay, lie   See p. 40.

Lead, led   *Lead* is an incorrect form for the past tense *led.*

Learn, teach   *Learn* means "to acquire knowledge." *Teach* means "to impart knowledge."
She could not *learn* how to work the problem until Mrs. Smithers *taught* her the formula.

Less   See **Fewer.**

Liable   See **Likely.**

Lie   See p. 40.

Like   Instead of *like* as a conjunction, prefer *as, as if,* or *as though.*

CONJUNCTION
She acted *as if* she had never been on the stage before.

PREPOSITION
She acted *like* a novice.

CONJUNCTION
She acted *like* she had never had a date before. (informal)

Such popular expressions as "tell it like it is" derive part of their appeal from their lighthearted defiance of convention.
Do not use *like* for *that* as in *feel like.*
Do not use *like* (the verb) for *lack.*

Likely, liable   Use *likely* to express probability; use *liable,* which may have legal connotations, to express responsibility or obligation.
You are *likely* to have an accident if you drive recklessly.
Since your father owns the car, he will be *liable* for damages.

Loose, lose   Frequently confused. *Loose* is an adjective; *lose* is a verb.
She wore a *loose* and trailing gown.
Speculators often *lose* their money.

Lot   See **A lot.**

Lot of, lots of   Informal in the sense of *much, many, a great deal.*

Lovely   See **Cute.**

May   See **Can.**

Most   Informal for *almost* in such expressions as the following:
He is late for class *almost* (not *most*) every day.

Myself, yourself, himself, herself, itself   These words are reflexives or intensives, not strict equivalents of *I, me, you, he, she, him, her, it.*

INTENSIVE
I *myself* helped Father cut the wheat.
I helped Father cut the wheat *myself.*

REFLEXIVE
I cut *myself.*

NOT
The elopement was known only to Sherry and *myself.*

BUT
The elopement was known only to Sherry and *me.*

NOT
Only Kay and *myself* had access to the safe.

BUT
Only Kay and *I* had access to the safe.

Nice   A weak substitute for more exact words like *attractive, modest, pleasant, kind,* and so forth.

Not hardly   Double negative. Avoid.

Nowheres   Dialectal. Use *nowhere.*

Nucular   A misspelling and mispronunciation of *nuclear.*

Number   See **Amount.**

Off of *Off* is sufficient.
He fell *off* (not *off of*) the water tower.

O.K., OK, okay Informal.

Percent (or per cent) Use after figures, as "50 percent." Do not use for *percentage:*
Only a small *percentage* (not *percent*) of the people had degrees.

Phenomena See **Criteria.**

Photo Informal.

Plus Avoid using for the conjunction *and.*

Principal, principle Use *principal* to mean "the chief" or "most important." Use *principle* to mean "a rule" or "a truth."
The *principal* reason for her delinquency was never discussed.
The *principal* of Brookwood High School applauded.
To act without *principle* leads to delinquency.

Quote A verb: prefer *quotation* as a noun.

Raise, rise See p. 40.

Real Informal or dialectal as an adverb meaning *really* or *very.*

Reason is (was) because Use *the reason is (was) that.* Formally, *because* should introduce an adverbial clause, not a noun clause used as a predicate nominative.

NOT
The *reason* Abernathy enlisted *was because* he failed in college.

BUT
The *reason* Abernathy enlisted *was that* he failed in college.

OR
Abernathy enlisted *because* he failed in college.

Respectfully, respectively *Respectfully* means "with respect"; *respectively* means "each in the order given."
He *respectfully* thanked the president for his diploma.
Crossing the platform, he passed *respectively* by the speaker, the dean, and the registrar.

Revelant A misspelling and mispronunciation of *relevant.*

Sensual, sensuous *Sensual* connotes the gratification of bodily pleasures; *sensuous* refers favorably to what is experienced through the senses.

Set, sit See p. 40.

Shall, will In strictly formal English, to indicate simple futurity, *shall* is conventional in the first person (I *shall*, we *shall*); *will*, in the second and third persons (you *will*, he *will*, they *will*). To indicate determination, duty, or necessity, *will* is formal in the first person (I *will*, we *will*); *shall*, in the second and third persons (you *shall*, he *shall*, they *shall*). These distinctions are weaker than they used to be, and *will* is increasingly used in all persons.

So For the use of *so* in incomplete constructions, see pp. 88–89. The use of *so* for *so that* sometimes causes confusion.

Sometime, some time *Sometime* is used adverbially to designate an indefinite point of time. *Some time* refers to a period or duration of time.
I will see you *sometime* next week.
I have not seen him for *some time*.

Sort of See **Kind of.**

Sort of a See **Kind of a.**

Super Informal for *excellent.*

Sure Informal as an adverb for *surely, certainly.*

INFORMAL
The speaker *sure* criticized his opponent.

FORMAL
The speaker *certainly* criticized his opponent.

Sure and, try and Use *sure to, try to.*
Be *sure to* (not *sure and*) notice the costumes of the Hungarian folk dancers.

Suspicion Avoid as a verb; use *suspect.*

Teach See **Learn.**

Than, then Do not use one of these words for the other.

Their, there Not interchangeable: *their* is the possessive of *they; there* is either an adverb meaning "in that place" or an expletive.
Their dachshund is sick.
There it is on the corner. (adverb of place)
There is a veterinarian's office in this block. (expletive)

These (those) kinds, these (those) sorts *These (those)* is plural; *kind (sort)* is singular. Therefore use *this (that) kind, this (that) sort; these (those) kinds, these (those) sorts.*

Thusly   Prefer *thus.*

Try and   See **Sure and.**

Unique   Means "one of a kind"; hence it may not logically be compared. *Unique* should not be loosely used for *unusual* or *strange.*

Use   Sometimes carelessly written for the past tense, *used.*
Thomas Jefferson *used* (not *use*) to bathe in cold water almost every morning.

Wait on   Unidiomatic for *wait for. Wait on* correctly means "to serve."

Ways   Prefer *way* when designating a distance.
a long *way*

   NOT
a long *ways*

When, where   See **Is when, is where.**

Where   Do not misuse for *that.*
I read in the newspaper *that* (not *where*) you saved a child's life.

Whose, who's   *Whose* is the possessive of *who; who's* is a contraction of *who is.*

Wicked   Slang when used for *excellent* or *masterly.*

-wise   A suffix overused in combinations with nouns, such as *budgetwise, progresswise,* and *businesswise.*

Wonderful   See **Cute.**

Glossary of
Grammatical Terms

50 Glossary of Grammatical Terms *gl/gr*

This is by no means a complete list of terms used in discussing grammar. See "Grammar" (pp. 2–26), the index, other sections of this book, and dictionaries.

Absolute phrase   See **20L.**

Active voice   See **Voice.**

Adjective   A word that modifies a noun or a pronoun. (See pp. 8–9).
Her young horse jumped over *that high* barrier for *the first* time.

Adjective clause   See **Dependent clause.**

Adverb   A word that modifies a verb, an adjective, or another adverb. (See pp. 9–10).

Adverbial clause   See **Dependent clause.**

Antecedent   A word to which a pronoun refers.

          antecedent   *pronoun*
              ↓   ↓
When the ballet *dancers* appeared, *they* were dressed in pink.

Appositive   A word, phrase, or clause used as a noun and placed beside another word to explain it.

      appositive
           ↓
The *poet John Milton* wrote *Paradise Lost* while he was blind.

Article   *A* and *an* are indefinite articles; *the* is the definite article.

Auxiliary verb   A verb used to help another verb indicate tense, mood, or voice. Principal auxiliaries are forms of the verbs *to be* and *to do.* (See p. 7.)
I *am* studying.
I *do* study.
I *shall* go there next week.
He *may* lose his job.

Case   English has remnants of three cases: subjective, possessive, and objective. Nouns are inflected for case only in the possessive *(father, fa-*

ther's). An alternative way to show possession is with the "of phrase" *(of the house).* Some pronouns, notably the personal pronouns and the relative pronoun *who,* are still fully inflected for three cases:

SUBJECTIVE (acting)
I, he, she, we, they, who

POSSESSIVE (possessing)
my (mine), your (yours), his, her (hers), its, our (ours), their (theirs), whose

OBJECTIVE (acted upon)
me, him, her, us, them, whom

Clause A group of words containing a subject and a predicate. See **Independent clause; Dependent clause.** See pp. 24–25.

Collective noun A word identifying a class or a group of persons or things. See p. 3.

Comparative and superlative degrees See **10a** and **10b.**

Complement A word or group of words used to complete a predicate. Predicate adjectives, predicate nominatives, direct objects, and indirect objects are complements. See pp. 19–20.

Complex, compound, compound-complex sentences A *complex sentence* has one independent clause and at least one dependent clause. A *compound sentence* has at least two independent clauses. A *compound-complex sentence* has two or more independent clauses and one dependent clause or more. See p. 26.

Compound structures See p. 16.

Conjugation The inflection of the forms of a verb according to person, number, tense, voice, and mood. See the abbreviated form of the conjugation of the verb *walk* in **4.**

Conjunction A word used to connect sentences or sentence parts. See also **Coordinating conjunctions, Correlative conjunctions, Subordinating conjunctions,** and pp. 11–12.

Conjunctive adverb An adverb used to relate two independent clauses that are separated by a semicolon: *however, therefore, moreover, then, consequently, besides,* and so on (see **22a**).

Coordinate clause See **Independent clause.** When there are two independent clauses in a compound or a compound-complex sentence, they may be called coordinate clauses.

Coordinating conjunction   A simple conjunction that joins sentences or parts of sentences of equal rank *(and, but, or, nor, for, yet, so)*. See p. 11.

Correlative conjunctions   Conjunctions used in pairs to join coordinate sentence elements. The most common are *either—or, neither—nor, not only—but also, both—and.*

Declension   The inflection of nouns, pronouns, and adjectives in cases, number, and gender. See especially **9**.

Degrees (of modifiers)   See **10a** and **10b**.

Demonstrative adjective or pronoun   A word used to point out *(this, that, these, those).*

Dependent (subordinate) clause   A group of words that contains both a subject and a predicate but that does not stand alone as a sentence. A dependent clause is frequently signaled by a subordinator *(who, which, what, that, since, because,* and so on) and always functions as an adjective, adverb, or noun.

ADJECTIVE
The tenor *who sang the aria* had just arrived from Italy.

NOUN
The critics agreed *that the young tenor had a magnificent voice.*

ADVERB
When he sang, even the sophisticated audience was enraptured.

Diagramming   Diagramming uses systems of lines and positioning of words to show the parts of a sentence and the relationships between them. Its purpose is to make understandable the way writing is put together. (See the example below.)

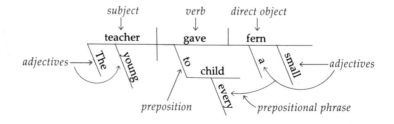

Direct object   A noun, pronoun, or other substantive receiving the action of the verb. (See page 19.)
The angler finally caught the old *trout.*

Elliptical clause   A clause in which one or more words are omitted but understood.

understood

The director admired no one else as much as *(he admired* or *he did)* her.

Expletive   See **7h.**

Faulty predication   Errors occur in predication when a subject and its complement are put together in such a fashion that the sentence is illogical or unmeaningful.

FAULTY
A reporter taking pictures meant that there would be publicity.

BETTER
Since a reporter was taking pictures, we knew that there would be publicity.

It is illogical to say that the reporter *meant.*

Gender   The clauses of nouns and pronouns that determine whether words are masculine, feminine, or neuter.

Gerund   See **Verbal.**

Indefinite pronoun   A pronoun not pointing out a particular person or thing. Some of the most common are *some, any, each, everyone, everybody, anyone, anybody, one* and *neither.*

Independent (main) clause   A group of words which contains a subject and a predicate and which grammatically can stand alone as a sentence.

Indirect object   A word which indirectly receives the action of the verb. (See p. 20.)
The actress wrote the *soldier* a letter.

Infinitive   See **Verbal.**

Inflection   A change in the form of a word to indicate its grammatical function. Nouns, adjectives, and pronouns are declined; verbs are conjugated. Some inflections occur when *-s* or *-es* is added to nouns or verbs or when *'s* is added to nouns.

Intensive pronoun   A pronoun ending in *-self* and used for emphasis. The director *himself* will act the part of Hamlet.

Interjection   A word used to exclaim or to express an (usually strong) emotion. It has no grammatical connections within its sentence. Some common interjections are *oh, ah,* and *ouch.* See p. 14.

Interrogative pronoun   See **9i.**

Intransitive verb   See **Voice.**

Inversion   A change in normal word order, such as placing an adjective after the noun it modifies or placing the object of a verb at the beginning of a sentence.

Linking verb   A verb that does not express action but links the subject to another word that names or describes it. See p. **7** and **10c.** Common linking verbs are *be, become,* and *seem.*

Modifier   A word (or word group) that limits or describes another word. See pp. 98–101.

Mood   The mood (or mode) of a verb indicates whether an action is to be thought of as fact, command, wish, or condition contrary to fact. Modern English has three moods: the indicative, for ordinary statements and questions; the imperative, for commands and entreaty; and the subjunctive, for certain idiomatic expressions of wish, command, or condition contrary to fact.

INDICATIVE
Does she *play* the guitar?
She *does.*

IMPERATIVE
Stay with me.
Let him stay.
The imperative is formed like the plural present indicative, without *-s.*

SUBJUNCTIVE
If I *were* you, I would go.
I wish he *were* going with you.
I move that the meeting *be* adjourned.
It is necessary that he *stay* absolutely quiet.
If this *be* true, no man ever loved.

The most common subjunctive forms are *were* and *be.* All others are formed like the present-tense plural form without *-s.*

Nominative case See **Case.**

Noun A word which names and which has gender, number, and case. There are proper nouns, which name particular people, places or things *(Thomas Jefferson, Paris,* the *Colosseum);* common nouns, which name one or more of a group *(alligator, high school, politician);* collective nouns (see **7d** and **8c**); abstract nouns, which name ideas, feelings, beliefs, and so on *(religion, justice, dislike, enthusiasm);* concrete nouns, which name things perceived through the senses *(lemon, hatchet, worm).*

Noun clause See **Dependent clause.**

Number A term to describe forms which indicate whether a word is singular or plural.

Object of preposition See **Preposition, 9b,** and p. 20.

Objective case See **Case.**

Obsolete words Not used in modern English, for example, *jump* for "exactly" and *shrewd* in the sense of "bad" or "evil."

Participle See **Verbal.**

Parts of speech See pp. 2–14.

Passive voice See **Voice.**

Person Three groups of forms of pronouns (with corresponding verb inflections) used to distinguish between the speaker (first person), the person spoken to (second person), and the person spoken about (third person).

Personal pronoun A pronoun like *I, you, he, she, it, we, they, mine, yours, his, hers, its, ours, theirs.*

Phrase A group of closely related words without both a subject and a predicate. There are subject phrases *(the new drill sergeant),* verb phrases *(should have been),* verbal phrases *(climbing high mountains),* prepositional phrases *(of the novel),* appositive phrases (my brother, *the black sheep of the family),* and so forth. See pp. 21–22.

Predicate The verb in a clause (simple predicate) or the verb and its modifiers, complements, and objects (complete predicate). See pp. 17–18.

Predicate adjective An adjective following a linking verb and describing the subject (see p. 19 and **10c**).
The rose is *artificial.*

Predicate nominative   A noun following a linking verb and naming the subject.

Predication   See **Faulty predication.**

Preposition   A connective that joins a noun or a pronoun to the rest of a sentence. A prepositional phrase may be used as either an adjective or an adverb. See pp. 13, 22.

Pronominal adjective   An adjective which has the same form as a possessive pronoun (*my* book, *their* enthusiasm).

Pronoun   A word which stands for a noun. See **Personal pronoun; Demonstrative adjective or pronoun; Reflexive pronoun; Intensive pronoun; Interrogative pronoun; Indefinite pronoun; Relative pronoun.**

Reflexive pronoun   A pronoun ending in *-self* and indicating that the subject acts upon itself. See **Myself** (Glossary of Usage).

Relative pronoun   See **9i.**

Simple sentence   A sentence consisting of only one independent clause and no dependent clauses. See p. 26.

Subject   A word or group of words about which the sentence or clause makes a statement. (See pp. 15–16).

Subjective case   See **Case.**

Subordinate clause   See **Dependent clause.**

Subordinating conjunction   A conjunction that joins sentence parts of unequal rank. Most frequently these conjunctions begin dependent clauses. Some common subordinating conjunctions are *because, since, though, although, if, when, while, before, after, as, until, so that, as long as, as if, where, unless, as soon as, whereas, in order that.* See pp. 11–12.

Substantive   A noun or a sentence element that serves the function of a noun.

Superlative degree   See **10a** and **10b.**

Syntax   The grammatical ways in which words are put together to form phrases, clauses, and sentences.

Transitive verb   See **Voice.**

Verb   A word or group of words expressing action, being, or state of being. (See p. 7).
Automobiles *burn* gas.
What *is* life?

Verb phrase See **Phrase.**

Verbal A word derived from a verb and used as a noun, an adjective, or an adverb. A verbal may be a gerund, a participle, or an infinitive. See pp. 22–23.

Voice Transitive verbs have two forms to show whether their subjects act on an object (active voice) or are acted upon (passive voice). See pp. 46–47.

Appendix: The APA Style of Documentation

An alternate method of documentation—used widely in the sciences and the social sciences—is that explained in the *Publication Manual of the American Psychological Association* (APA), 1983. For examples of the forms of parenthetical reference that follow the *Publication Manual of the American Psychological Association* (APA), see below.

Note that the list of works at the end of the paper is not called "Works Cited" but "References," that in the entries the date of publication comes immediately after the author's name, that initials are used instead of given names, that only the first word of a title is capitalized (except where there is a colon), that no quotation marks are used for titles, and that there are other differences from the method recommended by the Modern Language Association.

Follow the preferences of your instructor as to which method you use. Compare the entries below with those for the same works in the list of Works Cited, p. 381.

REFERENCES

Auden, W. H. (1940, January 13). The icon and the portrait. *Nation*, p. 48.

Bernstein, B. (1975). *Thurber: A biography*. New York: Dodd.

Elias, R. H. (1958). James Thurber: The primitive, the innocent, and the individual. *American Scholar, 27*, 355–363.

Hasley, L. (1975). James Thurber: Artist in humor. *South Atlantic Quarterly, 73,* 504–515.

NOTE: If more than one work by a single author appears in the list of References, they should be arranged *chronologically,* the work published earliest coming first.

FORMS OF PARENTHETICAL REFERENCE

The following examples are quotations from the model research paper, with parenthetical documentation recommended by the *Publication Manual of the American Psychological Association* (APA). Compare these examples to the research paper, on pp. 373 and 375, which shows the system of the Modern Language Association of America.

If an artist distrusts the world, Auden suggests, he will reproduce as little of its details as possible in his art (1940, pp. 60, 61).

In spite of his discontent, however, he thought of himself as an optimist rather than as a pessimist, and he believed that a sensitive audience would detect this positive note in his works (Hasley, 1982).

There is both danger and promise in human existence. He "insisted that the menace to the individual lurks in the world of man-made systems, whether mechanical or mental, and that the promise waits in the uncircumscribed realms of the instinct and the imagination" (Elias, 1958, p. 356).

Index

Bad, badly, 390
Balanced sentences, 110–111
B. C., A. D., capitalized, 181
Because, 390
Begging the question, 223–224
Being as, being that, 390
Beside, besides, 390
Between, among, 389
Between you and I, 390
Bible
  books of, not underlined, 165
  citing, 336
Bibliographical entries, colon in,
  144
Bibliography, 312–320
Bibliography cards, 321–323
Bibliography, working, 312–320
Blocked quotations, 147, 338–339,
  354–355
Body of paper, 275
Brackets
  for interpolations, 146, 350, 358,
    359
  for parentheses, 146
Bug, 390
Bunch, 390
Bureaucratic language, 198
Business letters
  envelopes for, 164
  folding, 164
  paragraphing in, 162
  proper stationery for, 162
  salutations of, 162
Bust, busted, 390

Can, may, 390
Capital, capitol, 390
Capital letters
  for *B. C.* and *A. D.,* 181
  for days of the week, 181
  for first words of sentences, 179
  for holidays, 181
  for interjection *O,* 179
  for months of the year, 181

for names of specific courses, 181
for pronoun *I,* 179
for proper nouns, 178, 180–181
for sacred books, 181
for words of family relationship,
  180
in direct quotations, 179
in literary titles, 179
in personal titles, 179
not *a, an, the* in titles, 179
not for conjunctions in titles, 179
not for prepositions in titles, 179
not for seasons of the year, 181
not with parenthetical sentence
  within another sentence, 145
to designate religious denominations, 181
to designate the Deity, 181
with degrees, 180
Card catalog, 312–316
Case
  after *as,* 71
  after *than,* 71
  defined, 3, 400–401
  objective, 68–69, 70
  of appositives, 71
  of indefinite pronouns, 72–73
  of interrogative pronouns, 73–74
  of personal pronouns, 72
  of phrase for possession, 71
  of pronouns, 68–74
  of relative pronouns, 73–74
  possessive, 71–72
  subjective, 68–69
Cause and effect, 225, 250–251
Center around, 390
Character, confusing with author in
  literary work, 292
Character analysis, in literary
  paper, 292
Characterization, confusing with
  character in literary work, 292
Checklist for papers, 274–275, 280
Choppy sentences, 82

Abbreviations Used in Marking Papers

Numerals refer to page numbers.